Tasting Paradise III

Restaurants & Recipes of the Hawaiian Islands

THIRD EDITION

Written and Illustrated by

Karen Bacon

COASTAL
IMPRESSIONS
PRESS, LLC

Tasting Paradise III
Restaurants & Recipes of the Hawaiian Islands
Third Edition

Illustrations and book design by Karen Bacon
Cover photography © 2003 David Watersun

Maps courtesy of Wizard Publications and Karen Bacon
Editing and proofreading by Juaneva Smith

ISBN 0-9644327-2-2
Library of Congress Catalog Card Number 2003095687
Includes index.
Printed in China

Published by:
Coastal Impressions Press, LLC
Post Office Box 1006
Kula, Maui, Hawai'i 96790-1006
Fax and Phone: 808-878-3855
kbacon@maui.net
www.tastingparadise.com

Cover photographs represent recipes for macadamia nut crusted fish (we selected 'ahi) with a tropical fruit salsa, cheesecake, and a fruit smoothie.

Please send any comments, questions or suggestions to the above address.

Grateful acknowledgment made to Pali Jae Lee and Night Rainbow Publishing Co. for permission to reprint the excerpts on page 11, from *Tales from the Night Rainbow*. Copyright 1988 by Pali Jae Lee and Koko Willis.

The author and publisher have made every effort to ensure that the information was accurate at press time; however, we assume no responsibility for errors or inconsistencies. The recipes have not been kitchen tested by the author. While the sources of the information contained in this book are believed to be reliable, changes in price, days open, menu items, etc. are inevitable and are therefore not guaranteed.

To Carol and Rich who graciously help make possibilities become realities.

ACKNOWLEDGEMENTS

I offer my grateful acknowledgement to all the chefs and restaurant owners who have taken the time out of their busy schedules to contribute their recipes and participate in this project. Thank you for sharing your talent and providing inspiration to many cooks. Rich and Carol Keith, thank you for your partnership in this endeavor. I greatly appreciate your patience and support with the timing, planning and creation of this book. Cora Puliatch, my beautiful daughter, thank you for your understanding, interest and valuable feedback during the day to day creation of this project. Your presence in my life is a gift. David Watersun, thank you for sharing your ideas, creativity and talent, for enhancing the beauty of the book with your exceptional photographs on the cover, and for making me laugh. Juaneva Smith, thank you for polishing the manuscript with your thoughtful suggestions, attention to detail, and working diligently to honor the time line. Kevin Puliatch, your flexibility, love and support as Cora's papa continues to be a blessing in my life. Sherri Green, thank you for listening and offering your support and dear friendship. Sophie Schweitzer, I appreciate your warmth, hospitality and suggestions for restaurants; thank you dear friend. Rendy Rosario, you went way beyond the call of duty as a Bed and Breakfast host! Thank you for your interest and restaurant suggestions. Thank you Barbara Williams for the original inspiration and concept for this book. Kaniela Akaka, Jr., thank you for sharing about the blessing with graciousness and humor. I offer my deep gratitude to Sylvia for teaching me about life, creating and crazy wisdom. To all my family and friends who have lovingly offered support, belief and encouragement, you are greatly appreciated. To all the greater powers that be and the beauty and spirit of aloha that surrounds us in Hawai'i, mahalo. It is an honor to be here.

TABLE OF CONTENTS

Letter from Chef James McDonald 9
Author's Note 10
The Spirit of Aloha 11
The Hawaiian Blessing 12

Kaua'i 14–45
Map 14
List of Restaurants, Cuisines and Recipes 15
Bali Hai, Princeville 16
The Beach House, Po'ipu 18
Brennecke's, Po'ipu 20
Dondero's, Po'ipu 22
Gaylord's at Kilohana, Lihu'e 24
The Hanalei Gourmet, Hanalei 26
Hawaiian Classic Desserts Restaurant & Bakery, Lihu'e 28
Hawai'i's Java Kai, Hanalei and Kapa'a 30
Hukilau Lanai, Kapa'a 32
Kalaheo Coffee Co. & Café, Kalaheo 34
Koke'e Lodge, Koke'e 36
Lemongrass Grill and Seafood & Sushi Bar, Kapa'a 38
Plantation Gardens Restaurant & Bar, Po'ipu 40
Roy's Restaurant, Po'ipu 74
Tidepools, Po'ipu 42
Wrangler's Steakhouse, Waimea 44

Oahu 46–81
Map 46
List of Restaurants, Cuisines and Recipes 47
Aaron's atop the Ala Moana, Honolulu 48
Alan Wong's Restaurant, Honolulu 50
Bali by the Sea, Honolulu 52
Buona Sera Italian Restaurant, Kailua 54
Crouching Lion Inn, Ka'a'awa 56
Golden Dragon, Honolulu 58
Hale'iwa Joe's Seafood Grill, Hale'iwa and Kaneohe 60
Hawai'i's Java Kai, Honolulu 30
Hy's Steakhouse, Honolulu 62
Jameson's by the Sea, Hale'iwa 64
Le Bistro, Honolulu 66
Lucy's Grill 'n Bar, Kailua 68

L'Uraku Restaurant, Honolulu 70
The Pineapple Room, Honolulu 72
Roy's Restaurant, Hawai'i Kai/Honolulu 74
Sansei Seafood Restaurant & Sushi Bar, Honolulu 116
Sarento's top of the "I", Honolulu 76
Tiki's Grill & Bar, Honolulu 78
The Willows, Honolulu 80

Maui 82–123

Map 82
List of Restaurants, Cuisines and Recipes 83
The Bay Club, Kapalua 84
CJ's Deli & Diner, Ka'anapali 86
Café Sauvage, Lahaina 88
Capische?, Kihei/Wailea 90
David Paul's Lahaina Grill, Lahaina 92
The Feast at Lele, Lahaina 94
Grandma's Coffee House, Keokea 96
Hula Grill, Ka'anapali 98
I'o, Lahaina 100
Kula Lodge & Restaurant, Kula 102
Ma'alaea Grill & Café O'Lei, Ma'alaea, Makawao, Lahaina, Wailuku 104
Mañana Garage, Kahului 106
Moana Bakery & Café, Pa'ia 108
Nick's Fishmarket Maui, Wailea 110
Pacific'O, Lahaina 112
The Plantation House Restaurant, Kapalua 114
Roy's Restaurant, Kahana and Kihei 74
Sansei Seafood Restaurant & Sushi Bar, Kapalua and Kihei 116
Sarento's on the Beach, Wailea 118
Stella Blues Café, Kihei 120
The Waterfront Restaurant, Ma'alaea 122

Lana'i 124–131

Map 124
List of Restaurants, Cuisines and Recipes 125
The Challenge at Manele Clubhouse, Manele Bay 126
Henry Clay's Rotisserie, Lana'i City 128
The Lodge at Koele, Lana'i City 130

TABLE OF CONTENTS

Hawai'i 132–163
Map 132
List of Restaurants, Cuisines and Recipes 133
Aioli's Restaurant, Kamuela 134
Aloha Angel Café, Kainaliu 136
Bamboo Restaurant, Hawi 138
Café Pesto, Hilo and Kawaihae 140
Coast Grille, Kohala Coast 142
The Coffee Shack, Captain Cook 144
Daniel Thiebaut Restaurant, Kamuela 146
Donatoni's, Kohala Coast 148
Hualalai Club Grill, Kailua-Kona 150
Imari, Kohala Coast 152
Jameson's by the Sea, Kailua-Kona 64
Kamuela Provision Company, Kohala Coast 154
Kilauea Lodge, Volcano 156
Kirin, Kohala Coast 158
Merriman's Restaurant, Kamuela 160
Roy's Restaurant, Waikoloa 74
Sibu Café, Kailua-Kona 162

Bonus Section Featuring Selected Recipes
from the First Edition 164–189
List of Recipes 164

Glossary 190
Index of Recipes 192
Index of Restaurants 199
Mail Order Sources 200

Letter From Chef James McDonald

As a chef, I feel very fortunate to live and cook on a gorgeous tropical island that is known world-wide. I am passionate about the beauty and bounty that we chefs get to work with on a daily basis here in Hawai'i where there are countless great restaurants, many of which are featured in this book.

Over the last several years, we have seen a transition in the cuisine of Hawai'i that continues to evolve daily. There was a time when continental dining was the norm and the majority of produce was imported. That's not to say there wasn't anyone growing veggies for small markets and personal consumption and pleasure. There were. But fresh, unique island foods were not reaching mainstream visitors. Now—we the chefs, are net-working with micro farms and aqua culture farmers and are able to deliver same day picked salads or fish directly to you, our guests. When the products are fresh and perfect, it is unbelievable! And here we are, chefs from all over the planet, with our different styles and knowledge, just having the time of our lives creating spectacular fusion dishes, as well as recreating traditional dishes using fresh island products. You get to enjoy the benefits of this when you visit our restaurants or try some of the recipes in this book that reflect this new and distinctive approach.

It isn't difficult becoming inspired to create unique dishes, when there are so many unique foods at our disposal. Think about this—a fisherman calls from his cell phone on his boat to tell you what he just caught and the next thing you know there's a beautiful fresh fish delivered at your front door. And then someone shows up with fresh picked avocado and star fruit. Well, you just chop up a Maui onion with that, and you have a fresh tropical salsa to put over that just-seared *papio*.

Life for the modern day chef isn't only cooking though. With so much popularity surrounding Hawaiian Regional Cuisine, we are often asked to go out and promote, and share our love with the rest of the world. In fact, I appeared on national TV with Karen Bacon to do a cooking demonstration when her last edition of *Tasting Paradise* was featured on the home shopping network QVC. Whether it's in the form of writing cookbooks, cooking at fund raisers, preparing menus for airlines, cooking abroad, cooking aboard luxury cruise ships, going on television and radio or doing joint cooking venues with other notable chefs, the bottom line is to do it with passion and consistency.

I hope that you will enjoy the recipes in this book and I look forward to saying *Aloha* to you in person.

Mahalo and a *Hui Hou,*

Chef James

Chef James McDonald is Executive Chef of I'o restaurant (page 100), Pacific'O restaurant (page 112) and The Feast at Lele, a gourmet luau (page 94).

(Since Chef James wrote this letter, he and his partners have created their own farm to grow and supply fresh choice produce for their restaurants.)

Author's Note

Many talented, creative people who are passionate about food and the abundant gifts and beauty found in Hawai'i have contributed to this book. The selection of enticing recipes and restaurants represent the cultural diversity that is found in Hawai'i. It is a rich experience to be in a community where people of many cultures live together and *Tasting Paradise* represents that unique richness by offering a sampling of many different cuisines within its pages. This allows you to share in this cultural diversity while dining out in Hawai'i and while creating in your own kitchen at home.

Chefs and restaurant owners chose the recipes they wished to contribute. Some represent items from the menu while others are specials that are served occasionally or seasonally. While putting the recipes together in this book, much effort has been made to make them clear, easy to follow and consistent in format. However, you may notice some differences in how the recipes are presented. I have allowed for this as a way of honoring the voice of each individual chef. For example, you may want to adjust the sizes of the recipes to meet your needs as some of them are in large quantities (a reminder that a chef cooks for many people).

The restaurants were selected primarily by word of mouth recommendations from residents of Hawai'i. A beautiful view, beachside location, a unique and fun atmosphere, a lovely and elegant setting, a creative, innovative menu and great food are some of the reasons that these restaurants were selected. Realizing that we all have different tastes, this book features a variety of restaurants allowing each individual to discover the cuisine and atmosphere that will delight and satisfy your preference. I also adjust my writing style to reflect the unique feeling and atmosphere of each restaurant.

On the facing page and following pages, you'll find the Stories of Aloha and a description of the Hawaiian Blessing. I have included these in the first two editions of the book and share them again in this third edition because many readers have enjoyed this taste of the Hawaiian culture as well as the flavors found in the food.

I invite you to try the delicious recipes, outstanding restaurants and your own experience of *Tasting Paradise*. Be adventuresome; experiment and enjoy!

> *Aloha,*
>
> Karen

How to Use Tasting Paradise

The book is divided into sections by island, including maps that will help you locate the general vicinity of a restaurant you would like to visit. The type of cuisine for each restaurant is listed on the bottom right hand side of the recipe page and also in the table of contents for each section. With a complete recipe index along with restaurant information and listings *Tasting Paradise* is easy to use as a cookbook and a restaurant guide.

Please be aware that many restaurants change continually. There are often daily menu changes; therefore, when an item is mentioned in a write up in this book, it will not necessarily be on the menu when you arrive at the restaurant. Prices, hours and days open are subject to change. Owners, chefs and staff may also change, which can result in a shift in quality or a restaurant may close its doors and a new one will open in the same location. It's an adventure. Be ready for surprises!

THE SPIRIT OF ALOHA

Aloha means the spirit of love, and is commonly used as hello and goodbye; it also means compassion, kindness and giving.

> *Aloha* is being a part of all
> and all being a part of me.
> When there is pain—it is my pain.
> When there is joy—it is mine also.
> I respect all that is
> as part of the Creator and part of me.
> I will not willfully harm anyone or anything.
> When food is needed I will take only my need
> and explain why it is being taken.
> The earth, the sky, the sea are mine
> To care for, to cherish and to protect.
> This is Hawaiian—This is *Aloha*![1]

This beautiful message is from the book *Tales from the Night Rainbow*, by Pali Jae Lee and Koko Willis. The book was inspired by stories shared by their big grandma, Kaili'ohe Kame'ekua. As with all cultures, there are many different versions and interpretations of the history of the Hawaiian people. Much of what is commonly known is the history of the Tahitian people after they came to Hawai'i (the *Ali'i*). But the true native Hawaiians that were here before the Tahitians came (pre *Ali'i*) have a different history and philosophy of life. They taught through stories and parables that were shared with children at an early age, such as the two examples shared on this page.

> "Each child born has at birth, a Bowl of perfect Light. If he tends his Light it will grow in strength and he can do all things—swim with the shark, fly with the birds, know and understand all things. If, however, he becomes envious or jealous he drops a stone into his Bowl of Light and some of the Light goes out. Light and the stone cannot hold the same space. If he continues to put stones in the Bowl of Light, the Light will go out and he will become a stone. A stone does not grow, nor does it move. If at any time he tires of being a stone, all he needs to do is turn the bowl upside down and the stones will fall away and the Light will grow once more."[1]

As we experience the people and the spirit of *aloha* throughout the islands, it enriches our experience and keeps the history alive to share these stories and others like them.

[1] *Pali Jae Lee and Koko Willis,* Tales from the Night Rainbow *(Honolulu, Hawai'i: Night Rainbow Publishing Co., 1988), pp. 18–19.*

THE HAWAIIAN BLESSING – A TRADITION

While the world is filled with people of different nationalities and cultures, religions and spiritual beliefs, there are things that tie us together—universal bridges such as food, which crosses language barriers, opens hearts, fills bellies and imparts a feeling of nourishment. In many cultures we bless our food and ask for it to serve us well; we also bless our babies with hopes that the blessing will help them have a happy, healthy and successful life. We want our relationships to be rewarding and harmonious, our ventures to be successful.

In Hawai'i, it is a tradition to bless new homes, boats, canoes, and new businesses, including restaurants, calling upon greater powers to assist in the safety, well being and success of the new creation. The blessing also cleanses and clears the way of any conflict or bad experience that may have occurred in the past. The ceremony is performed by a spiritual leader—a *kahuna*, priest, *kahu* or minister—and reflects the individuals own unique style and philosophy. Friends, family and members of the community are drawn together to participate in the ceremony of honoring a new beginning.

Kaniela Akaka, Jr., a Hawaiian historian explains, "When getting ready to perform a blessing you must prepare to be strong in mind and purpose, enough to combat seen or unseen obstacles that might be before you, including personalities present." With inspired chants and prayer and the request for all who are present to clear their minds and think only positive thoughts for the restaurant, Kaniela performs a blessing, as he did for Alan Wong's restaurant, The Pineapple Room. Kaniela explains that, for him, the chants are inspired in the moment. Each blessing is unique to fit the home or business it is for, and only with everyone's prayers along with his chants can the blessing and success of the restaurant be accomplished. Each person has a purpose and link to the whole. He relates it to a canoe voyage in which there are many roles and each one is vitally important to the success of the journey. In this case, the owner of the business is similar to the navigator who looks toward a goal, a guiding star. "We're all in this together and we need to work together and think as one. The restaurant, which is like a big canoe, needs everyone's helping hand—we will make it together. Each one of us is a part of this great wholeness," Kaniela says.

During the blessing, sea water is sprinkled on the four corners of the building or room, *pi kai* (salt) cleanses and purifies to clean out all the negative and unwanted elements, including what Kaniela refers to as "rascal spirits" who may make things hard. The prayers help the "rascals" move on and at the same time request other spirits who are present to help with their blessings. *Maile* (vines from the native Hawaiian shrub) are tied together to represent the *piko* (umbilical cord), or connection to the earth, which represents the mother. The *maile* is severed, as the umbilical cord is cut from the mother to enable the child to grow and move on without being held back. As part of the blessing, a lavish spread of food is presented—food that is a ceremonial feast, a commune with the gods, in which not only the physical world is invited to partake, but the spiritual world as well. The participants of the blessing are not only the witnesses of the event, but foster parents to help care for the new business—as there can be rough times, just as a canoe on a voyage can encounter rough seas or a child will go through challenging times. A blessing is a birth to a new spirit or life force and all who are there have the responsibility to help keep the life force alive.

As he begins his prayers and chants for the blessing, Kaniela asks for a feeling of love and *aloha* to bind everyone together as part of a family. He calls on spirits from the past to utilize the help of all considered part of nature and life, and they are invited to partake in the feasting—somewhat like a holy communion. He asks for silence, a conch shell is blown, and everyone brings their thoughts and *mana* (spiritual power) together as Kaniela and the owner of the new venture symbolically cut the *maile* and go from corner to corner sprinkling sea water as the blessing begins with the intention and awareness that our accomplishments will be much greater when we all work together as one.

Tasting Paradise is the result of many people contributing and working together to create a unique cookbook/restaurant guide for you to enjoy. It revolves around food, which is our lifeblood and, along with love, it nourishes us, brings us together and creates joy in our lives. Food is a creative expression, a way that we can share love and life with others; it is one of our greatest blessings.

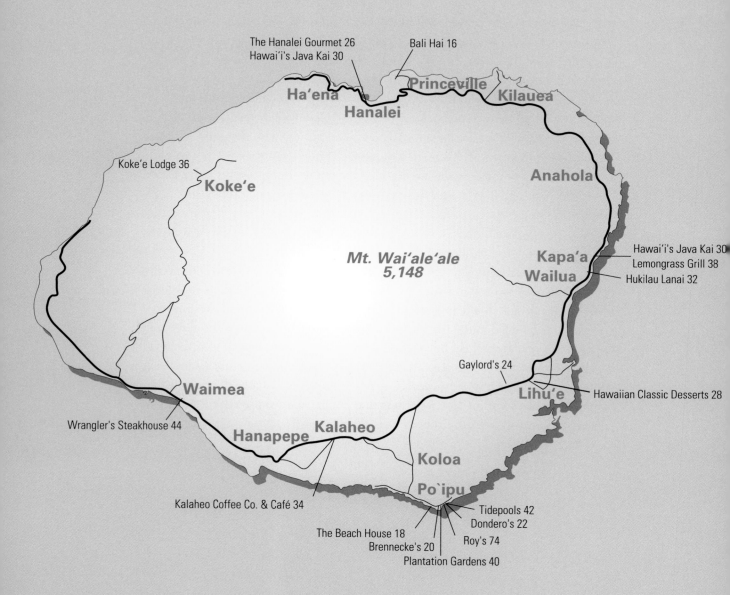

The Hanalei Gourmet 26
Hawai'i's Java Kai 30

Bali Hai 16

Ha'ena

Princeville

Hanalei

Kilauea

Koke'e Lodge 36

Koke'e

Anahola

Mt. Wai'ale'ale
5,148

Kapa'a
Wailua

Hawai'i's Java Kai 30
Lemongrass Grill 38
Hukilau Lanai 32

Gaylord's 24

Waimea

Lihu'e

Hawaiian Classic Desserts 28

Wrangler's Steakhouse 44

Hanapepe

Kalaheo

Koloa

Po`ipu

Kalaheo Coffee Co. & Café 34

Tidepools 42
Dondero's 22

The Beach House 18

Roy's 74

Brennecke's 20

Plantation Gardens 40

KAUA'I
THE GARDEN ISLE

Kauaʻi

Restaurant, Page, Type of Cuisine
Recipes Featured

Bali Hai Restaurant, 16, Pacific Rim
Curried Seafood and Saffron Rissotto with Achote Chili and Cilantro Chive Oils

The Beach House, 18, Pacific Rim
Mountain Apple Salad with Lilikoi Dijon Vinaigrette / Togarashi Calamari with Guava Cocktail Sauce

Brennecke's, 20, Steak & Seafood
Kamakazi Wrap

Dondero's, 22, Regional Italian
Veal Osso Buco / Chocolate Creme Brulée

Gaylord's at Kilohana, 24, Continental Pacific
Okinawan Potato Hash / Mascarpone Cheese Cake

The Hanalei Gourmet, 26, American
Curried Chicken and Grapes in a White Wine Cream Sauce / Macadamia Nut Breaded 'Ahi with Green Apple Guava Sauce

Hawaiian Classic Desserts Restaurant & Bakery, 28, Continental Island Style & Classic Bakery
Crispy Shrimp in a Blanket with Ogo Vinaigrette / Macadamia Cheese Mousse / Ginger Caramel Sauce

Hawaiʻi's Java Kai, 30, Specialty Coffee House
Keko Berry Fruit Smoothie / Papaya Salsa

Hukilau Lanai, 32, Fresh Kauaʻi
Okinawan Sweet Potato Ravioli / Lemon Grass Cream Sauce

Kalaheo Coffee Co. & Café, 34, Coffee House/Café/Deli
Oatmeal Fruit Scones / Chunky Chocolate Mac Nut Bars

Kokeʻe Lodge, 36, Fresh Local & American
Kokee Lodge Chili / Mokihana Coffee

Lemongrass Grill and Seafood & Sushi Bar, 38, Seafood and Sushi
Sautéed Jumbo Sea Scallops / Shiitake Mushroom Relish / Miso Vinaigrette / Buerre Blanc / Jade Sauce

Plantation Gardens Restaurant & Bar, 40, Hawaiian Fusion Pacific Rim
Plantation Gardens Seafood Lau Lau / Plantation Gardens Banana Lumpia / Chocolate Sauce / Creme Anglaise

Roy's Restaurant, 74, Hawaiian Fusian Style
Coconut Tiger Shrimp Sticks with a Thai Style Cocktail Sauce / Szechwan Baby Back Ribs with a Mongolian Marinade

Tidepools, 42, Creative Hawaiian/Pacific Rim
Wok-Seared Tiger Shrimp / Lemon Grass Coconut Curry Sauce / Coconut Lobster Soup

Wrangler's Steakhouse, 44, Steakhouse
Clam Chowder / Peach Cobbler

BALI HAI RESTAURANT

Majestic mountains and an exceptional view of Hanalei Bay and Bali Hai (the restaurant's namesake) provide a soothing and beautiful setting for **Bali Hai Restaurant**. Executive Chef Mark Burson uses fresh Kaua'i produce and herbs that are organically grown in the restaurant's own garden to keep the cuisine simple and fresh and the staff is taught about Hawaiian culture in order to share the special spirit of aloha and hospitality with guests.

Ambiance: A casual open-air and tropical setting where you'll be surrounded by stunning natural elements—verdant mountains with cascading waterfalls, sparkling ocean views and, in the evening, gorgeous sunsets. Many wedding dinners are celebrated at Bali Hai. You'll also find nightly entertainment and lighter fare served in the Happy Talk Lounge.

Menu: For a first course, try the outstanding Blackened Seared 'Ahi with Cajun spices. Recommended dinner entrées include Pan Seared Shrimp and Scallops with orange sherry beurre blanc, and Bali Hai Sunset—pan seared fresh fish served over a crispy crabcake with papaya ginger beurre blanc. Desserts feature Banana Cream Pie with macadamia nut crust, and a special cheesecake flavor each day. Breakfast items include Benedicts, Poi Pancakes, and a variety of omelettes such as Smoked Island Fish. Lunch features enticing salads, entrées, pasta and sandwiches.

Details: Open daily. Breakfast: $6.00–12.95. Lunch: $9.00–18.00. Dinner: $18.00–32.00. Reservations recommended for dinner. Ask for directions from the Princeville entrance information booth.

(808) 826–6522
HANALEI BAY RESORT, HONOIKI ROAD, PRINCEVILLE, KAUA'I, HI 96722

CURRIED SEAFOOD AND SAFFRON RISSOTTO
WITH ACHOTE CHILI AND CILANTRO CHIVE OILS

ACHOTE CHILI OIL

1 cup salad oil

1 tsp. achote powder or seed

½ fresh habañero pepper (no seeds or veins)

1 tsp. Hawaiian salt

1 pinch white pepper

CILANTRO CHIVE OIL

1 cup salad oil

1 Tbsp. fresh garlic chives (sliced)

1 Tbsp. fresh cilantro (chopped, no stems)

1 tsp. Hawaiian salt

1 pinch white pepper

In a blender mix all the ingredients for each oil separately. Blend on high until all ingredients are puréed completely, approximately 2 minutes. Season to taste with salt and pepper. Keep at room temperature for later use. Equals 8 1 ounce servings.

SAFFRON RISSOTTO

2 cups arborio rice

3 chopped shallots

4 Tbsp. olive oil

1 pinch saffron

1 tsp. cumin powder

2 tsp. curry powder

1 cup white wine

3 cups fish stock (or clam juice)

salt and pepper to taste

Sauté the shallots in olive oil until translucent. Add the saffron, cumin, curry powder, and then the arborio rice. Mix and coat the rice then add the white wine. Bring to simmer. Add the fish stock, bring to a simmer and cover with aluminum foil. Simmer approximately 20 minutes. Take off heat, fluff with fork, salt and pepper to taste. Keep warm and reserve for later use. Makes 8 portions.

CURRIED SEAFOOD

2 Tbsp. olive oil

2 – 16/20 shrimp (raw, peeled, deveined)

2 – 10/20 scallops

2 mussels (New Zealand green lip)

2 clams

¼ tsp. curry powder

3 oz. white wine

3 oz. heavy cream

3 oz. grated Parmesan cheese

salt and pepper to taste

In a very hot sauté pan, sauté all seafood in olive oil for approximately one minute. Add white wine and reduce by half. Add curry powder, then cream, then one cup cooked rissotto and mix well. Add Parmesan cheese and salt and pepper to taste. Place seafood mixture in a 6" ring mold in the center of the plate. Drizzle the two oils around the edge of the plate and sprinkle with Parmesan cheese. Garnish with fresh basil flower.

Executive Chef Mark Burson

PACIFIC RIM

THE BEACH HOUSE

Seduced by the soft sounds and scents of the sea, gracious service and superb food you are sure to enjoy dining at **The Beach House,** a uniquely special place on the lush garden isle of Kaua'i. A cherished favorite, The Beach House has been honored with the Hale 'Aina award for 6 consecutive years—1998 through 2003 and has also received excellent ratings from *Zagat Survey.* The Travel Network credits The Beach House as "One of the Most Romantic Restaurants in Hawaii." Executive Chef Scott Lutey, who is a native of Maui, is influenced by the cuisines of the many different cultures he grew up with in Hawai'i. Along with winning many awards throughout his career, in 2001 he was invited to "work his culinary magic" at the prestigious James Beard House in New York City.

Ambiance: A romantic and inviting open-air setting just steps from breaking waves, with a perfect sunset view over the glistening ocean.

Menu: Enjoy a bottle of fine wine and an enticing entrée such as Seared Crusted Macadamia Nut Mahi with citrus aka miso sauce, or Mint Coriander Marinated Lamb Rack with goat cheese roasted garlic crust. Recommended appetizers include Sea Scallops with green papaya salad; and 'Ahi Taster—'ahi poke sushi, 'ahi tostadas and 'ahi hash spring roll. A dessert sure to please chocolate lovers is Hawaiian Vintage Pyramid—a brownie nut crust with white chocolate mousse topped with chocolate fudge or try their signature Kahlua Taro Cheesecake.

Details: Dinner served nightly. Entrées: $22.00–29.00. Reservations recommended. When on Maui, visit sister restaurants, The Plantation House (page 114), and The SeaWatch.

(808) 742-1424 / WWW.THE-BEACH-HOUSE.COM
5022 LAWAI ROAD, PO'IPU, KAUA'I, HI 96756

MOUNTAIN APPLE SALAD
WITH LILIKOI DIJON VINAIGRETTE

Caramelized Macadamia Nuts
2 oz. butter

½ cup brown sugar
¾ cup macadamia nuts

Heat butter in a sauté pan, add macadamia nuts and brown sugar. Cook until sugar binds to nuts.

Lilikoi Dijon Vinaigrette
½ cup lilikoi concentrate
¼ cup sushi vinegar

2 Tbsp. whole grain Dijon mustard
1 cup canola oil
salt and pepper to taste

Place lilikoi concentrate, sushi vinegar and mustard in a blender and blend on high slowly adding the oil. Season to taste with salt and pepper.

Mountain Apple Salad
2 Mountain apples (or other type) cored
   and sliced
2 cups wild greens
4 oz. Gorgonzola cheese crumble

Garnish
½ cup cucumber strings
½ cup carrot strings

Mix wild greens, Caramelized Macadamia Nuts and Lilikoi Dijon Vinaigrette in a large salad bowl. Place salad on salad plate and sprinkle with gorgonzola cheese. Garnish with cucumber and carrot strings. Serves 4.

TOGARASHI CALAMARI WITH GUAVA COCKTAIL SAUCE

Togarashi Calamari
2 lbs. cleaned calamari tubes and tentacles
1 cup milk
3 cups all purpose flour
½ cup togarashi
2 Tbsp. kosher salt
1 cup corn meal

Garnish
4 ti leafs
½ cup sliced green onion
1 lemon cut into 4 wedges

Preheat fryer to 350 degrees. Soak calamari in milk for 1 hour. Combine flour, togarashi, kosher salt, and corn meal. Remove calamari from milk, letting any excess milk drain. Dredge calamari in togarashi flour. Fry calamari for 2 to 3 minutes or until golden brown. Remove from fryer and place on paper towel to drain excess oil. Place ti leaf on plate, arrange calamari on plate. Garnish with green onion and lemon wedge. Serves 4.

Guava Cocktail Sauce
2 cups chili tomato sauce
1 lime, juice from
1 cup guava syrup

¼ cup grated horseradish
salt and pepper to taste

Mix well.

Brennecke's

Named after the world famous body surfing beach next to Po'ipu Beach, **Brennecke's** is a great place to relax, have a cool one and a bite to eat. A landmark on the sunny South shore, Bob and Christine French opened this popular restaurant in 1983. Lining one of the walls at Brennecke's, you'll find photographs of a young woman dwarfed by mighty waves—this is their daughter, Rochelle Ballard, who is now wrapping up a successful career as a world class surfer.

Visit the Beach Center downstairs for activities and gifts, and Nukumoi Surf Shop next door, which is filled with great clothes and surf paraphernalia.

Ambiance: From your seat in the second story open-air location you'll have a view of blue sky, sparkling water, crashing waves, palm trees and people having fun in the sun at Po'ipu Beach Park.

Menu: Try one of their "World Famous" Mai Tais or an icy pitcher of coladas, margaritas or daiquiris to share. The salad bar features a wide variety of tasty items or enjoy an 'Ahi Caesar Salad or Kiawe Broiled Catch of the Day. A daily salsa is made with fresh fruit, such as: pineapple, papaya, mango, nectarine, and star fruit. A children's menu is offered that features child pleasing selections. Full dinner entrées include Fresh Island Fish, Cioppino or Prime Rib; they are known for their "killer" Alaskan King Crab Legs. For dessert try the enticing Layered Lilikoi (passion fruit) ice cream cake, or Chocolate Suicide Cake.

Details: Open daily. Lunch: $8.95–14.95. Full dinner: $16.95–29.95.

(808) 742-7588 / WWW.BRENNECKES.COM
2100 HOONE ROAD, PO'IPU, KAUA'I, HI 96756

Kamakazi Wrap

4 cups hot cooked medium grain rice
½ cup rice vinegar
½ cup sugar
1 tsp. salt
4 Tbsp. green wasabi tobiko (flying fish roe)
4 Tbsp. red spicy tobiko (it's not not too hot)
1 piece firm cucumber
1 piece ripe avocado
5 to 8 pieces ume (salted baby plums)
   remove seed and mince

2 Tbsp. roasted sesame seeds, black and white
6 5 oz. fresh 'ahi steaks
1 cup teriyaki sauce
6 12" Asian ginger wraps or flour tortillas
Garnish
purple savoy and pickled ginger, shredded
optional for fish:
wasabi paste
norikoumi furikaki (shredded nori or
   seaweed)

Fusion Sushi Rice: Combine vinegar, sugar and salt in a small sauce pan and heat until all ingredients are blended and make a clear sauce. **Do not boil.** Set aside and let cool. Place hot rice in a bowl and slowly add vinegar sauce. Mix well. Divide rice into three bowls of equal portions. Bowl #1: mix rice with spicy red tobiko. Place and spread evenly at the bottom of a 9x13" pan. Bowl #2: mix rice with green wasabi tobiko and spread evenly on top of bottom layer. Bowl #3: mix rice with ume and a little of the juice and sesame seeds. Add this mix on top of wasabi rice. Cover with plastic wrap and set aside.

Kamakazi Wrap: Cut cucumber in half, cut into strips and set aside. Either mash the avocado or cut into strips. Broil 'ahi steaks and baste with teriyaki sauce. Do not overcook fish. Heat wraps on open flame or in a pan. Cut wrap in half. Put 2 tablespoons of rice at a 45 degree angle on wrap. Cut fish steak in half, then into strips. Place fish on top of rice, following with cucumber and avocado. Gently roll into a cone shape. Proceed and do the same with the other half of wrap. Follow the same procedure for remaining five wraps.

Garnish with shredded purple savoy and a spoonful of shredded pickled ginger on the side. You may also add wasabi paste to the fish or sprinkle with norikoumi furikaki (shredded nori or seaweed). Enjoy!

Serves 6.

Dondero's

Whether you dine al fresco under the stars surrounded by beautiful gardens, or inside where the atmosphere is casually elegant, you will enjoy excellent service while savoring fine regional Italian cuisine at **Dondero's**. The chefs utilize fresh local ingredients to create award–winning fare and you may choose from an impressive selection of wines to find the perfect complement for your dinner. Private dining is available for up to 10 guests.

Ambiance: The restaurant's interior is graced with an inlaid marble floor, magnificent Franciscan murals and 2500 hand-painted seashells that decorate the walls. If you prefer dining outside in the balmy tropical night air, Dondero's offers a lovely piazza where the ambiance is enhanced by the sound of ocean waves.

Menu: For starters try the Insalata Alla Cesare (Caesar Salad) followed by Calamari Fritti, and Formaggio Caprino con Faggioline—warm goat cheese, roasted eggplant, cannellini beans and fried basil leaves. A favorite pasta is the Farfalle Pasta with Asparagus, fresh herbs, sun dried tomato and parmesan cheese. For your entrée try Roast Rack of Lamb with Herb Crust or Sautéed Sea Bass on couscous. The perfect finish is Chocolate Creme Brulée with fresh berries and an appealing after dinner drink.

Details: Please call for reservations. Appropriate resort wear required (no thongs or T-shirts). Dinner nightly. Entrées: $17.50–34.00.

(808) 742–6260
Hyatt Regency Kaua'i, Po'ipu, Kaua'i, HI 96756

Veal Osso Buco

5 pieces veal shank
flour, as needed
salt and pepper to taste
4 stalks celery, large dice
2 large carrots, large dice
1 oz. garlic
3 large onions, large dice
1 cup tomato paste

2 cups burgundy wine
¼ bottle port
½ gallon demi glace (brown sauce)
1 quart au jus, veal au jus
1 oz. herbs (mixed)
½ cup olive oil
1 lemon, zest from

Mix flour, salt and pepper to taste. Dust veal with flour mixture and brown on all sides in hot pan in olive oil. Add carrots, celery, garlic, onions, herbs and tomato paste. Cook for 3 minutes. Add burgundy and port, bring to boil. Add demi glace and au jus. Add lemon zest and veal, bring to boil, put in 550 degree oven for 3½ hours or until soft, or meat falling off bone. When cooked, remove veal, cool rapidly. Remove carrots; blend sauce in a blender or with a wand blender. Serve with sauce over and underneath Osso Buco.

Chocolate Creme Brulée

2 oz. milk
12 oz. heavy cream
4 egg yolks

3 oz. sugar
2.5 oz. semi-sweet chocolate

Cream the yolks with the sugar. Melt the chocolate with the cream and milk, then add to egg mixture. Pour into ramekin or small shallow bowls and bake at 300 degrees for 35 minutes. Using a torch, caramelize the top with additional sugar.

Makes 2 portions.

GAYLORD'S AT KILOHANA

Immerse yourself in gracious and comfortable elegance in the charming courtyard setting of **Gaylord's Restaurant.** Since opening in 1986, when Wally and Roberta Wallace "couldn't resist the challenge of creating a restaurant from scratch," Gaylord's has become a landmark favorite. With Wally's passing on Easter 2000, the Wallace's daughter and son-in-law, Paige and Russ Talvi, joined Roberta in carrying on the tradition of running this lovely restaurant. Recognized by Zagat's, Gaylord's has also received several Hale 'Aina Restaurant-of-Distinction Awards and is considered one of Hawai'i's most romantic restaurants. Gaylord's welcomes families and also hosts special occasions: parties, weddings and receptions, as well as presenting a Lu'au on the grounds (not at the restaurant) featuring quality food and a dynamic, fast-paced show suitable for the whole family. Call for nights the Lu'au is featured.

Ambiance: Beautiful gardens and a view of Kaua'i's lush hills leading to Mt. Wai'ale'ale (the rainiest spot on earth) enhance the warm welcoming atmosphere of the 16,000 square foot historic plantation owner's home where Gaylord's is located. Horse drawn carriage rides are available for tours of the 35-acre estate that surrounds the home, which was built in 1935 and also houses small boutiques.

Menu: Seafood Rhapsody is a long-standing dinner favorite: large tiger prawns, fresh fish, lobster tail, and plump sea scallops. Other favorites include Baby Back Ribs, and the Warm Crab and Artichoke Heart Dip. Tempting fresh fish and other specials are offered daily. An extensive wine list offers many fine choices by the glass. For dessert, try the decadent Kilohana Mud Pie or Mango Linzertorte with French pressed Kaua'i coffee.

Details: Open daily. Lunch: $8.95–11.95. Dinner: $18.95–33.95. Sunday Brunch: $9.95–16.95. Reservations recommended. Located just Southwest of Lihu'e on the main highway.

(808) 245-9593
KILOHANA PLANTATION ESTATE, KAUMAALII HWY., LIHU'E, KAUA'I, HI 96766

Okinawan Potato Hash

3 ¾ pounds purple sweet potatoes
¾ yellow pepper, diced
½ red pepper, diced
1½ yellow onion, diced
1 Tbsp. fresh ginger root, minced

1½ tsp. garlic, minced
¼ bunch cilantro, chopped
¼ batch Chicken for Hash (recipe below)
kosher salt to taste
fresh cracked pepper to taste

Wash sweet potatoes. Bake whole on a sheet pan until just done, then place in freezer to arrest cooking. Do not freeze! Peel and dice large. In a bowl, add all other ingredients, mix gently. Pan fry and serve with poached eggs and sauce maltaise.

Note: If potatoes freeze or overcook, they will become wet and mushy. It's best to mix all the ingredients together first, then add the potatoes.

Chicken for Okinawan Hash

5 6 oz. chicken breasts
⅝ cup Yamasa shoyu
1⅝ Tbsp. Thai sweet chili sauce

2 ⅜ tsp. sesame oil
3¼ Tbsp. oyster sauce

In a bowl, mix together shoyu, chile sauce, oil and oyster sauce. Place chicken in marinade and marinate for at least an hour. Flame broil until done, let cool. Dice large and mix with Okinawan hash recipe.

Note: Do not char or overcook the chicken as it will dry it out. We only want the flavor of the grill. It will be cooked again when tossed with the hash.

Chef Andy Althouse

Mascarpone Cheese Cake

1 cup sour cream
3½ eggs
1½ pounds cream cheese
¾ cup mascarpone cheese
½ pound white chocolate
3 oz. unsalted butter

2⅔ Tbsp. orange syrup
½ oz. cream de cacao
½ oz. orange curacao
1 oz. vanilla
½ tsp. salt
1½ cups sugar

Soften cream cheese, blend in food processor with butter and chocolate, which has been melted in a microwave. Combine with remaining ingredients, mix gently with processor. **Do not over mix.** Pour into Pistachio Crust (recipe below) in a ring mold or baking pan, about 1" to 1½" thick. Bake in preheated oven at 240 degrees for 20 minutes.

Pistachio Crust for Mascarpone Cheese Cake

1 cup egg whites
1 pound pistachio nuts, chopped
4 oz. melted butter

½ tsp. salt
1 Tbsp. sugar
1½ Tbsp. all–purpose flour (to bind)

Combine all ingredients in a bowl. Pack lightly onto bottom of mold, or pan of choice, about ⅛" thick.

Chefs Rob Chevlin and Andy Althouse

Continental Pacific

THE HANALEI GOURMET

Located in the Old Hanalei School building in the center of town, **The Hanalei Gourmet** has a deli, café, and a bar where you can sip a cool tropical drink. Owner Tim Kerlin (known as Big Tim) is proud of the talented chefs who invent creative daily specials with an international flair, which you can enjoy while dining in the café. If you're on your way to hike the Na Pali Coast, paddle up Hanalei River or just enjoy a day at the beach, stop by the deli and fill up one of their insulated backpacks or coolers with sandwiches, excellent pastries (by Suzi of Suzi's Date Bar) and drinks.

Ambiance: With live rock and roll or jazz music on most evenings and a sports bar atmosphere (with a happy hour) in the afternoon, The Hanalei Gourmet is a busy place to hang out and have fun. There are a few tables outside where you can enjoy watching the variety of tourists and North Shore locals passing by.

Menu: For lunch try the Oregon Bay Shrimp Sandwich or the Waioli Salad with chilled grilled veggies, Sonoma goat cheese and chef's mango vinaigrette (*Bon Appétit* requested the recipe for the mango vinaigrette, but Big Tim's not telling). The burgers are made with fresh beef. "Primo Pupus" include Crab Cakes, Coconut Shrimp, and Nachos. Dinners feature a Fresh Catch charbroiled and served with a soy caramel glaze, Beer Battered Fresh Fish and Chips with Asian coleslaw, specialty pastas, steak, chicken, and more.

Details: Open daily at 8 a.m. (so early birds can pick up picnic items and snacks). Lunch under $10.00. Dinner: $11.50–23.95.

(808) 826–2524
OLD HANALEI SCHOOL BUILDING, KUHIO HWY., HANALEI, KAUAʻI, HI 96714

Curried Chicken and Grapes
in a White Wine Cream Sauce

1 tsp. nutmeg
1 tsp. curry powder
1 tsp. salt
1 tsp. white pepper
2 tsp. fresh tarragon or 1 tsp. dry tarragon
2 oz. butter
5 oz. grapes

4-5 oz. heavy whipping cream
3 oz. dry white wine
1 8 oz. chicken breast
2 oz. apricot preserves or marmalade
1 tsp. minced garlic
3 oz. minced shallots or onion

Combine nutmeg, curry powder, salt, white pepper and tarragon to make a dry rub. Coat chicken with dry mixture. Heat sauté pan on medium heat. Add butter and let melt. Brown chicken on both sides, still on medium heat. After browned, remove chicken from pan and set aside. In same pan, add shallots and garlic, sauté until translucent. Add grapes and white wine. Reduce by half. Add apricot preserves and heavy cream, then place chicken back in pan. Cover and cook for another 5 minutes. Serve over jasmine rice.

Macadamia Nut Breaded 'Ahi
with Green Apple Guava Sauce

2 6 oz. Big Eye or Yellow Fin 'ahi fillets
½ cup macadamia nuts, finely chopped
1 cup panko or fresh bread crumbs
1 cup flour

2 eggs
¼ cup milk or half and half
salt and pepper to taste

In a bowl, mix together 2 eggs and milk. Season 'ahi with salt and pepper and lightly dust with flour. Dip 'ahi in egg wash and roll in the panko mixed with macadamia nuts. Reserve in refrigerator while preparing sauce or until ready to cook.

Fry the 'ahi fillets in enough oil to coat the bottom of the skillet. Sear both sides of fish until golden brown. Try not to over cook, keeping the center red to pink in color. Serve with sauce on the side or drizzle over fish while on plate. Serves 2.

Green Apple Guava Sauce

½ oz. oil
1 oz. shallots, minced
½ Tbsp. garlic, minced
½ Tbsp. ginger, minced
½ green apple, diced small

¼ cup white wine
1 cup guava puree
¼ cup butter
salt and pepper to taste

In a sauce pot, add oil and sauté shallots, garlic and ginger. Add green apple and white wine. Reduce wine by half. Add guava puree. Heat until guava puree starts to simmer. Remove from stove and purée entire mixture in a blender. Return sauce back to sauce pot and place on low heat. Whisk in butter a little at a time, stirring constantly. As soon as butter is incorporated, remove from stove and season with salt and pepper.

American

HAWAIIAN CLASSIC DESSERTS RESTAURANT & BAKERY

Raised on O'ahu and trained in Switzerland, Master Pastry Chef Fenton Lee has been creating delectable desserts for over 38 years. After devoting many years to the hotel industry, in June 1999 Fenton and wife Winona opened **Hawaiian Classic Desserts Restaurant & Bakery**. With Fenton as the creative genius in the kitchen, and Winona's gracious and warm personality greeting guests, they've come up with a winning restaurant that serves beautifully presented tasty food and special treats. "People eat with their eyes," Fenton says, and, as the artist, he uses fresh ingredients and cooks each item to order; Fenton enjoys making people happy.

Ambiance: When you walk in you'll be greeted by a pastry case full of luscious bakery goodies that you can enjoy right away or have packed up to savor later. The restaurant area is comfortable and stylish and offers open-air indoor dining or outdoor seating on the lanai.

Menu: Breakfast features omelettes, Loco Moco, pancakes or French Toast with Apple Smoked Chicken Sausage, and more. Sandwiches on freshly baked breads are served for lunch, along with fresh fish specials, and salads including a popular Chicken Oriental Salad. Malasadas, custard Danish, turnovers and muffins are some of the freshly baked pastries you'll find. Be sure to arrive early as they tend to sell out by mid to late morning. Awesome desserts include Lilikoi Chiffon Pie, Bread Pudding and Chocolate–Strawberry Decadence. Be sure to pick up some of their bottled sauces such as the delicious house salad dressing and the tangy buttery guava sauce for desserts or pancakes (careful, this sauce can be addictive!).

Details: Bakery, breakfast, lunch and desserts Monday through Saturday, closed Sunday. Breakfast and lunch, most items $7.95–12.95.

(808) 245–6967
4491 RICE STREET, LIHU'E, KAUA'I, HI 96766

CRISPY SHRIMP IN A BLANKET
WITH OGO VINAIGRETTE

4 pieces 21-25 tiger shrimp

4 bamboo skewers

1 small bunch rice sticks

½ gallon vegetable oil, for frying

Batter

½ cup all purpose flour

½ cup cornstarch

1 egg

¼ tsp. baking powder

1 cup water

salt and pepper to taste

Mix egg and water well. Combine rest of ingredients.

Sauce

1 cup granulated sugar

2 cups red wine or rice vinegar

1 Tbsp. ginger

1 bunch ogo, chopped

Reduce until thickened. Let cool. Add chopped ogo.

Season shrimp, heat vegetable oil in wok or other pan. Skewer shrimp and dip in batter. Roll battered shrimp in rice sticks. Deep fry until golden brown. Drizzle sauce on plate and set shrimp on top for presentation.

Serves 2.

MACADAMIA CHEESE MOUSSE

1 pound cream cheese

1⅓ cup sugar

3 oz. Kahana Royal

1½ oz. water

¾ oz. gelatin

2½ cups heavy cream

won ton wrappers

Whip cream. Beat until smooth cream cheese and sugar. Bloom gelatin in water and Kahana Royal. Melt gelatin over water bath. Add gelatin to cheese mixture. Fold in whipped cream. Chill until ready to scoop. Bake won ton wrappers.

GINGER CARAMEL SAUCE

Simple Syrup

½ cup sugar

½ cup water

1 oz. sliced ginger

Bring to a boil. Set aside to cool.

2 cups sugar

1 cup water

2 eggs

8 oz. butter

½ cup Simple Syrup (recipe above)

Boil sugar and water until caramel. Remove from heat and add (carefully) Simple Syrup. Stir until cooled a bit. Add slightly beaten eggs and melted butter.

Hawai'i's Java Kai

With curious drink names such as "Shark Bite" and "Lava Lust," **Hawaii's Java Kai** presents an impressive selection of awesome coffee drinks, smoothies, yummy baked goods and a few heartier items. The first Java Kai to lure customers in with the wonderful aroma of fresh coffee originated in Hanalei when Jennifer and Brent Hickman took over Old Hanalei Coffee Company in 1997. Running their own business in paradise is a dream come true for the husband and wife team who continue to roast and package Hawai'i's coffees and assist in opening more Java Kai locations (which could be trouble, just driving by makes me start craving a creamy iced Mocha Anu!).

Ambiance: Casual, funky and charming, Java Kai is a good place to people watch, chat with companions or grab a magazine to enjoy with your coffee drink or smoothie.

Menu: Their most popular coffee drink, the Mocha Anu, is a creamy iced blend of espresso and chocolate. You'll also find variations of familiar coffee favorites, some unique specialties and creative fruit smoothies such as "Lava Lust"—coconut milk, mango, and pineapple juice blended with raspberry sorbet. For breakfast try the Kaua'i Waffle—a Belgian waffle with bananas, papaya and whipped cream, topped with macadamia nuts. You can also feast on quiche, a Bali Hai Burrito and more. Scrumptious baked goods include their signature Aloha Bars with toasted coconut, mac nuts and chocolate chips on a shortbread cookie crust, Macaroons dipped in chocolate, Cinnamon Rolls and a variety of muffins and cookies.

Details: Open daily from early in the morning until late afternoon or evening, depending on the season. Most items under $10.00.

(808) 245-6704 / WWW.JAVAKAI.COM
(808) 823-6887 / 4-1384 KUHIO HWY., KAPAA, KAUA'I, HI 96746
(808) 826-6717 / 5-5183 C KUHIO HWY., HANALEI, KAUA'I, HI 96714
(808) 528-7061 / 1164 BISHOP STREET, HONOLULU, O'AHU, HI 96813

KEKO BERRY FRUIT SMOOTHIE

Small
½ banana
4 oz. orange juice
½ cup frozen strawberries
1 tsp. ginger

Large
¾ banana
6 oz. orange juice
¾ cup frozen strawberries
1 tsp. ginger

Fill drink cup ¾ full of ice. Blend with above ingredients for 30 seconds.

PAPAYA SALSA

3 cups diced papayas
¾ cup diced red onions
1 cup pineapple, diced and drained
2 Tbsp. chopped cilantro

2½ tsp. cumin
1 tsp. salt
½ tsp. black pepper
¼ tsp. cayenne

Toss all ingredients in a bowl.

HUKILAU LANAI

A frequently recommended wonderful restaurant on Kaua'i, **Hukilau Lanai** opened in May 2002 and quickly became a well-loved place to relax and enjoy fine food, wine and drinks. This successful venture was created by Paige and Russ Talvi, and Roberta Wallace, the owners of Gaylord's (see page 24), along with Executive Chef Ron Miller and significant other, Krissi Miller as manager and wine expert. Krissi is the inspiration behind the 20 wines for under $20 theme and suggestions of wine pairings to complement the chef's delicious "comfort food" made with

fresh Kaua'i ingredients. The tableware was pur-chased from the owner of Coco Palms (the famous site in Elvis Presley's *Blue Hawai'i* film); perhaps you'll drink from the same bamboo-style glass that Elvis used!

Ambiance: Dine under a canopy with the romance of tiki torches, palm trees, beautiful gardens and a peek-a-boo view of the ocean. There is indoor seating as well, a pupu bar, and live music on select nights in the lounge.

Menu: Start with the smooth Kaua'i Shrimp Bisque and the unique Sashimi Stack that bursts with flavor and a satisfying crunchy texture. The sublime Sweet Potato Ravioli's are festively presented and are nicely complemented by a glass of Gewürztraminer, or try the Sugar Cane

Skewered Shrimp & Mango Chicken Duet with Joseph Phelps Pastiche, or Pork Loin with Asian spiced mandarin orange demi-glace. The fresh focaccia bread served with olive oil for dipping is perfection. Chocolate lovers will swoon over the Warm Big Island Chocolate Cake, or set your taste buds sailing with a Goat Cheese Tart with fresh mango. Outrageous!

Details: Dinner and cocktails Tuesday through Sunday. Dinner: $10.95–23.95. Reservations recommended. Located behind the Coconut Marketplace.

(808) 822–0600
KAUA'I COAST RESORT, KUHIO HWY., KAPA'A, KAUA'I, HI 96746

OKINAWAN SWEET POTATO RAVIOLI

1 pound Okinawan (purple) sweet potatoes
3 Tbsp. brown sugar
2 Tbsp. chopped garlic
3 Tbsp. butter, melted
salt and pepper
1 egg
½ tsp. cinnamon
¼ tsp. nutmeg
½ cup Parmesan cheese

⅜ tsp. salt
1 kaffir lime leaf, powdered
2 tsp. coconut syrup
1 ½ Tbsp. heavy cream
½ tsp. white pepper
2 Tbsp. sweet chili sauce
For Assembly:
6 tsp. Feta cheese
24 won ton wrappers

In a large mixing bowl, combine brown sugar, garlic, melted butter, salt and pepper. Peel sweet potatoes. Place in cold water after peeling. Dice the potatoes about an inch square and toss them with the butter and brown sugar mixture. Place the potatoes in a casserole dish and cover. Bake for 25 minutes at 350 degrees or until soft.

Rice the potatoes (run through a food mill, or simply mash them as you would mashed potatoes) then mix in the remaining ingredients (from egg through sweet chili sauce). Refrigerate until chilled.

Lay out 12 won ton wrappers. Brush each wrapper with egg. Place a heaping tablespoon of the sweet potato mix on each wrapper. Place a ½ teaspoon of feta cheese on top of the sweet potato filling. Lay a won ton wrapper on top of each one. Press together tightly to seal. Crimp each ravioli around the edge with a fork to assure a tight seal. Boil in salted water until they float. Place on a plate and top with Lemon Grass Cream Sauce.

Serves 4.

LEMON GRASS CREAM SAUCE

¾ tsp. sesame oil
1 Tbsp. fresh peeled ginger
1 Tbsp. shallots (or onions)
1 Tbsp. chopped garlic
½ stalk lemon grass
2 Tbsp. mirin

1 ½ tsp. rice wine vinegar or white vinegar
¼ cup fish or chicken stock
1 cup heavy cream
1 cup coconut milk
4 oz. chopped butter
2 Tbsp. chopped cilantro

Sauté ginger, garlic, shallots and lemon grass in the sesame oil. Add mirin, vinegar, and stock, reduce by ½. Add cream and reduce by ½ again. Add coconut milk and bring back to almost a simmer. Whisk in butter. Strain through the chinoise. Add chopped cilantro.

You may use cilantro or sesame seeds for garnish.

Makes 8 servings.

Kalaheo Coffee Co. & Café

Who can resist the alluring aroma of freshly baked cinnamon rolls or in this case, awesome Cinnamon Knuckles? The bakers at **Kalaheo Coffee Co. & Café** begin creating their delicious baked goods before most of us are awake. Owned by John and Kristina Ferguson, this friendly neighborhood eatery and coffee store serves delicious food, pastries and coffee to the community and to travelers on their way to Waimea Canyon and Koke'e State Park. Choose some tasty picnic items to go or stock up on Hawaiian and international coffees sold by the pound. John enjoys exploring the different coffee flavors and makes his own house blends as well.

Ambiance: Casual and friendly with great food at reasonable prices, Kalaheo Coffee Co. is a good place to meet a friend for lunch or relax and read a book with a pastry and a cappuccino.

Menu: They start serving breakfast early with popular items such as Belgian Waffles, Very Veggie Omelette, or their Kahili Breakfast—Portuguese sausage, ham, green onions, tomatoes and melted Monterey Jack cheese scrambled with eggs. For lunch try the daily special, including fresh fish specials, or choose from a variety of tasty salads made with local produce. Wraps and deli sandwiches are also available. Favorites are: Grilled Cajun Tofu & Eggplant and the Chicken & Bulgar Salsa Wrap. Sweet temptations to enjoy with your coffee drink, tea or a smoothie include: Macnut Shortbread Cookies, Double Chocolate Macnut Brownies, a daily special Fruit Scone, Blueberry Muffin or if you get there early enough, one of their delectable Cinnamon Knuckles.

Details: Open weekdays 6 a.m. to 3 p.m., weekends 6:30 a.m. to 2 p.m. Breakfast: $3.50–7.25. Lunch: $4.95–8.95. You can purchase their coffee from their web site: kalaheo.com or call 1-800-255-0137.

(808) 332–5858 / WWW.KALAHEO.COM
2–2436 KAUMUALII HWY., KALAHEO, KAUA'I, HI 96741

Oatmeal Fruit Scones

9 cups flour	1½ pounds soft cool butter
1½ cups sugar	20 oz. buttermilk
2 Tbsp. baking powder	10 oz. orange juice
1 Tbsp. salt	32 oz. frozen or fresh fruit
1 Tbsp. baking soda	3 Tbsp. minced orange rind
7 cups oats	

Sift dry ingredients (except oats) into a bowl and reserve. Cut butter into dry ingredients until the size of small peas. Add oats and mix into flour mixture. Split into 2 bowls to make scones of 2 different flavors. Make a well in the center and add half of the buttermilk, orange juice, fruit and orange zest to each bowl. Pull ingredients together and mix until just combined. Batter will be sticky. Scoop with large scoop and portion approximately 15 to a sheet pan. Bake at 350 degrees for approximately 20 minutes until done. This recipe can also be cut down by half or quarter.

Makes 30 scones.

Chunky Chocolate Mac Nut Bars

Crust	¾ cup corn syrup
1½ cups all purpose flour	¾ cup granulated sugar
½ cup butter, softened	2 Tbsp. butter, melted
¼ cup brown sugar, packed	1 tsp. vanilla
Filling	1¾ cups chocolate chunks
3 large eggs	1½ cups macadamia nuts

Preheat oven to 325 degrees and grease 13 x 9" pan.

Crust: Beat flour, butter and brown sugar in a mixer until crumbly. Press into pan. Bake for 12 to 15 minutes or until lightly browned.

Filling: Beat eggs, corn syrup, sugar, butter and vanilla in medium bowl with whisk. Stir in chocolate chunks and nuts. Pour evenly over baked crust and bake for 25 to 30 minutes or until set. Cool on wire rack.

KOKE'E LODGE

For an enjoyable day trip, take a journey up to beautiful Koke'e State Park where you can explore forests, hiking trails and awe–inspiring vistas. At 3,600

feet elevation, the air is crisp

and cool

and

you'll

often

find

clouds

swirling

around the

tree tops. **Koke'e Lodge** is there to warm you up with some cozy comfort food or, if you're inspired to hit the trails, you can pick up snacks to take along such as organic chips and cookies, nutritious bars and gourmet ice cream. The gift shop features many Hawaiian made food products with a lot of mini sizes (great for tasting and travel). Examples are: macadamia honey, tropical fruit jams, spicy hot sauces, and papaya or mango BBQ sauce—all are made from Kaua'i grown ingredients. Koke'e Lodge bottles their own Hawaiian Pineapple Mustard that they serve on their sandwiches. Locally grown coffees are available, and they have an excellent selection of books on Kaua'i—flora and fauna, history, lore and legends from Kaua'i writers.

Ambiance: Casual and comfortable with large picture windows that present a view of the grounds, colorful strutting roosters and inviting forests.

Menu: Try a bowl of their popular Portuguese Bean Soup ("local soul food") or chili, vegetarian or meat. Don't miss the yummy hot corn bread; the recipe has been written up in several differ-ent languages! They also have sandwiches, fresh vegetarian selections, quiche, and some unique flavorful salads: Moroccan Salad, Blue Cheese and Pear Salad, Greek Salad. For dessert, enjoy homemade Lilikoi or Shredded Coconut Pie or Carrot Cake with some Kaua'i grown French roast coffee. Cocktails, Kaua'i brewed beers, and wine are served as well.

Details: Light breakfast and lunch daily. Under $10.00. If you want to have more time to hike and explore the area, cabins are available for overnight stays; call ahead for reservations.

(808) 335–6061
3600 KOKE'E ROAD, KOKE'E STATE PARK, KAUA'I, HI 96796

KOKEʻE LODGE CHILI

Chili Spice Mix
2 Tbsp. plus 2 tsp. dark chili powder
1 Tbsp. plus 1 tsp. garlic powder
1 Tbsp. basil
1 Tbsp. oregano
2 Tbsp. plus 1 tsp. sugar
1¾ tsp. salt
1¾ tsp. coarse ground black pepper

3¾ cups chopped onion
2-3 Tbsp. olive oil
3¾ pounds ground beef
1 can dark kidney beans (15-16 oz.)
 washed and drained
5 cups chili sauce
1½ cups tomato sauce
cheddar cheese and finely chopped onion

Mix dry spices for Chili Spice Mix.

Brown onions with dry spices. Add ground beef and brown. Add kidney beans. Add chili sauce and tomato sauce, then add 1 to 2 cups water. Cover and simmer 1 hour. Stir occasionally. Top each serving with 2 ounces of shredded cheddar cheese and 2 tablespoons finely chopped onion. Serve with crackers.

Makes 10 servings.

MOKIHANA COFFEE

1 shot macadamia nut liqueur
½ shot Tuaca

1 cup fresh coffee, a full-bodied bean
whipped cream

Warm mug; add liqueurs. Fill mug with fresh hot coffee and top with whipped cream.

LEMONGRASS GRILL AND SEAFOOD & SUSHI BAR

If you love sushi and fresh seafood, you'll be delighted to discover **Lemongrass Grill and Seafood & Sushi Bar** in Old Kapa'a town. The sushi bar is encircled by a waterway that transports each order of sushi to the customer after it's been placed on an individual surf board—the most unique idea I've ever seen for serving sushi! Executive Chef Wally Nishimura creates his delectable cuisine utilizing local produce with an emphasis on fresh seafood, which can be enjoyed with sake, Japanese or local beers, or house wines by the glass.

Ambiance: In the two–story pagoda–style building, you will enjoy a lovely setting decorated with Asian artwork, carvings and sculptures, and large vases bursting with fresh tropical flowers. You may also dine outdoors with the flickering light of tiki torches.

Menu: Choose from a full selection of sushi including Hand Rolls, Cut Rolls, Nigiri, Combos, and Sashimi. Starters include Fried 'Ahi Sushi Roll and Kalua Won Tons. For your next course, try the Shrimp and Moloaa Papaya Salad with Mango Thai Dressing or a Papaya Bisque, followed by a Lemongrass specialty of Huli Huli Chicken Breast served with fresh corn and spicy rice. Grilled Fresh Catch on Oriental Stir Fry, Grilled Pork Loin with Tropical Mango Pineapple Relish, or Grilled Salmon with Ginger Lemon Grass Aioli are also excellent choices.

Details: Open nightly. Starters, soups and salads from $5.00. Entrées: $12.95–21.00. Reservations recommended.

(808) 821–2888
4–885 KUHIO HIGHWAY, KAPA'A, KAUA'I, HI 96746

Sautéed Jumbo Sea Scallops

6 pieces sea scallops, individually quick frozen
3 oz. garlic mashed potatoes
2 oz. Shiitake Mushroom Relish (recipe below)
¼ cup Miso Vinaigrette (recipe below)

1 ½ oz. Buerre Blanc (recipe below)
½ tsp. tobiko
1 Tbsp. Jade Sauce (recipe below)
salt and cracked pepper corn to taste

Season scallops with salt and cracked pepper corn, then sauté on medium heat with olive oil until caramelized. Arrange on plate with garlic mashed potatoes in center, then around with Shiitake Mushroom Relish. Place 6 medium drops of Buerre Blanc with scallops on top. Add a small amount of Jade Sauce on scallops then tobiko. Garnish with a couple of pieces of deep fried long rice. Sprinkle a small amount of MIso Vinaigrette and black sesame seeds on dish.

Shiitake Mushroom Relish

1 shiitake mushroom, ¼" dice, and blanch
1 Tbsp. of 3 colors bell peppers, finely minced

Miso Vinaigrette, as needed to moisten

MIx all together.

Miso Vinaigrette

1 large egg
2 tsp. white vinegar
½ tsp. ginger juice

¼ tsp. peanut butter
⅛ tsp. sesame oil
½ cup olive oil

In blender combine egg, vinegar and ginger juice. Blend until incorporated, then add peanut butter, sesame oil, then olive oil until the right consistency is achieved.

Buerre Blanc

½ cup white wine
1 small piece bay leaf
4 Tbsp. white vinegar

1 Tbsp. whole black pepper corn
¼ cup heavy cream
¼ pound unsalted butter

Reduce wine, vinegar, bay leaf and black pepper corn until almost gone, then add cream. Reduce until ½ or thickened. Add salt and butter and additional salt as needed.

Jade Sauce

1 ½ oz. peeled fresh ginger
1 oz. diced green onion
1 ½ oz. cilantro
1 Tbsp. sugar

½ tsp. fish sauce (patis)
3 small drops sriracha (red hot sauce)
2 oz. olive oil

Blend all together well.

PLANTATION GARDENS RESTAURANT & BAR

A Zagat Survey award winner, **Plantation Gardens Restaurant & Bar** invites you to experience the flavors of Kaua'i in a beautifully restored plantation home built in 1932. Born and raised on Kaua'i, Chef Brenda Silva-Morando blends her "local girl" heritage, Portuguese background, love of Kaua'i and the ethnic diversity of the islands to create her unique Hawaiian Fusion Pacific Rim Cuisine. Originally inspired by her grandmother, Chef Brenda uses locally caught fresh fish and Kaua'i produce, including vegetables and herbs grown organically in the restaurant's garden.

Ambiance: Enjoy relaxed island elegance in this historic plantation home surrounded by enchanting gardens bursting with colorful orchids, succulents, cacti and koi ponds. Refurbished with rich Brazilian cherry wood floors and koa trim, the home now features a large open-air veranda for your dining pleasure.

Menu: Pupu selections include Kekaha Shrimp and 'Ahi Poke Wontons or Crab and Rock Shrimp Stuffed Shiitake Mushrooms. A favorite Fresh Catch is the Hawaiian Mixed Grill—fresh ono, lobster and shrimp with caper lemon butter cream sauce, or for a local flavor try the Seafood Lau Lau. House Smoked Pork Tenderloin, and Jumbo Scallops Stir Fry are also popular choices. For dessert try the irresistible Banana Lumpia or Warm Chocolate Cake.

Details: Dinner nightly. Reservations recommended. Dinner entrées: $15.95–27.95. Formerly named Piatti Kaua'i Restaurant.

(808) 742–2216
2253 Po'ipu Road, Kiahuna Plantation Resort, Po'ipu, Kaua'i, HI 96756

Plantation Gardens Seafood Lau Lau

8 oz. fresh mahimahi

8 fresh prawns

8 jumbo scallops

8 oz. julliened oriental vegetables

4 oz. fresh spinach

8 pieces ti leaves

Marinate seafood for 1 hour in:

¼ tsp. garlic

¼ tsp. ginger

⅛ cup oyster sauce

2 Tbsp. sesame oil

⅛ cup scallions

⅛ cup mirin rice vinegar

black pepper and salt to taste

Chili Pepper Lemon Grass Aioli

⅓ cup fresh mayonnaise

1 small Hawaiian chili pepper

1 tsp. minced lemon grass

1 tsp. shiso basil

1 Tbsp. lime juice

salt and pepper to taste

Lay 2 ti leaves down in a cross pattern and place the spinach first, then the julienned vegetables, then the seafood in the center. Grab the 4 ends of ti leaves making a pouch and, using one end, tie in a knot. Place in steamer for 5 minutes. Serve with Chili Pepper Lemon Grass Aioli, steamed sticky rice, cold beer and Hawaiian music.

Serves 4.

Plantation Gardens Banana Lumpia

4 bananas

2 tsp. Hawaiian brown sugar

½ tsp. cinnamon

1 vanilla bean

16 sheets lumpia wrappers

1 fresh egg

4 sprigs fresh mint

⅓ cup Chocolate Sauce (recipe below)

⅓ cup Creme Anglaise (recipe below)

1 scoop vanilla ice cream

Cut bananas in 4's. Add brown sugar, cinnamon, vanilla bean and mix lightly without breaking bananas. Lay 1 piece of banana on 1 corner of lumpia wrapper and fold 2 corners over. Roll until 1 corner is left at top. Brush with egg wash and fry until golden brown and crispy. Serve with vanilla ice cream, Chocolate Sauce, Creme Anglaise and fresh mint.

Serves 4.

Chocolate Sauce

3 oz. Hawaiian Vintage dark chocolate

¼ cup heavy whipping cream

Melt chocolate and whipping cream in a double boiler until melted. Mix well and keep warm.

Creme Anglaise

½ cup whipping cream

2 oz. sugar

3 egg yolks

½ vanilla bean

Mix ingredients in a stainless steel bowl and cook in double boiler on medium heat whipping constantly until thickened.

TIDEPOOLS

Lush and inviting, with ponds and meandering pathways, the beautifully landscaped grounds of the Hyatt will lead you to **Tidepools** where grass thatched huts appearing to float over a freshwater lagoon create a romantic tropical setting. Tidepools features Contemporary Regional Hawaiian Cuisine. Executive Chef David Boucher explains, "This type of cuisine is indigenous to Kaua'i and Hawai'i. Because of the island's diverse culture, we can use items made from Hawaiian ingredients, such as local somen noodles, local fish, bison, fruits, vegetables, taro chips and even taro ice cream. We are bringing to life the traditional Hawaiian cuisine and presenting it in a new way." Tidepools was honored with the 2003 Hale 'Aina Restaurant-of-Distinction Award.

Ambiance: A mesmerizing open–air setting with ocean breezes and a waterfall nearby. As evening sets in, the glow in the sky from the sunset is replaced by the flickering light of tiki torches reflecting across the shimmering lagoon.

Menu: For a tantalizing appetizer try Kimo's Crab Cake followed by the popular Big Island Baby Romaine Salad with goat cheese. Tidepools' signature dish is the Macadamia Nut Crusted Mahimahi with a Kahlua, lime, ginger butter sauce and Jasmine rice. You may also want to try one of the fresh fish specials. Local fishermen call in the catch of the day before the fish arrives so the chefs can begin planning the evening's specials. Desserts include a delicious Warm Apple Tart with ice cream or Coconut Creme Brulée. Enjoy!

Details: Dinner nightly. Entrées: $22.00–34.00. Reservations recommended. Resort wear acceptable.

(808) 742–6260
HYATT REGENCY KAUA'I, PO'IPU, KAUA'I, HI 96756

Wok–Seared Tiger Shrimp

5 pieces shrimp
pinch lemon grass
1 oz. red bell peppers, julienne
1 oz. yellow bell peppers, julienne
1 oz. onions, julienne
1 oz. shiitake mushrooms, julienne
pinch garlic
pinch ginger

2 oz. white wine
1½ oz. braising greens
2½ oz. Coconut Curry Sauce (recipe below)
2 oz. Jasmine Rice (recipe below)
Garnish:
miniature greens
red ginger
rice noodles, deep fried

In a hot sauté pan with oil, add shrimp, lemon grass, bell peppers, onion, shiitake mushrooms, garlic and ginger. Sauté for 30 seconds. Add white wine and cook until shrimp is ½ cooked. Add braising greens. Season with salt and pepper. Makes 1 serving.

Lemon Grass Coconut Curry Sauce

2 oz. butter
½ oz. lemon grass
½ oz. garlic
18 oz. coconut milk
8 oz. clam juice
6 oz. brown sugar
¾ oz. green curry
¾ oz. lemon juice

1 piece lime leaf
½ oz. fish sauce (patis)
3 oz. cornstarch
6 oz. water
Jasmine Rice
desired amount of jasmine rice
1 small stalk lemon grass
1 lime leaf

In sauce pan with butter, add lemon grass and garlic. Sauté for 10–15 seconds. Add coconut milk, clam juice, brown sugar, green curry, lemon juice, lime leaf and patis. Bring to a boil; simmer for 20 minutes. Thicken with cornstarch slurry to desired consistency.

Prepare jasmine rice; add lemon grass and lime leaf.

Coconut Lobster Soup

2 Tbsp. chopped ginger
2 Tbsp. chopped garlic
2 Tbsp. red curry paste (Thai)
2 stalks lemon grass
2 Tbsp. lobster base
2 Tbsp. tomato paste

1 cup white wine
6 cups clam juice
3 cups coconut milk
1 tsp. lime juice
3 oz. lobster meat

Cook in a sauce pot: ginger, garlic, red curry paste, lemon grass, lobster base and tomato paste. After 30 seconds add white wine and reduce by ½. Add the clam juice and coconut milk, bring to a boil then simmer for 10–15 minutes to infuse flavor. If you would like thicker soup, use a small amount of cornstarch to thicken. Strain through a fine strainer; adjust seasoning with salt and pepper and add lime juice. Steam the lobster meat ahead of time and then garnish the soup.

Serves 4.

CREATIVE HAWAIIAN/PACIFIC RIM

WRANGLER'S STEAKHOUSE

On the sunny and warm west side of Kaua'i, **Wrangler's Steakhouse** is a great place to stop for refreshments and a sizzling steak or fresh fish. The paniolo (Hawaiian cowboy) theme is authentic, owner Colleen Faye grew up riding horses—rodeos and herding cattle were part of her childhood. Her father made some of the saddles and bridles that now hang in Wrangler's, which also has a shop that features items by local artists.

Ambiance: Casual and friendly, Wrangler's is situated in a historic plantation–style building with open–beam ceilings, fans, wood floors and tables set on two levels. You can also enjoy dining on the shady lanai where you can sip your beer or Passion Fruit Margarita while watching the activity of the town.

Menu: Start with the Crab Cake with pineapple salsa or fresh 'Ahi Sashimi. The Pistachio Crusted Salmon Salad is popular for lunch and dinner. Try the "Kau Kau" Tin Lunch with beef teriyaki, shrimp and vegetable tempura, and kim chee, which is served in the traditional plantation worker tin. Dinner specialties include a New York cut Sizzling Steak, Pulehu Steak, Japanese Tempura and some seafood and vegetarian selections. For a fine finish, try the Peach Cobbler or Lilikoi Dream Pie.

Details: Lunch served Monday through Friday. Dinner served Monday through Saturday. (Closed Sundays.) Lunch: $7.95–14.95. Dinner: $12.95–35.00.

(808) 338–1218
9852 KAUMUALII HIGHWAY, WAIMEA, KAUA'I, HI 96796

CLAM CHOWDER

1 quart half and half

1 cup chopped clams

10 pieces of bacon

1 onion, medium dice

3 sticks of celery, medium dice

8 oz. flour

2 quarts clam stock

⅛ tsp. thyme

2 bay leaves

8 oz. butter

Sauté bacon, onion and celery until translucent. Add flour and cook for a few minutes. Add clam stock, thyme, bay leaves, chopped clams and simmer for a few minutes. Add half and half.

PEACH COBBLER

Crust

1 pound pastry flour

8 oz. shortening

2 oz. butter

¾ cup cold water (40 degrees F)

1 tsp. salt

1 Tbsp. sugar

Mix water, salt and sugar. Mix flour, shortening and butter with hands until small ball forms. Add water, don't over mix, then roll out.

Makes 2 9″ pie crusts.

Filling

2 pounds sliced peaches

1 cup sugar

½ tsp. cinnamon

½ tsp. salt

1 cup passion orange juice

½ cup cornstarch

¼ cup butter

Cook peaches, sugar, cinnamon and salt until mixture starts to simmer. Add passion orange juice and cornstarch to thicken. Then add butter, turn off stove and let cool. Fill oven proof bowl with peach filling and cover with crust making sure to press edges to seal. Slit top of crust to vent and bake at 350 degrees for 20 minutes or until golden brown.

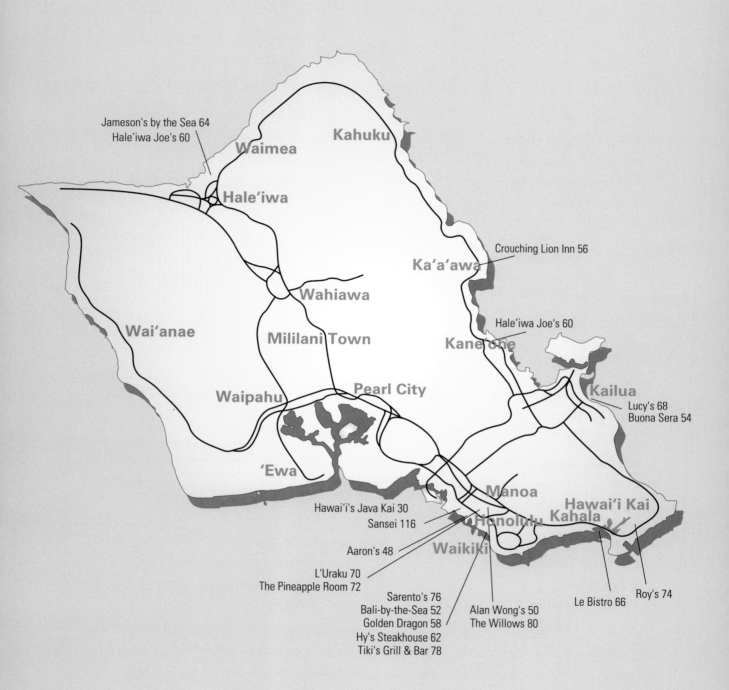

Jameson's by the Sea 64
Hale'iwa Joe's 60

Waimea

Kahuku

Hale'iwa

Crouching Lion Inn 56

Ka'a'awa

Wahiawa

Hale'iwa Joe's 60

Wai'anae

Mililani Town

Kane'ohe

Kailua

Waipahu

Pearl City

Lucy's 68
Buona Sera 54

'Ewa

Hawai'i's Java Kai 30
Sansei 116

Manoa

Hawai'i Kai
Kahala

Honolulu

Aaron's 48

Waikiki

L'Uraku 70
The Pineapple Room 72

Le Bistro 66

Roy's 74

Sarento's 76
Bali-by-the-Sea 52
Golden Dragon 58
Hy's Steakhouse 62
Tiki's Grill & Bar 78

Alan Wong's 50
The Willows 80

O'AHU
THE GATHERING PLACE

O'AHU

Restaurant, Page, Type of Cuisine
Recipes Featured

Aaron's Atop the Ala Moana, 48, Classic American Continental
Fresh Oysters with 'Ahi Tartare & Lilikoi Mignonette

Alan Wong's Restaurant, 50, Hawai'i Regional
Shrimp and Clams with Chili Lemon Grass Black Bean Sauce

Bali by the Sea, 52, Pacific Rim
Island Bouillabaisse / Baguette / Pepper Pineapple Dessert / Cream of Cocoa Sauce

Buona Sera Italian Restaurant, 54, Italian
Chicken Buona Sera / Linguine Diavola

Crouching Lion Inn, 56, American
Chicken Macadamia / Honey Garlic Shrimp

Golden Dragon, 58, Cantonese and Szechwan
Scallop Stir Fry with Baby Eggplant / Kung Pao Shrimp

Hale'iwa Joe's Seafood Grill, 60, Fresh Fish, Seafood & Steak
'Ahi Spring Rolls / Sesame Miso Dressing

Hawai'i's Java Kai, 30, Specialty Coffee House
Keko Berry Fruit Smoothie / Papaya Salsa

Hy's Steakhouse, 62, Prime Steak & Seafood
Caesar Salad / Banana Foster

Jameson's by the Sea, 64, Fresh Seafood & Steak
Baked Stuffed Shrimp

Le Bistro, 66, Continental
Salt Baked Moi / Roasted Sea Bass with Serrano Ham & Rosemary

Lucy's Grill 'n Bar, 68, Euro/Local
Lucy's Pick–it Salad / Lucy's Szechwan Prawns with Spicy Black Bean Cream Sauce

L'Uraku Restaurant, 70, Euro–Japanese
Garlic Shichimi 'Ahi with Ponzu Vinaigrette / Agedashi Tofu

The Pineapple Room, 72, Hawai'i Regional
Pineapple BBQ Ribs / Wok Charred Soy Beans with Garlic and Chilies

Roy's Restaurant, 74, Hawaiian Fusian Style
Coconut Tiger Shrimp Sticks with a Thai Style Cocktail Sauce / Szechwan Baby Back Ribs with a Mongolian Marinade

Sansei Seafood Restaurant & Sushi Bar, 116, Japanese-Based Hawaiian Regional
Macadamia Nut Crusted Tiger Prawn Temaki (Hand Rolled Sushi) / Sansei Seared Scallop and Foie Gras

Sarento's Top of the "I", 76, Multi–Regional Italian
Eggplant Tapenade / Tiramisu

Tiki's Grill & Bar, 78, South Pacific with Island Flavors
Five Spiced Seared Scallops / Saffron Coconut Clams

The Willows, 80, Hawaiian/American
The Willows Curry / Bacon Wrapped Shrimp with Lobster Cream Sauce

AARON'S ATOP THE ALA MOANA

An excellent choice for a stellar evening of celebration for any occasion, **Aaron's Atop the Ala Moana** features award-winning cuisine, outstanding views and first–rate service. Aaron's received the 2002 Hale 'Aina Award for Best Restaurant along with Ilima Awards for Best Service and Best View. The restaurant is named in honor of Aaron Placourakis who is President and CEO of Tri-Star Restaurant Group. Jiro Noguchi and Al Souza are also partners in this successful company that owns 3 outstanding sister restaurants. Corporate Chef George Gomes, Jr., a "culinary pioneer" oversees the four restaurants and is the creative genius behind the menus.

Ambiance: From this glorious vantage point on the 36th floor you will be awed by the stunning sunset, views of Magic Island Beach, and as the sky darkens, the sparkling lights of Honolulu. Aaron's features a unique private dining room—a glass-enclosed 2,000 bottle wine cellar. Enjoy live music Wednesday through Saturday.

Menu: For appetizers, choose from Crab Cakes to Caviar. The Greek Maui Wowie Special salad is a fabulous burst of fresh zesty flavors—Tomatoes, avocado, Maui onions, feta cheese and bay shrimp. Signature dishes include Live Kona Maine Lobster, Steamed Island Onaga and Opakapaka Gabriella. Prime steaks, veal, lamb and chicken favorites are also served. With a regal selection of fine domestic and imported wines, you are sure to find the perfect complement for your dinner.

Details: Open nightly. Entrées from $23.95. Late night supper menu and late night entertainment. Located on the top floor of the Ala Moana Hotel. Valet service or self parking. Sister Tri-Star restaurants are Sarento's Top of the "I", page 76, Nick's Fishmarket Maui, page 110, and Sarento's on the Beach Maui, 118.

(808) 955–4466 / WWW.TRI-STAR-RESTAURANTS.COM
410 ATKINSON DRIVE, ALA MOANA HOTEL, HONOLULU, O'AHU, HI 96814

Fresh Oysters with 'Ahi Tartare
& Lilikoi Mignonette

20 fresh oysters

½ pound 'ahi, sashimi grade, finely diced

1 Tbsp. fresh chives, chopped

1 Tbsp. white truffle oil

sea salt to taste

Lilikoi Mignonette

½ cup rice wine vinegar

1 Tbsp. sugar

1 finely diced shallot

¼ tsp. fresh thyme leaves, chopped

¼ cup lilikoi puree

sea salt to taste

fresh cracked pepper to taste

Avruga caviar, as garnish

Mignonette: Combine all ingredients and refrigerate for 2 hours before serving.

Tartare: Gently combine 'ahi, chives, truffle oil and season with salt.

To serve, place oysters on ice, spoon Tartare on top and drizzle with Lilikoi Mignonette. Top with caviar and serve immediately.

Serves 5, 4 pieces each.

Classic American Continental

ALAN WONG'S RESTAURANT

With Island roots, Asian heritage and classical training, Alan Wong, chef and owner of **Alan Wong's Restaurant**, has become a star attraction in the culinary world. One of the pioneers of Hawai'i Regional Cuisine, he utilizes fresh local ingredients to create food that is innovative, imaginative, and has even been referred to as witty. He is known for his humbleness, sense of humor and creativity. His exceptionally popular restaurant continues to gain national recognition and is a local favorite winning Hale 'Aina awards every year. In 1996 Chef Wong was honored with the prestigious James Beard Foundation "Best Pacific-Northwest Chef" award. Chef Wong, who loves to teach, shares his expertise in his own beautiful cookbook, *New Wave Luau*, which features his recipes along with photographs and other interesting information.

Ambiance: Alan Wong's Restaurant, on the third floor of an office building, offers a city view from the glassed-in lanai, the excitement of an exhibition kitchen and award-winning service.

Menu: Enjoy the flavorful Ginger Crusted Onaga with Miso Sesame Vinaigrette or Macadamia Nut-Coconut Crusted Lamb Chops. Outrageous appetizers include: Nori Wrapped Tempura 'Ahi, "Poki-Pines" crispy won ton ahi poke balls on avocado with wasabi sauce, and "Hot" California Rolls– baked Kona lobster mousse wrapped in nori with crab avocado stuffing. If you

still have room for dessert, try the artfully presented and aptly named "The Coconut" haupia sorbet in a chocolate shell served with tropical fruits and lilikoi sauce.

Details: Open nightly. Entrées: $26.00–38.00. Call for reservations. Another Alan Wong restaurant is The Pineapple Room, see page 72.

(808) 949-2526 / WWW.ALANWONGS.COM
1857 SOUTH KING STREET, 3RD FLOOR, HONOLULU, OAHU, HI 96826

SHRIMP AND CLAMS
WITH CHILI LEMON GRASS BLACK BEAN SAUCE

3 pieces 16/20 shrimp, peeled & deveined

3 pieces manila clams, washed

4 oz. penne pasta, cooked

½ tsp. garlic, minced

1 oz. onion, diced

½ tsp. ginger, minced

1 oz. lemon grass, sliced

1 tsp. Chinese black beans, rinsed & drained

1 oz. sherry wine

1 Tbsp. Thai chili sauce

2 oz. snow peas

1 oz. tomato, diced

1 oz. chicken stock

3 Tbsp. butter

salt and pepper to taste

With a hot sauté pan, sear shrimp and clams. Add garlic, onion, ginger, lemon grass and chinese black beans. Deglaze with sherry wine. Add Thai chili sauce, snow peas, tomato, pasta, chicken stock and butter. Cover pan and simmer until seafood is fully cooked and butter is melted. Season with salt and pepper. Add more Thai chili sauce for desired taste.

Serves 1.

HAWAI'I REGIONAL

BALI BY THE SEA

Romantic and alluring, **Bali by the Sea** will capture your imagination and please your senses with all the right elements—beauty, elegance and perfect service that is friendly and gracious and completely unpretentious. Selected as one of the top 14 restaurants on O'ahu, Bali received the 2003 Hale 'Aina award and Best Restaurant Wine List. With selections from Italy, France, Germany, and America, you're sure to find perfect wine to enhance your culinary experience. Chef Roberto Los Baños brings his unique island flair to the exquisite Pacific Rim cuisine; the food is artfully presented, the flavors outstanding.

Ambiance: Comfortable chairs, candlelight, orchids and large open windows that invite the soft sound and breeze from the ocean to come in and mingle, blend with a spectacular view of the sunset, palm trees, lit up cruise ships, and waves caressing the sand.

Menu: Begin with the sumptuous Trio of Fresh Island 'Ahi—'Ahi Avocado Cake, 'Ahi Lemon Grass Trap and Sashimi, or Bali by the Sea Sampler—Crispy Prawns, Seared Scallops, Beet Salad and 'Ahi Avocado. For a flavorful salad try the Roasted Beet and Maui Surfin' Goat Cheese Salad, then, for an entrée the Sautéed Island Opakapaka Crusted with Macadamia Nuts and Cilantro, Roast Rack of Sonoma Lamb with Orange Hoisin Glaze or Poached Kona Lobster served with truffle risotto, asparagus, baby carrots and lemon garlic butter.

Details: Dinner served Monday through Saturday, entrées: $17.50–44.00. Reservations are recommended. Complimentary valet and self parking.

(808) 941–2254 / WWW.HILTONHAWAIIANVILLAGE.COM
HILTON HAWAIIAN VILLAGE BEACH RESORT & SPA, 2005 KALIA ROAD, HONOLULU, O'AHU, HI 96815

ISLAND BOUILLABAISSE

2 oz. celery, cubed
3 oz. onion, cubed
3 oz. leeks, cubed
3 oz. carrots, cubed
3 oz. fennel, cubed
2 oz. olive oil
5 oz. potatoes, cubed
1 can whole peeled tomatoes, chopped

1 oz. garlic, chopped
bay leaves
⅛ oz. saffron
5 oz. cream
1 pound opakapaka
20 shrimp
20 scallops
fresh parsley for garnish

In a large pan, heat olive oil. Sauté all vegetables, except potato, for 5 minutes. Add potatoes, tomatoes, garlic, bay leaves, and saffron. Cook for 35 minutes. Add cream and seafood, simmer for 5 minutes. Add parsley for garnish.

BAGUETTE

1 oz. chopped parsley
4 oz. extra virgin olive oil
½ oz. garlic, chopped

5 egg yolks
20 baguettes
salt, pepper and saffron to taste

Combine olive oil, garlic, egg yolk, saffron and salt and pepper. Spread on baguette and toast. Cut into 3″ pieces and serve with Island Bouillabaisse.

PEPPER PINEAPPLE DESSERT

½ of a whole pineapple
2 oz. butter
¼ tsp. black pepper
½ cup cream of Cocoa Sauce (recipe below)

1 cup coconut ice cream
3 hippen
2 oz. raspberries
2 oz. strawberries

Core pineapple and cut large dice from meat. Heat sauté pan over high heat. Add butter and let brown slightly. Then add pineapple chunks and pepper. Caramelize meat. Next add the Cocoa Sauce and bring to a boil. Arrange in a ½ pineapple. Top with ice cream, hippen, fruit garnishes and drizzle sauce over warm pineapple.

CREAM OF COCOA SAUCE

1 Tbsp. butter
6 oz. brown sugar
1 cup orange juice

juice of 1 lemon
¼ cup cocoa liquor
½ cup heavy cream

Melt butter in sauce pan and brown lightly. Add brown sugar and mix well. Then add orange juice and lemon juice. Cook for 1 minute. Add cocoa liquor, heavy cream and cook for about another minute.

Chef Roberto Los Baños

PACIFIC RIM

BUONA SERA ITALIAN RESTAURANT

A new discovery for *Tasting Paradise*, **Buona Sera Italian Restaurant** is recommended by many residents of Kailua including several Bed and Breakfast hosts who enjoy sending their guests there.

Owners Kevin and Cammi Ma believe that running one small great restaurant is plenty; it allows them time to offer personal attention to their guests and still have time to spend with their three children. Kevin cooks with fresh ingredients and is careful to keep the cuisine light, which is something their customers appreciate. You'll also find consistent quality because Kevin prepares every meal while Cammi and crew graciously run the dining room.

Ambiance: Small and friendly, regular guests become friends and even vacationers return year after year! The personality of this intimate setting is enhanced by an abundance of Chianti bottles wrapped in straw baskets covering the ceiling and much of the walls. If you'd like to contribute your bit of history to their collection, order the Chianti to enjoy with your dinner. When you're finished, they'll provide markers for you to decorate and/or sign your bottle and it will be placed among the others.

Menu: A favorite appetizer is the Escargots Stagionale. House specialties include the popular Chicken Buona Sera sautéed with fresh spinach, roasted pepper, garlic, capers and Romano cheese, or Shrimp Veneziana sautéed with bacon, fresh basil and garlic, served with marinara sauce. They offer many vegetarian selections including Eggplant Sorrentino. Beer and wine served.

Details: Open nightly. Sunday through Thursday 5:30 to 9 p.m. Friday and Saturday 5:30 to 10 p.m. Dinner entrées: $9.00–13.00.

(808) 263–7696
131 HEKILI STREET, KAILUA, OʻAHU, HI 96734

CHICKEN BUONA SERA

7 oz. fresh chicken, cut into strips
1 Tbsp. garlic, chopped
1 Tbsp. extra virgin olive oil
½ Tbsp. capers
2½ Tbsp. roasted red bell pepper, chopped
½ cup spinach

½ cup chicken stock
¼ tsp. kosher salt
⅛ tsp. ground black pepper
½ Tbsp. dried basil
¼ pound linguine pasta

Sauté chicken five to 10 minutes with garlic in extra virgin olive oil. Add capers, roasted red bell pepper, spinach and chicken stock. Season with salt, ground black pepper, and dried basil. Sauté for another 3 minutes. Serve over cooked pasta.

LINGUINE DIAVOLA

2½ Tbsp. black olives, sliced
2½ Tbsp. pepperoncini, chopped
2½ Tbsp. sun-dried tomatos, chopped
1 Tbsp. garlic, chopped
1 Tbsp. extra virgin olive oil

¼ tsp. kosher salt
⅛ tsp. ground black pepper
½ Tbsp. dried basil
2½ Tbsp. fresh basil leaf
¼ pound linguine pasta

Sauté black olives, pepperoncini, sun-dried tomato and garlic in extra virgin olive oil for 5 minutes. Season with salt, ground black pepper and dried basil. Add fresh basil. Sauté for another minute. Serve over cooked pasta.

CROUCHING LION INN

The spectacular scenery you'll find on the way to **Crouching Lion Inn** will surround you with impressive natural elements—vertical verdant mountains towering above you on one side and the glistening turquoise sea on the other. Nestled behind the inn, notice the landmark rock formation in the form of a crouching lion. If you'd like to know the legend of the crouching lion, ask at the restaurant. The Inn was originally built as a family residence in 1926, and was converted to a restaurant in 1957. Be sure to explore the gallery downstairs featuring "gifts of aloha" and a beautiful selection of art by well-known artists of Hawai'i.

Ambiance: Hawaiian hospitality has been experienced here for many years, and you will definitely feel the spirit of aloha when you are greeted by Frances "Fattie" Bryant, who is the manager and has worked there for 20-something years. Dine indoors or outside on the lanai with ocean breezes and a great view of Kahana Bay, a perfect place to sip a Polynesian drink.

Menu: Entrées include: Shrimp Salad, Rotisserie Chicken, Kalua Pork and fresh Island fish purchased daily at local fish auctions. Also, there are hamburgers, sandwiches, salads and their own homemade buns. Dinner choices include seafood, steak, vegetarian selections, and their specialty Slavonic Steak. Desserts are prepared daily in their bakery; try the outrageous Mile High Pie (another house specialty).

Details: Open daily. Lunch: $4.95–12.95. Dinner: $11.95–29.95. Early bird dinner from 5 to 7 p.m. nightly (except on holidays) $10.95.

(808) 237-8511
51–666 KAMEHAMEHA HIGHWAY, KA'A'AWA, O'AHU, HI 96730

Chicken Macadamia

20–25 pounds chicken breasts

diced macadamia nuts

Sweet and Sour Sauce

1 quart ketchup

1 quart cider vinegar

1 cup sweet and sour mix

1½ pounds brown sugar

4 oz. cornstarch

1 clove garlic

1 oz. ginger

3 quarts water

Chicken Batter

7 eggs

4 oz. salad oil

4 oz. shoyu

4 oz. brandy

4 oz. cornstarch

1¾ pounds flour

¼ onion

1 oz. ginger

4 cups water

Sweet and Sour Sauce: Boil all ingredients in a pot for an hour.

Chicken Batter: Mix ingredients in a bowl until smooth.

Cut chicken breasts in half, dip in batter. Deep fry until golden brown. Place on paper towel to absorb excess oil. Top chicken with Sweet and Sour Sauce, then sprinkle with diced macadamia nuts.

Honey Garlic Shrimp

4 pounds shrimp

Sauce

5 pounds honey

½ cup sherry

2 Tbsp. sesame seeds

2 Tbsp. chopped garlic

Batter

6 cups flour

1 cup baking powder

6 eggs

4 cups water

Mix sauce ingredients together and heat. Whisk batter ingredients together. Dip shrimp in batter and deep fry. Serve with sauce.

GOLDEN DRAGON

If you're looking for a unique and memorable dining experience, enjoy an evening at the award-winning **Golden Dragon** where you will be pampered with exceptional service while feasting on Chef Steve Chiang's authentic Cantonese and Szechwan cuisine. The Golden Dragon was honored with the Hale 'Aina award 2003 Restaurant of Distinction, adding to the continual list of awards this superb restaurant has accumulated. Beginning his career by training under famous cooking masters in Taiwan over 30 years ago, Chef Chiang has been in charge of some of the finest Chinese restaurants in the United States and Canada.

Ambiance: Golden Dragon is elaborately decorated with traditional Asian touches creating a sense of place to match the food. You may also enjoy your dining experience outside on the lanai with a sunset view over a serene lagoon. Lovely tea ladies will visit your table offering exotic Chinese teas and an intriguing description of each person's Chinese horoscope, which can be extremely entertaining.

Menu: The extensive menu features many tempting items: Crispy Crab Meat Won Ton, Hot and Sour Soup, Szechwan Tenderloin of Beef, Scallops with Lychees and Asparagus, and Abalone with Shiitake Mushrooms. If you can plan ahead, indulge in a feast for two with Imperial Beggar's Chicken or Imperial Peking Duck. Both are prepared with such care that a 24 notice is required. Top off your meal with a Banana Fritter with Coconut Ice Cream or choose from the pleasing selection on their dessert cart.

Details: Dinner served Tuesday through Sunday. Entrées: $13.00–33.00. Full dinners: $34.00–50.00. Please call for reservations. Complimentary valet and self parking.

(808) 946–5336 / WWW.HILTONHAWAIIANVILLAGE.COM
HILTON HAWAIIAN VILLAGE BEACH RESORT & SPA, 2005 KALIA ROAD, HONOLULU, O'AHU, HI 96815

Scallop Stir Fry with Baby Eggplant

8 oz. scallops

2 Tbsp. egg white

1 tsp. cornstarch

3 Tbsp. + 1 tsp. salad oil

2 Tbsp. garlic

2 Tbsp. sugar

1 Tbsp. hoisin sauce

1 Tbsp. soy sauce

1 Tbsp. ginger

1 Tbsp. brandy

1 Tbsp. equal parts cornstarch and water

1 tsp. sesame oil

1 tsp. chili bean sauce

3 oz. chicken stock

½ tsp. white pepper

4 oz. baby eggplant, 8" diagonal cut pcs.

Marinate scallops with egg white, cornstarch and salad oil. Heat wok, then add 3 tablespoons of salad oil. Sauté scallops until 80% done. Remove scallops from pan. Place garlic and ginger in wok. Add scallops and remaining ingredients, except eggplant. Deep fry eggplant for 2 minutes. Serve stir fry with fried eggplant on top. Enjoy!

Serves 4.

Kung Pao Shrimp

15 pieces fresh shrimp

1 Tbsp. egg white

1 tsp. cornstarch

3 Tbsp. + 1 tsp. salad oil

5 pieces dried chili pepper

6 1" pieces white portion of green onion

2 Tbsp. hoisin sauce

1 Tbsp. ketchup

1 Tbsp. soy sauce

1 Tbsp. white vinegar

1 Tbsp. sugar

1 Tbsp. brandy

1 Tbsp. sesame oil

Marinate shrimp with egg white, cornstarch and 1 teaspoon salad oil. Heat wok, then add 3 tablespoons of salad oil. Sauté shrimp until 80% done. Remove shrimp. Place dry chili pepper in wok. Sauté until color becomes black. Add remaining ingredients, then add partially cooked shrimp and stir fry. Enjoy!

Serves 4.

Chef Steve Chiang

HALE'IWA JOE'S SEAFOOD GRILL

The North Shore is a mecca for surfers and other ocean sport enthusiasts and the owners of **Hale'iwa Joe's Seafood Grill** are no exception. Created by Joe Lazar, John Creed, Tim York, Steve McGilland and Moe Lerner, Hale'iwa Joe's is a place to have fun and fill up on fresh tasty food with portions that are intentionally large enough to satisfy the big appetites of surfers and they're offered at a good price.

Ambiance: At the North Shore location you can relax and enjoy a view of Hale'iwa Harbor from the lanai or the dining room, which is deco-rated with surf boards and big wave/surf photos. The lovely open-air Ha'iku Gardens site offers an exceptional view of lush gardens and mountains. Live music on alternating Friday nights at both restaurants.

Menu: Lunch includes: Grilled Cajun Fish Sandwich, Sticky Ribs and tasty specials. Both lunch and dinner menus feature tempting "small plates" of Thai Fried Calamari, Joe's Tempura Crab Roll (yum!) and other choices. For a salad, try the popular Grilled Salmon Spinach Salad or Sumatran Grilled Beef Salad. For dinner, Joe recommends the Fresh Whole Hawaiian Moi, Crunchy Coconut Shrimp or Prime Rib. For dessert: Burnt Caramel Macadamia or the sublime Love Cake. Full bars at both locations.

Details: Hale'iwa location open daily for lunch, $6.25–18.50 and dinner, $9.75–22.95. The Ha'iku Gardens location serves dinner and Sunday brunch (no lunches). Dinner reservations recommended.

(808) 637–8005 / 66–011 KAMEHAMEHA HWY., HALE'IWA, O'AHU, HI 96712
(808) 247–6671 / 46–336 HAIKU ROAD, KANEOHE, O'AHU, HI 96744

'AHI SPRING ROLLS

3¾ pounds 'ahi

1 gallon Napa cabbage, shredded

1 quart red cabbage, shredded

2 cups carrots, grated

2 pkgs. enoki mushrooms, cut in thirds

1 cup green onions, ⅛" slice

2 Tbsp. sesame oil

1 Tbsp. ginger, minced

1 Tbsp. garlic, minced

1 Tbsp. chili paste (Sambal Olek)

bean thread, softened

60 lumpia wrappers

Place all ingredients, except 'ahi and lumpia, in a large mixing bow. Toss until evenly mixed. Place two lumpia wrappers in the shape of a baseball diamond. Place 4 ounces of the mix in the middle (horizontally). Top with a 2 ounce piece of 'ahi. Fold the bottom edge of wrapper over mixture and roll half–way up the wrapper. Tuck both ends inward and finish rolling forward. Dab a small amount of egg wash on the end of wrapper to seal. Fry in hot oil.

Makes approximately 30 rolls.

SESAME MISO DRESSING

2½ quarts lemon juice

3⅓ cups sugar

2½ quarts miso

1¾ cups black sesame seeds

2½ quarts sesame oil

5 quarts salad oil

Mix lemon juice, sugar and miso with wire whisk until smooth and creamy. Add sesame seeds, sesame oil and salad oil and mix for 2 minutes.

Makes 3 gallons. Refrigerate for up to 2 weeks.

HY'S STEAKHOUSE

Hy's Steak House was recommended by a friend on Maui who said it was his favorite place to eat in Honolulu. Reminiscent of a private gentlemen's club, this award-winning restaurant offers something unique in the Hawai'i dining scene. The spectacular centerpiece is in the "Broiler Room" where you will be entranced watching Executive Chef Alma Arcano and his staff in action as they prepare orders over native Hawaiian Kiawe wood in a brass and copper caldron enclosed by glass. Wednesday through Sunday you can also enjoy the sweet sounds of Audy Kimura's live music wafting through the restaurant.

Ambiance: With walls of books, art, antiques, ornately carved wood moldings and a Tiffany stained glass ceiling (circa 1905) you may feel as if you're dining in an old English mansion. Waiters wearing tuxedos expertly prepare Caesar Salad, carve Chateaubriand for two and flambè sensational desserts right at your table.

Menu: Specialties include the prime grade New York Strip, Porterhouse T-Bone, Delmonico and Filet Mignon. They explain that "the kiawe wood sears the steaks with an intense heat, while complementing the flavor of the fine beef perfectly." Appetizers feature Angel Hair Pasta with Scallops, basil and garlic, or Blackened 'Ahi Sashimi with enoki mushrooms and wasabi tobiko, or Beluga Caviar. Other entrées include Hy's "Thai-style" scallops and succulent New Zealand lobster tails, or roast Rack of Lamb. Select a fine wine from their *Wine Spectator* award-winning wine list.

Details: Dinner nightly from 6 p.m. and from 5:30 p.m. on Saturdays and Sundays. Entrées begin at $17.95. Call for reservations. Valet parking.

(808) 922–5555 / WWW.HYSHAWAII.COM
2440 KUHIO AVENUE, HONOLULU, O'AHU, HI 96815

CAESAR SALAD

8 to 10 oz. romaine lettuces, cut bite sized   ½ lemon, juice
2 cups croutons   1 tsp. Worcestershire sauce
1 Tbsp. garlic, minced   ½ tsp. course grind pepper, to taste
1 egg yolk   ½ cup Parmesan cheese
1½ Tbsp. Grey Poupon mustard   ¼ olive oil
1 Tbsp. anchovy paste   2 Tbsp. red wine vinegar

Rinse and dry lettuce. Place garlic in a wooden salad bowl, mash it to a paste. Add egg yolk, mustard and anchovy paste. Keep mashing it to blend mixture well. Add lemon juice, Worcestershire sauce, pepper and Parmesan cheese. Slowly add olive oil while whisking, then add the red wine vinegar. Add romaine lettuce and croutons and toss until the leaves are evenly coated. Garnish with more Parmesan cheese on top.

Makes 2 servings.

BANANA FOSTER

¼ cup butter   4 bananas, cut 1″ thick
1 cup brown sugar   rum
½ lemon, juice   ¼ tsp. cinnamon
½ orange, juice   4 scoops vanilla ice cream (preferably
¼ cup orange Curacao   Haagen-Dazs)
¼ cup banana liquor

Combine the butter, brown sugar, lemon juice, and orange juice in a flambé pan. Cook over medium heat stirring frequently until sugar dissolves. Stir in orange Curacao and banana liquor. Place the bananas in the pan. When bananas soften and begin to brown, carefully add the rum. Continue to cook the sauce until rum is hot, then tip the pan slightly to ignite the rum. When the flames subside, lift the bananas out of the pan and place over each portion of ice cream. Generously spoon warm sauce over the top of ice cream and serve immediately.

Serves 4.

JAMESON'S BY THE SEA

For spectacular sunsets, a great ocean view and a relaxing place to enjoy good food and have a cool one, **Jameson's** is a long-standing favorite on the North Shore of O'ahu. When those famous North Shore waves are really cranking, a seat on the lanai provides an excellent view of the excitement. The Jameson's Gift Shop features a quality selection of crafts by local artists, and delicious creamy fudge from The Fudge Works. Ed Greene opened the first Jameson's in 1975. Along with the Hale'iwa location, you'll find Jameson's in Kailua-Kona on the Big Island of Hawai'i.

Ambiance: Casual and open-air, the Hale'iwa location offers dining indoors, with views of a Hawaiian fish pond and the ocean, or on the lanai where you'll be closer to the ocean and the action outdoors.

Menu: Daily specials include an assortment of fresh seafood entrées such as Mahi Mahi panko sauté with macadamia nuts. The house specialty is Opakapaka poached in white wine, topped with garlic hollandaise sauce or try the Baked Stuffed Shrimp, another popular dinner item. For lunch the Jameson's hamburger is a favorite. Try the chiffon pies (made on the premises) with tempting flavors such as Kona Coffee and Chocolate Mousse. Weekend breakfast items include pancakes, benedicts and omelettes.

Details: Open daily. Lunch: $7.00–15.00. Dinner: $16.00–25.00. Call for dinner reservations (808) 637-4336. Breakfast $3.00–10.00, served 9 a.m. to noon on Saturday and Sunday only. For dinner reservations at the Kailua-Kona location call: (808) 329-3195.

(808) 637-4336
62-540 KAMEHAMEHA HIGHWAY, HALE'IWA, O'AHU, HI 96712

BAKED STUFFED SHRIMP

48 large shrimp, butterflied

Stack 2 shrimp on top of each other. Place wedges of Crab Stuffing (recipe below) on top of shrimp and place in baking pan. Bake for 5 minutes or until shrimp are cooked. Top with Hollandaise Sauce (recipe below).

CHEESE SAUCE

12 oz. milk
dash salt
dash white pepper
dash Worcestershire sauce

2 oz. flour
dash dry mustard
2 oz. butter
14 oz. sharp cheddar cheese

Heat milk, salt, pepper and Worcestershire sauce in a large pot. Mix flour and mustard together, set aside. Add butter to pot. Mix well. When milk mixture comes to a boil, add flour mixture. Mix in well. Turn stove off. Add shredded cheese; mix well.

CRAB STUFFING

2 oz. onion, minced
1 oz. celery, minced
¼ cup butter
¼ oz. parsley, minced
¼ oz. sherry

¼ pound Dungeness crab meat
¼ pound white fish, steamed
½ pound bread crumbs
1 pint Cheese Sauce (recipe above)

Sauté together, onions and celery in butter until tender. Add parsley and sherry; mix well. In a large mixing bowl, combine all other ingredients. Mix together well. Portion and form mix into 24 wedges.

HOLLANDAISE SAUCE

5 egg yolks
24 oz. drawn butter

⅛ tsp. cayenne pepper
1 Tbsp. lemon juice

In a double boiler, heat egg yolks while stirring. Remove from heat and then slowly add butter while mixing. Add pepper and lemon juice. Mix in well.

LE BISTRO

After growing up in Niu Valley on O'ahu, Alan Takasaki, looking for adventure, traveled to New Orleans, New York, Los Angeles, France and Brussels. Now home again, his menu creations at **Le Bistro** represent flavorful influences from these diverse locals. Alan and wife Debbie (a former teacher) opened the successful eatery in September 2001; it is located in the area where he used to play after school as a boy. Their goal was to "create something for the neighborhood where people in the community can have a home base and see friends" and, of course, devour the tasty cuisine that Alan creates. He smiles as he describes how guests will go from table to table happily visiting with friends and neighbors, a rewarding moment to see the goal realized. Le Bistro was honored with the Hale'Aina Award for "Best New Restaurant" in 2003.

Ambiance: A friendly and charming neighborhood bistro with white linen table cloths, tile floors and European art, Debbie adds an inviting element with her fresh and dried flower arrangements and other thoughtful touches.

Menu: For starters try the Onion Soup or Escargot De Bourgogne. Favorite entrées include Barbequed Lamb Chops glazed with balsamic vinegar and honey, or Slow & Low Short Ribs. Alan prepares 6 nightly specials such as Opakapaka steamed in Prosseco (Italian Sparkling Wine) and on Thursdays Roast Long Island Ducking with Grand Marnier. Enjoy a glass of fine wine and for dessert try the delicious Caramelized Apple Tart.

Details: Open Wednesday through Monday 5:30 to 9 p.m. A la carte entrées, available in petite and regular portions, range from $12.80–23.80. Reservations recommended.

(808) 373–7990
NIU VALLEY SHOPPING CENTER, 5730 KALANIANAOLE HWY., HONOLULU, O'AHU, HI 96821

SALT BAKED MOI

1 1 pound whole moi, cleaned	Sauce
1 lemon, zested	¼ cup extra virgin olive oil
4 cups Hawaiian salt	1 Roma tomato, peeled and seeded
2 cups amaranth leaves	1 tsp. chives
1 cup sage	salt and pepper to taste

Cut 2 diagonal slits into moi; rub lemon zest into cuts. Pour 2 cups of salt into long copper pan, top salt with amaranth leaves, then ½ of the sage. Place moi on sage and cover with more sage and amaranth, then cover with remainder of salt. Bake for 25 minutes in 350 degree oven. Remove fish from salt and carefully brush salt off herbs. Peel herbs away from fish (skin will come off with herbs). Fillet meat onto plate and finish with sauce.

ROASTED SEA BASS WITH SERRANO HAM & ROSEMARY

5 oz. sea bass	1 Tbsp. butter
1 Tbsp. serrano ham, julienne	1 tsp. chives
white wine, to deglaze	salt and pepper to taste
1 sprig rosemary	

Place sea bass on oiled pie tin and bake in 375 degree oven for 12 minutes. When done, place fish on plate and deglaze pan with white wine. Add rosemary, ham, butter and chives. Bring to a boil and pour over fish.

LUCY'S GRILL 'N BAR

Lively and boisterous, **Lucy's Grill 'n Bar** is the popular new restaurant in Kailua that everyone is recommending. Lucy is the

Great Grandmother of owners Christian and Jiffy Schneider (brother and sister) who grew up in Lanikai and also in the restaurant business. Their parents own the legendary Buzz's Lanikai and Buzz's Pearl City. They definitely know how to please their guests, after opening the restaurant in December 2000, Lucy's won the Hale 'Aina award for the Best New Restaurant 2002, Restaurant of Distinction.

Ambiance: Fresh air and tiki torches will complement your dinner on the lanai. The interior decor is complete with mahogany tables, bubbling fish tanks, Hawaiiana paintings, an exhibition kitchen and many interesting Hawaiian artifacts that Christian has collected over the years.

Menu: Christian is the mastermind behind the mouth-watering Euro-local menu creations in which everything is made from scratch. For starters try the Spicy 'Ahi Tower, Crispy Kalua Pig Triangles, or a thin crust pizza. Along with nightly specials, dinner entrées feature the popular Szechwan Spiced Jumbo Black Tiger Prawns and Black Pan Rib Eye. They also prepare nightly dessert specials or you can try Coconut Macadamia Nut Tart or Sonia's Belgium Chocolate Walnut Brownie served ala mode. Ooh la la!

Details: Dinner nightly from 5 to 10 p.m. Entrées: $14.00–30.00. Wednesday evenings all bottles of wine are half price with the purchase of an entrée. Lucy's is also available for private parties and will cater events.

(808) 230–8188
33 AULIKE STREET, KAILUA, O'AHU, HI 96734

LUCY'S PICK-IT SALAD

romaine hearts

gorgonzola cheese

Candied Walnuts (recipe below)

Red Wine Vinaigrette (recipe below)

Prepare Candied Walnuts and Red Wine Vinaigrette. Separate leaves from romaine hearts, arrange on platter. Sprinkle Candied Walnuts and gorgonzola cheese in the middle of the romaine leaves. Drizzle with Red Wine Vinaigrette. Pick-It up and enjoy!!

Serves 4.

CANDIED WALNUTS

1 cup sugar

1 cup water

2 cups walnuts

Place walnuts on a sheet pan. Brown in 350 degree oven for 5 minutes. Let cool. In a small sauce pan bring sugar and water to a boil. Let boil until it comes to a simple syrup consistency. In a stainless steel mixing bowl, add nuts and simple syrup. Mix with wooden spoon until crystallized.

RED WINE VINAIGRETTE

pinch garlic

½ cup red wine vinegar

pinch fresh basil, chopped

pinch fresh oregano, chopped

½ cup olive oil

1 Tbsp. Dijon mustard

salt and pepper to taste

Mix all ingredients with a wire whisk until emulsified.

LUCY'S SZECHWAN PRAWNS
WITH SPICY BLACK BEAN CREAM SAUCE

5 pieces U-12 shrimp

2 tsp. black beans (Chinese)

½ tsp. garlic, chopped

½ tsp. ginger, chopped

2 tsp. scallions, chopped

2 tsp. basil, chiffonade

2 tsp. cilantro, chiffonade

pinch chili flakes

1 oz. brandy

1 oz. white wine

½ oz. oyster sauce

3 oz. heavy cream

7 oz. penne pasta, cooked

Heat sauté pan. Add shrimp and cook approximately three to four minutes. Add black beans, garlic, ginger, scallions, basil, cilantro and chili flakes. Add brandy to deglaze. Add white wine, oyster sauce and heavy cream. Let boil until sauce thickens. Add pasta and toss.

Enjoy! Serves 1.

EURO/LOCAL

L'Uraku Restaurant

Filled with creative inspiration, Chef Hiroshi Fukui of **L'Uraku** combines fresh island ingredients with his traditional Japanese training and European influences to create award-winning contemporary cuisine. He enjoys the creative process of turning basic ingredients into extraordinary creations. "I believe in layers of freshness, not layers of complicated flavors. The end result should be light and subtle, yet complex and intriguing," he explains. Recognized on the national culinary scene for his talent, Chef Hiroshi received rave reviews for the dinner he prepared at The James Beard House in New York in 2002. L'Uraku has also won the acclaimed Hale 'Aina award for 7 consecutive years, indicating their standing as one of O'ahu's top restaurants.

Ambiance: Playful and artistic, the restaurant itself is a creative inspiration filled with colorful whimsy—festive umbrellas covered with spontaneous brush strokes by expressionist painter Kiyoshi adorn the ceiling in an upside down fashion. His expression is also evident on the wall frescos, lamps, ceramics and stools filling the restaurant with an air of celebration.

Menu: Lunch includes Almond Crusted Catch of the Day served on pasta with L'Uraku's famous light miso cream sauce, Garlic Steak with steamed vegetables, arugula salad and light teriyaki sauce, Crunchy Soft Shell Crab "BLT" and Tender Greens with Grilled Salmon. Dinner features Fresh Island fish, lamb, beef and even a "Vegetarian's Dream." Signature recipes include Steamed Onaga with roasted garlic-tomato bacon vinaigrette, truffled Nalo micro greens and basil oil, and L'Uraku Style Cioppino. Enjoy their award-winning wine list recognized for "friendliness, ease of use and originality."

Details: Open daily. Lunch from $9.50. Dinner from $16.95. Reservations recommended. Located next to Ala Moana Center.

(808) 955–0552 / WWW.LURAKU.COM
1341 KAPIOLANI BOULEVARD, HONOLULU, O'AHU, HI 96814

Garlic Shichimi 'Ahi with Ponzu Vinaigrette

1 pound 'ahi filet
2 Tbsp. garlic, minced
½ tsp. salt
½ cup shichimi
1 Tbsp. onion chive, minced
2 Tbsp. daikon radish, grated

½ tsp. momiji oroshi (Japanese chili paste)
½ tomato, vine–ripened
mixed greens
½ cup ponzu sauce
¼ cup olive oil

Place 'ahi filet on cutting board and brush on minced garlic. Sprinkle salt on both sides. Roll the 'ahi in shichimi and place on a skewer. Hold the 'ahi over the open flame of the stove until it is nicely roasted. the inside should be rare. (You can also quickly sear in a hot skillet or under a broiler.)

For presentation: Slice the 'ahi thinly and lay it around the plate nicely, leaving the middle of the plate open.

Mix the grated daikon and momiji oroshi. Garnish each 'ahi slice with the daikon mixture and minced onion chive. Thinly slice the half tomato and form into a ring. Place the tomato ring in the center of the plate. Garnish with greens in the middle. Blend ponzu sauce and olive oil. Pour around the edge of the 'ahi.

Agedashi Tofu

1 piece soft tofu
½ cup potato starch
4 cups vegetable oil
2 Tbsp. grated ginger
2 Tbsp. grated daikon

1 Tbsp. ume puree
2 Tbsp. thinly sliced green onion
9 oz. Dashi (recipe below)
2 oz. light shoyu
2 oz. mirin

Bring Dashi, light shoyu and mirin to a boil in a pot and set aside. Cut the tofu into 8 square blocks. Coat them lightly in potato starch and deep fry in 350 degree oil for 4 to 6 minutes, until outside is crispy and inside warm. Place the tofu in a bowl and garnish the top with ¼ tablespoon of ginger and daikon and a dab of ume puree topped with green onions. Pour the sauce from the side until the middle of the tofu is covered with sauce. Serve immediately.

Serves 8.

Dashi

4 cups water
1 piece konbu, 2"x2" square

small handful of bonito flakes

Put the water in a pot, add konbu and start to boil, just when the water is ready to boil (you'll see small bubbles coming out from the konbu) pull out the konbu and continue to boil. When the water comes to a full boil, add the bonito and stop the fire right away. Let sit for a minute or so and strain.

THE PINEAPPLE ROOM

Since opening just in time to be included in the last edition of *Tasting Paradise*, **The Pineapple Room** has become an easy favorite featuring Alan Wong's (see page 50) fresh innovative Hawai'i Regional Cuisine. You can savor local flavors and comfort foods with a twist, in a pleasing and comfortable location on the third floor of the Ala Moana Macy's. Over 15 wines by the glass and full bar selections are available to enjoy with your lunch or dinner or at the Pineapple Room Bar, which also serves coffee drinks and features tempting pastries.

Ambiance: The Pineapple Room combines touches of old plantation days with a contemporary feel utilizing hanging lights in fish shapes, a dropped ceiling resembling the shape of a pineapple top, a lava rock enclosed pizza oven and an exhibition kitchen with a bar where guests may dine while watching the chefs.

Menu: The lunch menu includes: Crab Cakes, Kalua Pig "BLT" with half Caesar salad, Furikake and Wasabi Crusted Ahi Steak, Kiawe Grilled Kalbi Short Ribs and wood oven pizzas. Dinner offers some of the delicious lunch items mentioned plus Coconut and Macadamia Nut Crusted Lamb Chop and Ginger Crusted Opakapaka with miso sesame vinaigrette. "Grinds" (food) offered with their "Pau Hana" (after work) Drink Special include Crab and Cream Cheese Won Tons with lilikoi sweet and sour sauce and the awesome Nori Wrapped Tempura Salmon. Fabulous desserts include Fresh Fruit Tart or Chocolate Decadence.

Details: Lunch daily: $9.75–$19.50. Dinner: $10.00–30.00, Pau Hana Grinds most items under $10.00, both served Monday through Saturday. Breakfast served Saturday and Sunday only.

(808) 945-6573 / WWW.ALANWONGS.COM
MACY'S AT ALA MOANA, 3RD FLOOR, HONOLULU, O'AHU, HI 96814

Pineapple BBQ Ribs

4 cups Pineapple BBQ Sauce (recipe below)
1 (slab) baby back pork ribs
1 quart water
salt and pepper to taste

Season ribs with salt and pepper. Grill ribs (preferably over a wood burning flame for approximately 30 minutes or until fully cooked and caramelized), then place ribs into a roasting pan, add water and cover with foil. Bake in 400 degrees oven for 1hour and 45 minutes (be sure to check water level periodically; add if necessary). Remove ribs from pan and let cool. For best results, marinate ribs overnight and reheat in oven, basting with additional sauce if necessary.

Pineapple BBQ Sauce

3 cups ketchup
1 Tbsp. white vinegar
2 Tbsp. whole grain mustard
¾ cup molasses, dark
⅓ cup brown sugar
1 Tbsp. salt
2 Tbsp. Sombal
1 Tbsp. Worcestershire Sauce
2 cups grilled pineapple puree

Mix all ingredients together well. Use for marinades, basting and barbeques.

Wok Charred Soy Beans
with Garlic and Chilies

8 oz. soy beans, cooked with the shell on
1 tsp. ginger, minced
1 tsp. garlic, minced
1 piece Hawaiian chili pepper, minced
1 Tbsp. soy sauce
1 tsp. oyster sauce
½ tsp. sesame oil

In a hot wok, sauté garlic and ginger until golden brown. Then add soy beans and continue to cook until hot. Add chili, soy, oyster sauce, and sesame oil. Stir fry for additional minute and serve immediately.

Hawai'i Regional

73

ROY'S RESTAURANT

Internationally-acclaimed for his award-winning innovative Hawaiian Fusion cuisine, Chef Roy Yamaguchi, who opened the first **Roy's Restaurant** in Honolulu in 1988, has expanded his talent to become a highly successful restaurateur. With exciting, artistic and flavorful cuisine, a cutting-edge wine list, and "aloha" style service, Roy's Restaurants are wowing foodies with locations across the country. You may also catch Chef Yamaguchi on *Hawai'i Cooks with Roy Yamaguchi* aired nationally on Public Broadcast System.

Ambiance: A lively atmosphere centered around Roy's signature exhibition kitchen creates a sense of excitement and energy in each location. In the spirit of aloha, the staff is there to "totally please and indulge" every guest.

Menu: To sample Roy's definitive Hawaiian Fusion dishes, start with Hawai'i Kai Style Crispy Crab Cakes or Seared Shrimp on the Stick with Spicy Wasabi Cocktail Sauce. Favorite entrées include Hibachi Grilled Salmon, Roy's Original Blackened Island 'Ahi, and Char Broiled Honey Mustard Short Rib of Beef or try a mixed plate.

Details: Open nightly. Dinner entrées: $15.50–39.50. Reservations recommended.

WWW.ROYSRESTAURANT.COM
(808) 396–7697 / 6600 Kalanianaole Highway, Honolulu, O'ahu, HI 96825
(808) 669–6999 / 4405 Honoapiilani Hwy., Kahana, Maui, HI 96761
(808) 669–5000 / 4405 Honoapiilani Hwy., Kahana, Maui, HI 96761
(808) 891–1120 / 303 Piikea Avenue, Kihei, Maui, HI 96753
(808) 742–5000 / 2360 Kiahuna Plantation Drive, Poipu, Kaua'i, HI 96756
(808) 886–4321 / 250 Waikoloa Beach Drive, Waikoloa, (Big Island) Hawai'i, 96738

Coconut Tiger Shrimp Sticks
with a Thai Style Cocktail Sauce

16 large tiger prawns, peeled, deveined
6x6" bamboo skewers
1 cup all purpose flour
4 large eggs
1 cup coconut flakes
1 cup panko bread crumbs
3 cups vegetable oil
2 cups tomato ketchup
½ cup brown sugar

¼ cup saracha chili sauce
2 Tbsp. fish soy
2 Tbsp. soy sauce
2 Tbsp. rice wine vinegar
4 limes, juiced
½ cup cilantro, chopped
4 large kaffir lime leaves, minced
1 stalk fresh lemon grass, minced
1 cup fresh mint, chopped

Shrimp Sticks: Starting at the tail end of the shrimp, run the bamboo skewers through the shrimp until it reaches the end. In three separate bowls: place the flour in one, scramble the eggs in another, then place the coconut and panko together in the third bowl. Dust the shrimp individually into the flour, shake off excess, dredge through the egg wash, roll the sticks in the panko coconut mix. Repeat for all of the shrimp sticks.

Thai Cocktail Sauce: In a large mixing bowl, combine ketchup, brown sugar, saracha chili, fish soy, soy sauce, rice wine vinegar, lime juice, chopped cilantro, minced kaffir lime leaves, minced lemon grass and mint. Mix well, consolidate into smaller container and refrigerate.

To assemble: In a large cast iron skillet at medium-high heat, pour in the vegetable oil, make sure that it's hot by dropping a bit of panko into it to see if the shrimp sticks will fry. Cooking no more than 5 sticks at a time, cook until golden brown, remove from heat and place on paper towels to remove excess oil. Repeat until all sticks are cooked. On a large plate spoon the cocktail sauce flat onto the surface with the stick end facing outside. Arrange the shrimp sticks around the plate. Garnish with spots of fresh coriander. Serves 4.

Szechwan Baby Back Ribs
with a Mongolian Marinade

3 slabs of baby back ribs, cut in ½
2 cups hoisin sauce
2 Tbsp. minced garlic

2 Tbsp. minced ginger
2 Tbsp. Chinese chili paste
½ cup honey

Mongolian Marinade: In a medium large bowl, combine all ingredients (except ribs), mix well then refrigerate.

To assemble: In a very large stock pot of boiling water, place the ribs and cook on a slow rolling boil for about 1½ hours or until tender (the meat must have shrunk down from the top of the bone by at least ½"). Remove from heat and let stand for about 10 minutes until warm but not hot. Evenly spread the Mongolian sauce onto both sides of the ribs. In a preheated 450 degree oven, place the marinated ribs on a large cookie sheet with cookie rack. Cook for no more than 10 to 15 minutes until the ribs are shiny and the marinade has been baked into the meat. Remove the ribs and let them cool; cut into individual pieces. Take what is left of the marinade and brush onto unmarinated sides of ribs. Finish ribs by cooking on an outdoor grill. Turn them evenly on the grill until crispy brown on all sides. Serve immediately. Serves 4.

Sarento's Top of the "I"

Beckoning with an air of romance and style, **Sarento's Top of the "I"** is a celebrated place to savor superb Italian cuisine and "old-country warmth." The second of 4 acclaimed restaurants in the Tri-Star Restaurant Group, Sarento's is named after the grandfather of Aaron Placourakis (President and CEO of the company). A unique feature of Sarento's is the beautiful private dining rooms, which can be reserved for a special dinner occasion such as a custom wine tasting and cigar dinner at the Chef's Table in Jiro's Cellar. Sarento's offers an impressive selection of fine domestic and imported wines to enhance your dining pleasure.

Ambiance: After gliding up to the 29th floor of the Renaissance Ilikai Waikiki Hotel in a glass elevator, you'll enter Sarento's where you'll be inspired by breathtaking views of Diamond Head, Waikiki Beach and the twinkling lights of the city. You'll also be pampered by exceptional service in a comfortable, elegant atmosphere.

Menu: Feast on homemade pastas, veal specialties, fresh Hawaiian fish such as Opakapaka Portofino sautéed with rock shrimp, asparagus tips and mushrooms served in a lemon dill butter sauce or enjoy prime steaks, Lobster Ravioli or Seafood Fra Diavolo—lobster, shrimp, scallops, mussels and calamari in a zesty marinara sauce. For the grand finale, indulge in a decadent Italian dessert.

Details: Dinner nightly. Entrées: $16.95–32.95. Call for reservations. Check out the other Tri–Star restaurants: Aaron's Atop the Ala Moana, page 48, Nick's Fishmarket Maui, page 110, and Sarento's on the Beach on Maui, page 118.

(808) 955–5559 / www.tri-star-restaurants.com
1777 Ala Moana Blvd., 30th Floor of the Renaissance Ilikai Hotel, Honolulu, O'ahu, HI 96815

Eggplant Tapenade

3 pounds large round eggplant

1 oz. garlic, chopped

3 oz. basil leaves, torn

3 oz. pitted Sicilian green olives, chopped

2 oz. capers, chopped

2 oz. extra virgin olive oil

2 oz. canola/olive oil blend

2 oz. sun dried tomatoes, chopped

sea salt and fresh cracked pepper to taste

Halve eggplant, score, brush with olive oil and salt. Roast in oven until soft. Combine with remaining ingredients in processor and blend until coarsely chopped. Check for seasoning.

Tiramisu

2½ pounds Italian mascarpone cheese

8 egg yolks

15 Tbsp. sugar

6 Tbsp. kahlua

2 cups whipped cream

6 Tbsp. Myers rum

1 quart double strength coffee

imported Italian ladyfingers, as needed

Mix eggs and sugar; whisk until pale and frothy. Add mascarpone cheese and combine well. Whisk in kahlua and fold in whipped cream. Combine coffee with rum and dip ladyfingers for a few seconds. Form a ladyfinger layer in 2" pan and spread marscapone mixture on top. Repeat with ladyfingers and finally with marscapone mixture. Chill for 24 hours. Dust top generously with unsweetened cocoa powder, spoon and serve.

Serves 15.

TIKI'S GRILL & BAR

Some are mischievous, some are lovers; they definitely like to have fun, and legend says they come alive at night. **Tiki's Grill & Bar** is full of them—tiki's, that is. Representing all the islands of Polynesia they line the walls and pop out of corners. Opened in October 2002, Tiki's is the fruition of an idea that began with 3 friends who were fraternity brothers in college and are now partners, Bill Tobin, Kelly McGill and Greg Montgomery. The fourth partner is Chef Fred DeAngelo who says he likes to "give people flavors that they're familiar with and add a twist of surprise" creating "an approachable level of sophistication." Breads and desserts are baked from scratch on the premises by Pastry Chef Ron Viloria.

Ambiance: Casual, open-air and above street level, Tiki's provides a great view of Waikiki Beach and is a wonderful place to be lulled by Hawaiian music, a sunset, and a tropical drink. Along with the abundance of tiki's, the decor includes shells and other items from the beach that are suspended from the ceiling in a fish net. Live music nightly begins with relaxed Hawaiian sounds and moves into high energy music later in the evening.

Menu: Lunch and dinner share some of the same menu items: Crab Cakes, Kalua Pig Quesadilla, Pan-Seared 'Ahi in a wasabi mushroom soy beurre blanc sauce, tender Braised Beef Short Ribs or Grilled Mahi Mahi with a spicy seafood salsa. Or try the Chef's Signature King Salmon glazed with special seasonings and caramelized cane sugar. You can even get a Tiki's Cheeseburger or Island Nachos. There's something to please everyone. Dessert selections include the enticing and beautiful Creme Brulee Trio and zesty Lilikoi Glazed Cheesecake.

Details: Lunch and dinner daily. Lunch: $7.95–15.95. Dinner: $7.95–29.95. Valet parking.

(808) 923–8454 / WWW.TIKISGRILL.COM
2570 KALAKAUA AVENUE, HONOLULU, O'AHU, HI 96815

FIVE SPICED SEARED SCALLOPS

12 U–10 size "diver" scallops
2 cloves roasted garlic, rough chop
4 oz. cooked orrechette (ear lobe) pasta
2 oz. sun dried tomato, julienne ¼"
2 oz. snow peas, string removed
2 oz. shiitake mushrooms, julienne ¼"
2 oz. asparagus, cut 2" long
2 oz. vine ripe local tomato, diced, no seeds
1 oz. fish stock, may substitute clam juice

1 oz. white wine
2 oz. sweet butter, room temperature
½ tsp. gremolata (lemon zest and Italian parsley chopped, 1:1)
2 tsp. total 5 spice season blend (5 spice, salt, white pepper, 1:1:½)
1 Tbsp. macadamia nut oil
pinch of salt and pepper to taste

Heat sauté pan over medium high heat for 1 minute. Season scallops with 5 spice seasoning. Place scallops, seasoned side down, into heated **dry** sauté pan. Once down, season other side with salt and pepper. Sear for approximately 45 seconds to insure good brown color, then add in order: macadamia nut oil, shiitake mushrooms, vine ripe tomato, roasted garlic, sun dried tomato, asparagus, snow peas and pre–cooked pasta. Season with salt and pepper. Deglaze with white wine, then fish stock, toss together, insure scallops do not over cook. Remove from heat. Fold in room temperature butter to the dish and top with gremolata. Enjoy!

Serves 2.

SAFFRON COCONUT CLAMS

1 pound fresh clams
1 tsp. salad oil
½ tsp. minced garlic
½ tsp. green curry paste
pinch crushed chilies
1 oz. fish stock, may substitute clam juice
1 oz. white wine
2 oz. coconut milk
4 oz. Lemon Grass Saffron Cream Sauce
1 tsp. fresh sweet basil, julienne
1 tsp. diced red bell peppers, ¼"

Lemon Grass Saffron Cream Sauce
1 tsp. olive oil
1 Tbsp. shallots, minced
½ Tbsp. finely grated fresh lemon grass
1 Tbsp. finely grated fresh ginger
½ cup fish stock, or clam juice
1 tsp. saffron threads
1 tsp. turmeric
1½ cups heavy cream
pinch salt and white pepper

Sauce: Heat oil over medium heat in a sauce pan. Sweat shallots, ginger and lemon grass—**do not burn**. Add fish stock, saffron, turmeric and heavy cream. Bring to a simmer. Reduce heat and allow to simmer for about 5 minutes. Using an immersion blender, mix sauce and continue to simmer until mixture is reduced to about a cup. Reserve.

Clams: In a heated sauté pan, add oil, clams, garlic, green curry paste and crushed chilies. Toss over medium heat. Deglaze your pan with fish stock, white wine, coconut milk. Add Lemon Grass Saffron Cream Sauce and bring to a simmer, cover. Allow all clams to open; toss in basil and diced red bell peppers. Enjoy!

Serves 2.

THE WILLOWS

As you relax in the serene setting of **The Willows** you may feel the long-ago presence of Hawaiian royalty dining under the hau trees and swimming in the ponds, or the Kama'aina who have enjoyed luau's and other celebrations there since the 1940's. After being closed for six years during the 1990's, this historical site re-opened in 1999 and is once again a Kama'aina favorite for celebrations and a place to enjoy Hawaiian/American cuisine by Executive Chef Jay Matsukawa.

Ambiance: A lovely garden setting with covered dining areas, graceful willow trees, plumerias and palms, a dancing water fountain, waterfalls, and a pond complete with a Hawaiian double canoe set up with a dining table on a platform—the most requested table! A variety of banquet rooms are available to host private parties and special occasions.

Menu: Lunch and brunch buffets include: caesar salad, lomi lomi salmon, "The Willows Famous Curry," prime rib, seafood and more. On specific days a sushi bar, saimin station, kalua pork, lau lau and other favorites are offered. "The Willows Roasted Portabello Mushrooms" is their dinner buffet specialty. The ala carte specialty is Kauai Prawns Wrapped with Smoked Bacon served with lobster cream. Each buffet offers a dessert station; be sure to try their popular deep fried haupia.

Details: Open daily. Lunch buffet: $15.95, on Saturday $18.95. Dinner buffet: $25.95. Sunday brunch buffet: $25.95. (Keikis are half-price.) Ala carte dinner in the Rainbow Room Wednesday through Sunday, "Small Plate" tasting menu, courses from $5.00–9.00 each (3 to 5 courses recommended. Located on Hausten Street, one block off of University Ave, via Date Street. Valet or self park in lot $3, either choice.

(808) 952-9200 / WWW.WILLOWSHAWAII.COM
901 HAUSTEN STREET, HONOLULU, O'AHU, HI 96826

THE WILLOWS CURRY

½ cup granulated sugar
2 cups brown sugar
¾ cup curry powder
3 quarts chicken stock

2 cups coconut milk
½ pound unsalted butter
1½ cups flour

In a stock pot, melt the butter then whisk in flour. Cook the mixture for 3 to 4 minutes and place aside. In another stock pot, add all the remaining ingredients and bring to a boil. When the mixture comes to a boil, whisk in the "roux" (the butter and flour mixture) until fully incorporated. Reduce to medium heat and simmer for ten minutes. Let cool and refrigerate.

You may add any type of protein or vegetable that you prefer to the curry.

BACON WRAPPED SHRIMP WITH LOBSTER CREAM SAUCE

"Best seafood dish at the Taste of Honolulu 2002"

5 pieces shrimp, peeled and deveined
5 slices bacon

salt and pepper

Score the shrimp, then salt and pepper lightly. Starting from the top of the shrimp, wrap with bacon while slightly overlapping each layer until you reach the bottom. Trim bacon if necessary. Hold and set aside. Meanwhile, heat a sauté pan on medium high heat for one minute. Place the shrimp into the pan and leave for about two minutes (depending on the size of the shrimp). Flip over and repeat the process on the other side. Remove from the pan and serve.

LOBSTER CREAM SAUCE

1 quart Lobster Stock (recipe below)
2 cups heavy cream

salt and pepper to taste

In a heavy saucepan, reduce lobster stock to half its volume. Add heavy cream and reduce by twenty-five percent or until it coats the back of a spoon. Taste and adjust seasoning if necessary.

Lobster Stock

2 quart water
2 oz. olive oil
1 onion, peeled and quartered
1 carrot, peeled and quartered

3 stalks celery, large chop
1 cup white wine
½ cup tomato paste
2 pounds lobster bodies

In a large stock pot, heat olive oil. Add the vegetables and sauté for two minutes. Add the lobster bodies and tomato paste and cook for two minutes. Deglaze the pan with white wine. Make sure to rub the bottom of the pan to get off all the caramelized pieces. After about two minutes, add the water to the pot and let simmer for about one hour. Strain the stock and cool until ready to use.

HAWAIIAN/AMERICAN

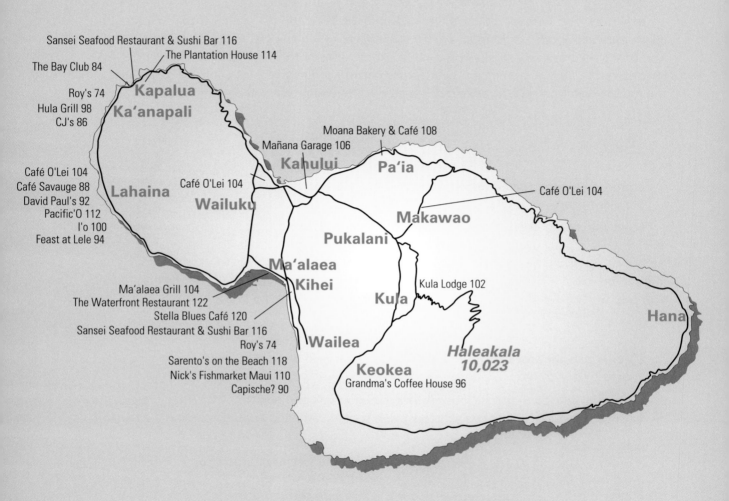

Sansei Seafood Restaurant & Sushi Bar 116
The Plantation House 114
The Bay Club 84
Roy's 74
Hula Grill 98
CJ's 86

Kapalua
Ka'anapali

Moana Bakery & Café 108
Mañana Garage 106

Kahului
Pa'ia

Café O'Lei 104
Café Savauge 88
David Paul's 92
Pacific'O 112
I'o 100
Feast at Lele 94

Lahaina
Café O'Lei 104
Wailuku

Café O'Lei 104
Makawao

Pukalani

Ma'alaea
Kihei

Kula Lodge 102

Ma'alaea Grill 104
The Waterfront Restaurant 122
Stella Blues Café 120
Sansei Seafood Restaurant & Sushi Bar 116
Roy's 74

Kula

Hana

Wailea

Sarento's on the Beach 118
Nick's Fishmarket Maui 110
Capische? 90

Keokea
Grandma's Coffee House 96

Haleakala
10,023

Maui
The Valley Isle

MAUI

Restaurant, Page, Type of Cuisine
Recipes Featured

The Bay Club, 84, Seafood with a Local Flair
Pan Seared Opakapaka and Kona Prawns Sweet Chili Beurre Blanc, Green Papaya Slaw and Fermented Black Beans
Lobster and Hearts of Palm Salad

CJ's Deli & Diner, 86, Comfort Foods
Garlic Prawn Pita with Mango Dressing / Hawaiian Grilled Beef Papadam

Café Sauvage, 88, Contemporary American
Seared Peppered 'Ahi With Wasabi Aioli / Creme Brulee

Capische?, 90, Italian with French Influence
Lamb Osso Bucco / Quail Saltimboca

David Paul's Lahaina Grill, 92, New American with Island Influence
Tequila Shrimp with Firecracker Rice

The Feast at Lele, 94, Contemporary Polynesian
Hawaiian 'Ahi Poke / Octopus Lobster Salad

Grandma's Coffee House, 96, Island Style
Grandma's Banana Macadamia Nut Scones / Uncle Chris's Sweet and Sour Spareribs

Hula Grill, 98, Hawaiian Regional Seafood
Macadamia Nut Crusted Mahi Mahi / Firecracker Fish Soup

I'o, 100, Pacific Rim
Island Carpaccio du jour / Citrus Herb Vinaigrette / Goat Cheese Crab Cakes

Kula Lodge & Restaurant, 102, Fresh Country
Papaya Shrimp Salad / Braised Lamb Shank (Osso Buco)

Ma'alaea Grill & Café O'Lei, 104, American with Island Influence
Manoa Lettuce Wrap / Thai Seafood Curry

Mañana Garage, 106, Latin American
'Ahi Ceviche / Adobo Pulled Pork with Eddie's Latin Dip

Moana Bakery & Café, 108, Euro–Asian
Crispy Veggie Spring Rolls with Sweet Chili Sauce and Namasu

Nick's Fishmarket Maui, 110, Innovative Classic
'Ahi "Poi Pounder"

Pacific'O, 112, Contemporary Pacific
Thai Chicken Coconut Soup / Oysters / Shiso Miso Mignonette

The Plantation House, 114, Maui–Mediterranean
Pepper Rubbed 'Ahi Tuna with Heirloom Tomatoes, Arugula and Mediterranean Tomato-Caper Berry Salsa
Jumbo Diver Scallops with Spinach and Herb Butter

Roy's Restaurant, 74, Hawaiian Fusian Style
Coconut Tiger Shrimp Sticks with a Thai Style Cocktail Sauce / Szechwan Baby Back Ribs with a Mongolian Marinade

Sansei Seafood Restaurant & Sushi Bar, 116, Japanese-Based Hawaiian Regional
Macadamia Nut Crusted Tiger Prawn Temaki (Hand Rolled Sushi) / Sansei Seared Scallop and Foie Gras

Sarento's on the Beach, 118, Multi–Regional Italian
Kaua'i Shrimp Wrapped in Pancetta with Fire Roasted Sweet Pepper Sauce & Leeks

Stella Blues Café, 120, Homemade American Comfort Food
Stella's Ancho Chicken Chili

The Waterfront Restaurant, 122, Fine Seafood
Maui Onion Dressing / Upside-Down Apple Pecan Pie

THE BAY CLUB

Tropical breezes and the sound of the surf mingle with live piano or jazz and set the tone for an evening of dining pleasure with exquisite food and impeccable service at the **Bay Club**. Utilizing fresh, local ingredients, the chef changes the menu seasonally and serves fresh, well-prepared and beautifully presented fare. To find the right wine accompaniment, the staff will assist you with your selection from their award-winning wine list.

Ambiance: In an elegant open-air setting with a view of Kapalua Bay and Moloka'i just across the channel, the feeling of the upscale urban ambiance is enhanced with natural island elements. After an exquisite sunset, watch the waves as they are lit up by a spot light each time they explode to a height where they catch the light and are illuminated against the darkness of night.

Menu: Start with award winning Crab and Rock Shrimp Cake—a delicious combination of flavors that burst onto the taste buds. For lovers of lobster try the three course Lobster Sampler, or have their chef prepare a five-course tasting of signature dishes. Fabulous dessert specials include Island Fruit Tart with Vanilla Bean Custard and Grand Marnier Ice Cream or one of their luscious chocolate creations.

Details: Dinner nightly. Entrées start at $32.00. Reservations recommended. Direct access and parking for the restaurant are located off Lower Honoapiilani Road or, from the hotel, you may follow the paved beachfront walkway that leads to the restaurant.

(808) 669–5656 / WWW.KAPALUABAYHOTEL.COM
ONE BAY DRIVE, KAPALUA, MAUI, HI 96761

Pan Seared Opakapaka and Kona Prawns
Sweet Chili Beurre Blanc, Green Papaya Slaw and Fermented Black Beans

2 6 oz. opakapaka fillets	¼ cup Hawaiian chili water
4 large Kona prawns	3 Tbsp. rice wine vinegar
2 Tbsp. canola oil	salt and pepper to taste
1 Tbsp. unsalted butter	½ cup green pea shoots
¼ cup white wine	**Sweet Chili Beurre Blanc**
3 Tbsp. chopped fresh herbs	¾ cup white wine
Papaya Slaw	4 Tbsp. unsalted butter
2 cups shredded green papaya	2 Tbsp. sweet chili sauce
¾ cup shredded carrots	**Garnish**
¾ cup sliced red onion	fresh ogo
½ cup sliced tri–color pepper	1 Tbsp. fermented black beans

Heat sauté pan over medium heat and add canola oil. Season the opakapaka with salt and pepper. Sear face down until golden brown then turn. Add the prawns and cook for about 30 seconds on each side or until slightly crispy. Add 1 tablespoon of butter, ¼ cup white wine and chopped fresh herbs. Bring to a boil and put in 400 degree oven for 4 to 6 minutes or until fish is cooked through. Serves 2.

Papaya Slaw: Combine papaya, carrots, onion and pepper; mix. Pour in chili water and rice vinegar. Season with salt and pepper and let sit. Just before serving add the pea shoots and place mixture in the middle of the plate.

Beurre Blanc: Reduce the wine by ¾ at medium heat. Whisk in butter and season. Finish with sweet chili sauce and pour over prawns and fish while it is still warm. Garnish with black beans and ogo.

Lobster and Hearts of Palm Salad

Vinaigrette	juice of ½ lime
2 Tbsp. miso	1 Tbsp. chopped herbs
1 tsp. chopped garlic	1 tsp. honey
1 cup chopped shallots	1 cup canola oil
¼ cup sherry vinegar	salt and fresh pepper to taste

Whisk together all ingredients except oil. Slowly whisk in canola oil and season with salt and fresh cracked pepper.

1½ pounds lobster, cooked, removed from shell	½ cup corn shoots
	½ cup pea shoots
½ head shredded radicchio	½ cup julienne tomato
½ cup sliced hearts of palm	1 Tbsp. chopped herbs

In a large bowl, mix the lobster and all ingredients except vinaigrette. Lightly drizzle with vinaigrette to taste. For garnish, scatter a few lobster chunks around with a little vinaigrette and put one claw on top of the salad.

CJ's Deli & Diner

Who can resist delicious comfort food at a reasonable price? You can enjoy exactly that to your heart's content at **CJ's Deli & Diner**, the brainchild of Chef/Owners Christian Jorgensen and Darren LeMoss. Their instincts have served them well. From the day CJ's opened in January 2003 their diner has been bustling with happy customers. Both partners bring many years of culinary experience and most recently worked at the Westin Maui where Christian was Executive Chef and Darren, Executive Sous Chef. Grab a menu or stand back and read the items in colored chalk on the board; either way you'll find plenty of favorites to entice your tastebuds.

Ambiance: Wood floors and high ceilings are accented with rich warm Tuscan tones on walls adorned with colorful Island art. Order at the counter and have a seat inside where you'll stay cool with air conditioning, or outside under the shade of an umbrella.

Menu: Breakfast features Omelettes, a Breakfast Wrap, Classic Eggs Benedict, Hot Cakes, and much more. Bakery items include "To Die For Malasadas" (Portuguese doughnuts), Cinnabuns and muffins. For lunch choose from a great selection of plate lunches such as their signature Pot Roast, deli and hot sandwiches and Paninis (Italian Style Grilled Sandwiches on Focaccia). I'm very excited to have found a place on Maui that serves Paninis—try the Caprese with Buffalo mozzarella, vine ripened tomatoes and herbs. You can also choose from several refreshing salad options or try the delicious flavors of the Garlic Prawns in Pita with Mango Dressing. For those with a sweet tooth: awesome Chocolate Cake, cheesecakes, ice cream sundaes and more.

Details: Open daily from 6:30 a.m. to 7:30 p.m. Breakfast $3.00–7.95. Lunch, most items $5.50–8.95. Keiki meals $4.95. Dinner under $12.95. CJ's also offers "Chefs to go."

(808) 667–0968 / WWW.CJSMAUI.COM
THE FAIRWAY SHOPS, 2580 KEKAA DRIVE, KA'ANAPALI, MAUI, HI 96761

Garlic Prawn Pita with Mango Dressing

1½ pounds prawns, peeled, tail off

2 cups mixed greens

1 cup Mango Dressing (recipe below)

6 each pita bread

2 tsp. chopped garlic

4 tsp. olive oil

1 cup diced tomato

1 cup diced mango

1 cup diced cucumber

1 cup Mandarin orange

Marinate prawns in olive oil and garlic for 2 hours. Sauté prawns in olive oil with remaining garlic. Season with salt and pepper. Combine all ingredients (except pita bread) in a bowl and toss with the Mango Dressing. Cut pita bread in half and stuff salad into pocket. Serve immediately.

Makes 6.

Mango Dressing

1 cup fresh mango

1 cup rice wine vinegar

½ cup sugar

¼ cup Thai chili sauce

2 cups olive oil

Blend all ingredients together until smooth.

Hawaiian Grilled Beef Papadam

1 pound beef sirloin

Kalbi Marinade

10 each papadams (Indian crackers)

Cajun spice

1 cup arugula

2 vine ripe tomatoes

fresh pepper

chopped herbs

⅛ cup balsamic vinegar

2 tsp. furikake

Marinate beef in Kalbi Marinade for 12 to 18 hours. Sear beef over char grill or barbecue. Remove from grill and let rest for 10 minutes. Toast papadams over charcoal until golden brown and slightly bubbled. Season with Cajun spice. Slice tomatoes and season with fresh pepper and chopped herbs. Toss tomatoes and arugula with balsamic vinegar. Place a small portion onto the papadams. Slice the beef very thin and portion on top of arugula–tomato mix. Sprinkle furikake on top.

Makes 10.

Comfort Foods

CAFÉ SAUVAGE

The first of many recommendations I received for **Café Sauvage** came from a hot Maui chef, which, of course, is a very good sign! In January 2002, owners Chef Dean Louie and Jeff Felice opened this wonderful little eatery, which has been embraced by the community and frequented by visitors ever since. Chef Dean prepares everything from scratch and explains, "We're all about the food and quality and value." After earning a degree in art, his fascination for cooking lead him to apprentice as a chef and he found that his artistic sensibility translated well into the culinary arts.

Ambiance: In this casually intimate bistro you can relax in a lovely open-air courtyard setting or cool off in the air-conditioned dining rooms decorated with the chef's quality art collection.

Menu: To taste a variety of nightly appetizers try the Appetizer Trio; the tender Crispy Calamari is another popular starter. Featured fares include Chef Dean's Duck Specials, Black-Sesame Tempura Prawns and the Taste of Lahaina Award-winning Plum-Glazed Lamb "Lollichops." If you can't decide, The Sauvage Mixed Grill allows you to indulge in smaller portions of 3 top-notch entrée items of the chef's choice. Complement your dinner with a "hand-selected, reasonably priced" bottle of wine. And, for the grand finish try the Mascarpone Tiramisu or homemade ice cream or sorbet.

Details: Dinner nightly, entrées: $13.95–25.95. A special $19.95 Prix Fixe Menu with 3 courses is served between 5 and 6:30 p.m. nightly. Dinner reservations recommended on weekends.

(808) 661–7600 / WWW.CAFESAUVAGE.COM
844 FRONT STREET, LAHAINA, MAUI, HI 96761

SEARED PEPPERED 'AHI
WITH WASABI AIOLI

Residents living in the tropical Pacific have the benefit of exceptionally fresh fish throughout the year. This simple dish hits your taste buds with the sensations of spicy, sweet and salty — all combined with the rich smoothness of the popular and abundant Yellowfin Tuna. It has the healthy benefit of zero fat and cholesterol without sacrificing great taste, and has been a hit on our menu since we've opened.

Cook the fish quickly just to caramelize the peppery crust and make sure there is plenty of ventilation in the kitchen when searing it!   —Chef Dean Louie

2 each center-cut 'ahi tuna 2x2x6"
    (sashimi size)
1 Tbsp. fresh crushed black peppercorns

2 Tbsp. sugar (can be omitted for dietary reasons)
1 tsp. kosher salt
1 tsp. crushed red chilies

Crush peppercorns with the back of a sauté pan or pulse with coffee grinder. Mix all 4 dry spices together. Heat a large sauté pan to high heat. Lightly roll the ahi logs in the dry-spice mixture. When the pan is smoking, add a little salad oil and sear the logs one side at a time. The finished 'ahi should be nicely brown on the outside and raw in the middle. Cool in the refrigerator uncovered.

WASABI AIOLI

1 Tbsp. wasabi (Japanese horseradish paste)
½ cup mayonnaise

½ tsp. finely minced garlic
juice of one lemon

Mix all of the ingredients together and keep cold. Slice the cooled Seared 'Ahi into thin even pieces (against the grain) and dip into the Wasabi Aioli or your own fine sauce. Garnish with grated daikon and/or ginger if desired.

Garnish
grated daikon radish
carrot curls

thinly sliced green onion
¼ tsp. wasabi (Japanese horseradish paste)

CREME BRULEE

8 egg yolks
1 quart cream
1 cup milk

8 oz. sugar
1 oz. vanilla bean extract

In heavy bottomed sauce pan, scald cream and milk with ½ cup sugar. Separate yolks and mix in remaining sugar. Temper hot cream with yolk mixture a little at a time. Strain and add vanilla. Pour evenly into ramekins set flat in 2" deep baking pan. Pour hot water in the pan half-way up to surround the ramekins. Bake at 300 degrees in Bain Marie until custard is set. Cool.

To serve, sprinkle sugar on top of the cooled custard and place under broiler until sugar is caramelized. Makes 12 4 ounce ramekins.

CONTEMPORARY AMERICAN

CAPISCHE?

A quintessential place for a romantic candlelight dinner al fresco, **Capische?** will capture your imagination with the views, the food, the fine wine and intimate setting. Award-winning Chef Brain Etheredge describes himself as a hands-on chef/owner. He appreciates the advantage of such a small restaurant as it allows him to give more personal attention to the preparation of each plate. Capische? means Understand? in Italian. The name arose from the quizzical situation of a British chef, trained in classic French cuisine, cooking Italian. Capische? Based on the popularity of his restaurant and first-rate food, he's doing an excellent job of it.

Ambiance: Capische? showcases a breathtaking panoramic view that stretches from Makena Beach to the island of Lanai. With only 9 dining tables spaciously lined up along the lanai, you are assured excellent service and privacy. The air of romance is enhanced by the wafting sound of jazz being played on the baby grand piano in the lounge.

Menu: Using organic meats and produce as much as possible, Chef Etheredge prepares favorite appetizers such as: Quail Saltimboca—apple-smoked bacon wrapped quail with sage and pinenut brown butter and Beef Carpaccio. You may also try the fresh flavors of Caprese—buffalo mozzarella, local Heirloom tomatoes, baby basil, Maui onions and coriander vinaigrette. Recommended entrées are Cioppino, Veal Three Ways: picatta, marsala and parmesan, and the Lamb "Osso Buco" with Maui onion gremolata and lemon risotto. Choose your wine from a nice variety of Italian or California selections, or splurge for a very fine French wine.

Details: Dinner nightly, entrées: $29.00–49.00. Please call for reservations.

(808) 879–2224 / WWW.CAPISCHE.COM
555 KAUKAKI STREET, KIHEI, MAUI, HI 96753

Lamb Osso Buco

4 lamb shanks
1 onion, small dice
4 stalks celery, small dice
2 carrots, small dice
1 fennel bulb, small dice
¼ tsp. coriander seed
4 oz. butter

4 thyme sprigs
2 oz. tomato paste
8 oz. Chianti (Sangiovese blend)
to taste salt and fresh black pepper
equal parts veal and chicken stock
    to cover shanks

Season lamb heavily. Sear over high heat until well caramelized on all sides. Remove and reserve. Add butter and caramelize vegetables. Add tomato paste and cook for 3 to 5 minutes stirring frequently. Deglaze with wine and add lamb shanks, coriander, and thyme. Use equal parts veal and chicken stock to cover shanks. Cover pot and simmer on very low heat for 3 to 8 hours. Do not boil as it will cause the shanks to fall apart. To serve: Reduce the lamb broth. Place lamb in bowl with potatoes or risotto (recommended). Garnish with Gremolata (recipe below).

Maui Onion Gremolata

1 small Maui onion, shaved thin
1 oz. basil, chiffonade
juice from 2 lemons

1 oz. extra virgin olive oil
to taste salt and pepper

Shave onions and basil. Combine all ingredients.

Quail Saltimboca

1 whole quail, deboned, salted & peppered
1 piece apple smoked bacon
1 small bunch sage
½ tomato, small dice
2 Tbsp. pine nuts
1 oz. olive oil

2 oz. butter
2 cloves garlic, minced
1 shallot, minced
juice of ½ lemon
2 oz. white wine

Wrap quail in the piece of apple smoked bacon. Add oil to medium hot pan. Brown the quail on all sides. Place quail in 300 degree oven for about 5 minutes. Drain oil from pan, add butter and cook until lightly brown. Add and brown pine nuts (be careful not to burn), then add garlic and shallots, then white wine, lemon juice and tomatoes. Reduce until most of the liquid is gone. Add salt and pepper and a pinch of chopped sage. Serve quail on a bed of your pine nut and brown butter sauce. Serve with a very crisp Pino Grigio.

Serves 1.

DAVID PAUL'S LAHAINA GRILL

Exuding vitality and style while serving exceptional food, **David Paul's Lahaina Grill** has inspired rave reviews from a local and national audience. In addition to a long list of accolades, the Lahaina Grill has won the Hale 'Aina Award as one of Maui's best restaurants for 10 consecutive years! This successful bistro has wowed guests from day one with the innovative culinary artistry of Chef David Paul Johnson.

Now, proprietor Jurg Munch brings his wealth of experience and, collaborating with David Paul and Executive Chef Arnulfo Gonzalez, continues to offer the fresh blend of island flavors and extraordinary dining experience of this well-loved restaurant.

Ambiance: An elegant and spirited bistro on the first floor of the lovely historic Lahaina Inn, jazz and the hum of happy diners mingle with excellent service while splashes of colorful Jan Kasprzycki paintings lead to intimate tables set in alcoves.

Menu: Excellent appetizers include The Cake Walk—petite servings of Kona lobster crab cake, sweet Louisiana rock shrimp cake and seared 'ahi cake, and the Reconstructed California Roll. The Warm Pecan Crusted Goat Cheese and Baby Arugula Salad is fresh and zesty. For the main course I relished the light and delicious flavors of the Maui Onion Crusted Seared 'Ahi with an apple cider-soy butter vinaigrette, or try their signature Tequila Shrimp and Firecracker Rice, or Kona Coffee Roasted Rack of Lamb. Thankfully, the dessert sampler provides a miniature selection of divine tastes: Triple Berry Pie, Lime Tart, a Creme Brulée and some sinfully luscious chocolate cakes.

Details: Dinner nightly. Most entrées: $23.00–39.00. Please call for reservations.

(808) 667–5117 / WWW.LAHAINAGRILL.COM
127 LAHAINALUNA ROAD, LAHAINA, MAUI, HI 96761

TEQUILA SHRIMP WITH FIRECRACKER RICE

Tequila Shrimp & Marinade
1½ pounds 13/15 shrimp, deveined
¾ cup corn oil
1½ tsp. chili paste
1½ tsp. cilantro, chopped
1½ tsp. lime juice
¼ tsp. salt

½ tsp. pepper
1 Tbsp. brown sugar
½ tsp. toasted cumin
⅛ cup tequila
½ tsp. Worcestershire sauce
1 Tbsp. Dijon mustard
⅛ tsp. cayenne pepper

Tequila Butter
4 oz. butter
1 Tbsp. tequila
1½ tsp. brown sugar
1½ tsp. cilantro, chopped
⅓ tsp. chili paste

1 tsp. lime juice
¼ tsp. white pepper
¼ tsp. salt
½ tsp. cumin
pinch cayenne
¼ tsp. Worcestershire sauce

Tequila Beurre Blanc
7 oz. tequila
½ tsp. ground cumin
1 tsp. chili paste

½ tsp. cilantro, chopped
½ tsp. garlic, chopped
½ tsp. brown sugar
6 oz. tequila butter

Tequila Shrimp: Butterfly back side and thoroughly wash shrimp. Layer in container and marinade for at least 1 hour. Take directly from marinade and place in single layer in a sauté pan and cook over medium heat until the shrimp are cooked through.

Marinade: Combine all ingredients in large bowl and whisk to combine.

Tequila Butter: In a mixer with a paddle on medium speed, whip butter separately. Add all ingredients except lime juice and tequila. Thoroughly mix then add tequila and lime juice; mix until blended. Do not over mix as you will lose the stability of the blend.

Tequila Beurre Blanc: In a heavy bottomed sauce pan, combine all ingredients except the tequila butter. Reduce by 90 percent. Off the heat, whisk in the tequila butter. Process in a blender for 10 seconds. Store in a warm water bath for service.

Chili Rice
21 oz. Jasmine rice
⅔ dried Anaheim chili
1 Tbsp. corn oil
1 oz. garlic, minced

3 Tbsp. annato paste
3 Tbsp. Mulatto Butter
pinch cayenne pepper
16 oz. chicken stock

Vanilla Rice
21 oz. Jasmine rice
1½ Tbsp. butter
1 oz. shallots, chopped

2 vanilla beans
1 tsp. vanilla extract
16 oz. clam juice
⅓ cup white wine

Mulatto Butter
⅛ oz. dried Anaheim chili
⅛ tsp. garlic, minced

1½ oz. butter
1 Tbsp. chicken stock
salt and pepper to taste

Mix ingredients together for Mulatto Butter. For the Chili Rice, heat annato, Mulatto Butter, garlic and Anaheim chilies in oil. Add the rice and sauté, stirring constantly. Add chicken stock and cook at a simmer until done. For the Vanilla Rice, melt butter and sweat the shallots. Add rice and sauté for 5 to 10 minutes, stirring constantly. Deglaze with white wine and reduce. Add vanilla beans, extract, clam juice, salt and pepper. Simmer until rice is fully cooked. Serve a portion of each rice as a bed for the shrimp. Serves 4.

NEW AMERICAN WITH ISLAND INFLUENCE

THE FEAST AT LELE

Feel your heart beating to the rhythm of the drums and the island breeze on your face while exotic flavors burst in your mouth. Provocative and sensual, **The Feast at Lele** is an innovative venue that blends dynamic Luau performances with gourmet island dining. It is executed brilliantly by the creators of Pacific'O, I'o and the Old Lahaina Luau. You will experience the cultures and cuisines of Hawai'i, Tonga, Tahiti and Samoa. Each act is accompanied by a sampling of dishes representing the culture, which have been researched and created by Executive Chef James McDonald. *Travel & Leisure* says, "This is the most fabulous cooking on Maui, which is saying a lot."

Ambiance: As you become entranced by the powerful music, chants and dance, you'll feel like royalty dining so close to the beach at your own reserved table complete with white linens. As the sun sinks into the horizon, a canoe arrives with performers; a young native man carries a beautiful princess to the grass stage where she performs her hypnotic, erotic dance that mesmerizes and captures the imagination of all.

Menu: Indulge in fine wines, tropical drinks and outstanding dishes such as: Steamed Moi—fresh delicate fish (historically only for Hawaiian royalty) garnished with crispy ogo seaweed and tobiko caviar. Tonga features Salati Feke 'Uo Limu, watercress and fresh seaweed; and Tunu Pulu, grilled strip steak. The third course represents Tahiti: Fafa—chicken wrapped in taro leaf baked in coconut milk, chicken stock, ginger and lemongrass; and E'iaota-poisson cru. The Samoan course includes Fresh grilled fish wrapped in banana leaf, and Shrimp, avocado and passion fruit, and more. Macadamia Nut Tart, Hawaiian Chocolate Truffles and tropical fruits are the finishing touches.

Details: Open nightly. Call for prices and reservations. Private parties and weddings are usually booked 3–5 days in advance.

(808) 667-5353 / WWW.THEFEASTATLELE.COM
505 FRONT STREET, LAHAINA, MAUI, HI 96761

Hawaiian 'Ahi Poke

1 pound fresh yellowfin tuna, diced

1 cup fresh ogo seaweed, chopped

1½ Tbsp. fresh ginger, minced

½ tsp. crushed red chili flakes

¼ cup green onion, chopped

1½ oz. sesame oil

3 oz. low salt soy sauce

sea salt to taste

Combine all ingredients and keep chilled until ready to "grind" (eat).

Octopus Lobster Salad

1 pound octopus, cooked

1 pound lobster meat, cooked, chopped

2 cups ogo seaweed, rough chopped

½ cup rice wine vinegar

fish sauce to taste

½ pound watercress, chopped

1 Maui onion, julienne

1 tomato, diced

¾ cup canola oil

salt and pepper to taste

Grill the octopus and allow to cool. Slice the octopus into slivers and mix with the other remaining ingredients. Chill until ready to serve.

GRANDMA'S COFFEE HOUSE

After you meander through the scenic pastoral landscape of Kula where you'll be amazed by the panoramic view and bird's-eye perspective of the island, you'll discover a tiny, winsome town called Keokea. Picturesque white churches, a park, a couple of neighborhood stores, an art gallery, and **Grandma's Coffee House** complete the town. Set at about 3,000 feet elevation, the area is home to many small coffee farms that provide the organic coffee beans that owner Al Franco roasts and brews at Grandma's. Inspired by his grandmother and the many generations in his family who have grown and processed coffee, Al continues with the family tradition. He recently shared this legacy on national television when the film crew from Emeril Live (The Food Network) arrived in Keokea to feature him roasting the hand-picked beans in an 1885 roasting machine that has been in his family for many years.

Ambiance: Small, relaxed and friendly. Order at the counter and have a seat inside or on the lanai where you can enjoy the expansive view.

Menu: Breakfasts feature Belgian Waffles with tropical fruit in season, bacon and eggs, omelettes and eggs benedict. For lunch try the daily special, such as Al's Oriental BBQ Chicken, or a Taro Burger, BLT, or Lasagna. A changing selection of goodies include: Banana Mango Bread, Cherry, Peach or Apple Cobbler, and Carrot Cake or a Pineapple Banana Mac Nut Cake (both cakes are incredible!) or with a smoothie, cappuccino or mocha, feast on cheesecake or Tiramisu.

Details: Under $10.00. Open daily 7 a.m. to 5 p.m. You can also purchase coffee by the pound at Grandma's, on their web site, or call 1-800-375-7853.

(808) 878–2140 / WWW.GRANDMASCOFFEE.COM
9232 KULA HIGHWAY, KEOKEA, MAUI, HI 96790

GRANDMA'S BANANA MACADAMIA NUT SCONES

6 cups four
1 cup Hawaiian raw sugar
3 Tbsp. baking powder
1 tsp. salt
1 cup softened butter

4 eggs
1 cup buttermilk
1 cup fresh squeezed lemon juice
2 cups chopped apple bananas
¾ cup chopped macadamia nuts

Mix flour, sugar, baking powder and salt. Cut in butter. In separate bowl blend eggs, buttermilk and lemon juice. Gently fold together with dry mix and add bananas and macadamia nuts. Place scones on a greased pan, sprinkle with cinnamon sugar. Bake at 400 degrees for 20 minutes.

Makes 24 scones.

UNCLE CHRIS'S SWEET AND SOUR SPARERIBS

5 pounds cubed pork spareribs
2 Tbsp. apple cider vinegar
1 cup dark brown sugar
1 cup raw sugar
4 cups shoyu

1 cup water
½ cup grated Hawaiian ginger
½ cup chopped garlic
¼ tsp. Chinese five spice
1 whole pineapple, cubed

Boil the spareribs for 45 minutes. Drain water and rinse. Add remaining ingredients, except pineapple, to pot along with the ribs. Cook for one hour over medium heat, then add pineapple and enjoy!

HULA GRILL

Hula Grill is a favorite place for Maui residents to unwind and pretend we're tourists and for visitors to luxuriate in the quintessential good life of the tropics. Soothed by the ocean breeze and swaying palm trees, you can sip a tropical drink and listen to the mellow groove of live music during the afternoon. For lunch and dinner, you can experience the exceptional food of talented Chef Peter Merriman (see page 160), one of the founders of Hawai'i Regional Cuisine—a group of chefs dedicated to working with farmers and utilizing fresh local ingredients. Merriman combined talents with T S Restaurants to open Hula Grill in 1994.

Ambiance: With a design inspired by a plantation-style beach house, the restaurant offers open-air seating, a view of the glistening ocean, passing boats and parasailors backed by Lana'i and Molokai'i. For cocktails and an all-day menu where you can curl your toes into the sand under grass thatched umbrellas, the irresistible Barefoot Bar serves patrons who may be bikini clad and dripping from a dip in the ocean.

Its slogan—"No shoes, no shirt, no problem."

Menu: Popular menu items include: Wood Grilled Ono with pineapple salsa, Screamin' Sesame Opah roasted Szechwan style, Big Island Goat Cheese, Macadamia Nut and Shrimp Quesadilla and BBQ Pork Spare Ribs. The favorite dessert is the Homemade Ice Cream Sandwich: vanilla ice cream, macadamia nut brownies, raspberry sauce and whipped cream.

Details: Open daily. Lunch: $8.00–14.00. Dinner entrées: $16.00–29.00. Live contemporary music and hula dancers in the evening. Dinner reservations recommended. Dining room open from 5:00 p.m. to 9:30 p.m. Barefoot Bar open from 11 a.m. to 11 p.m. daily.

(808) 667–6636 / WWW.HULAPIE.COM
WHALERS VILLAGE, 2435 KA'ANAPALI PKWY., KA'ANAPALI, MAUI, HI 96761

MACADAMIA NUT CRUSTED MAHI MAHI

6 6 oz. pieces mahi mahi fillet
2 cups finely ground unsalted
    macadamia nuts
½ cup vegetable or sterling salad oil
4 cups finely ground unsalted
    macadamia nuts

2½ cups mayonnaise
1 Tbsp. Worcestershire sauce
2 tsp. garlic powder
1 tsp. salt
1 tsp. pepper

Combine second two ingredients in a food processor and mix until a butter forms. In a medium size bowl combine the rest of the ingredients (except fish). Add the macadamia nut butter and mix thoroughly by hand.

On a greased baking sheet season the fish of your choice* with salt and pepper. Spread the mixture evenly over fish. Bake at 350 degrees until the crust is a golden brown.

*Mahimahi and snappers work well. Avoid large game fish such as ono, 'ahi, or marlin as they tend to dry out.

Serves 6.

FIRECRACKER FISH SOUP

6 6" corn tortillas
¼ cup olive oil
2 Tbsp. seeded jalapeños, pureed in
    processor
1 large onion, pureed in a processor
3 Tbsp. garlic, pureed in a processor
1 tsp. chili powder
1 tsp. coriander
1 tsp. cumin
9 Tbsp. fresh seeded tomato, pureed in
    processor

9 Tbsp. canned tomato puree
¼ cup cilantro with stems, chopped
2 Tbsp. chicken base mixed with 9 cups
    water
1 cup boneless fish, cut into 1" cubes
½ cup corn
salt and pepper to taste
¼ cup basil chiffonade (cut into thin
    strips the size of a match)
sour cream for garnish

In a medium size sauce pot over medium heat add olive oil. Sauté tortillas until crispy. Turn heat to low. Add jalapeños, onion, and garlic and sauté for 2 minutes. Add chili powder, cumin and coriander; sauté for 3 minutes. Add fresh and canned tomato, and cilantro; sauté for 3 minutes. Add the chicken stock and bring to a boil. Remove from heat. Salt and pepper to taste and stir in basil chiffonade. Sauté fish cubes and corn in 1 tablespoon vegetable oil then add to soup. Garnish with sour cream, fried tortilla strips and a sprig of cilantro.

Serves 6.

I'o

"**I'o** is exciting, exotic and adventurous, yet maintains a level of quality and class that any five star restaurant should offer, with a staff that is knowledgeable, not stuffy." These are the words of Executive Chef James McDonald describing the cutting edge restaurant that he and partners Louis Coulombe and Stephan Bel-Robert created. Their other successful ventures include Pacific'O (page 112) and Feast at Lele (page 94). Each venue offers the artistic Chef McDonald a unique outlet for his creative ingenuity and a distinctive and extraordinary dining experience for guests. I'o has been honored with *Honolulu Magazine's* Hale 'Aina Restaurant of Distinction Award, "A Taste of Lahaina" Best Seafood/Best of Show, and *Wine Spectator's* Award of Excellence.

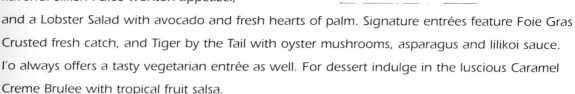

Ambiance: A futuristic, post-modern-funk theme juxtaposed with a chic sophisticated feeling that you'd be likely to find in New York or San Francisco, yet you're on Maui and just steps from the beach. The exhibition kitchen is highlighted behind lit etched-glass panels and the curved custom "Martini" bar is an artistic showpiece. You may also enjoy dining outside under the stars with tropical ocean breezes.

Menu: For starters try the smooth and flavorful Silken Purse wonton appetizer, and a Lobster Salad with avocado and fresh hearts of palm. Signature entrées feature Foie Gras Crusted fresh catch, and Tiger by the Tail with oyster mushrooms, asparagus and lilikoi sauce. I'o always offers a tasty vegetarian entrée as well. For dessert indulge in the luscious Caramel Creme Brulee with tropical fruit salsa.

Details: Dinner served nightly. Entrées: $22.00–59.00. Call for reservations. Catering is also available.

(808) 661-8422 / WWW.IOMAUI.COM
505 FRONT STREET, LAHAINA, MAUI, HI 96761

ISLAND CARPACCIO DU JOUR

½ pound fresh fish fillet
3 cups Kula greens
1 Tbsp. sea salt
½ Tbsp. course ground pepper
pink peppercorns (optional)

Citrus Herb Vinaigrette (recipe below)
6 won ton skins, julienne, deep fried
1 Tbsp. chili paste
1 cup extra virgin olive oil
plastic wrap

Mix chili paste and oil together and reserve. Cut fish into 18 slices. Lay slices between plastic wrap and gently pound out into thin sheets. Arrange 3 slices per plate; ladle some vinaigrette over fish, arrange a small bouquet of Kula greens in center and top with some won ton. Drizzle a light amount of oil on fish, sprinkle with sea salt and pepper, and serve.

CITRUS HERB VINAIGRETTE

1 cup orange juice
½ cup lemon juice
½ cup lime juice
½ cup mirin
1 Tbsp. jalapeño pepper, minced

2 Tbsp. mint, chopped
2 Tbsp. Thai basil, chopped
2 Tbsp. dill, chopped
2 Tbsp. cilantro, chopped
2 Tbsp. tarragon, chopped

Mix all ingredients and reserve chilled. Vinaigrette will hold for 5 days.

GOAT CHEESE CRAB CAKES

5 pounds crab meat (blue crab preferred)
⅛ cup Sambal chili paste
3 cups mayonnaise
salt and pepper to taste
2 cups cilantro, chopped

2 lemons, juiced
2 cups goat cheese crumbles
flour
egg wash
3 cups panko

Mix crab, sambal, cilantro, lemon juice, mayonnaise, goat cheese and seasoning together. Form into 3 ounce portions and roll in flour, then egg, followed by the panko. Refrigerate until ready to use. Cook in oil at 350 degrees until golden brown. Serve with Maui Onion Miso dressing.

Yield 25 to 30 crab cakes.

KULA LODGE & RESTAURANT

On the scenic slopes of Maui's Haleakala crater, you will discover the **Kula Lodge & Restaurant** nestled amongst majestic trees and rolling hills at 3,200 feet elevation. Surrounded by a beautiful private garden with a lovely terrace, the restaurant also hosts weddings and private parties. Hundreds of varieties of protea, trees and flowers grace the grounds. Fresh herbs grown on the property and other organic produce, provided by local farmers, are used in the restaurant. Browse through the Curtis Wilson Cost Art Gallery, the Upcountry Harvest gift shop featuring Maui grown protea flowers, and the new Kula Marketplace, which includes an artisan gallery and food pantry featuring items from Hawaii. Owned by Fred Romanchak, the property also offers overnight accommodations—charming chalets that provide the perfect place to begin an early sojourn to see the spectacular sunrise on Haleakala.

Ambiance: Comfortable and rustic with a cozy fireplace and sweeping views of Maui and the Pacific. The Garden Terrace Restaurant invites you to dine at outdoor tables situated on varying levels of the terrace and features items from the wood-burning oven (such as pizzas).

Menu: My favorite breakfast items are the Smoked Salmon Eggs Benedict with a tangy Kula orange hollandaise sauce, and the Cinnamon French Toast. Lunch fare features the refreshing Thai Summer Rolls and flavorful Grilled Catch Sandwich with basil pesto aioli, also burgers and a variety of sandwiches and entrées. Dinners include ribs, steak and Fresh Island Fish—dragon seared, macadamia nut crusted or grilled with lemon caper butter sauce, along with vegetarian specials and more.

Details: Open daily. Breakfast: $4.00–13.00. Lunch: $6.00–16.00. Dinner entrées: $14.00–28.00. For the Garden Terrace Restaurant, call for days and times.

(808) 878-1535 / WWW.KULALODGE.COM
15200 HALEAKALA HIGHWAY, KULA, MAUI, HI 96790

PAPAYA SHRIMP SALAD

1 medium papaya, ripe
8 oz. bay shrimp, 50 count
1 tsp. red onion, finely diced
2 tsp. celery, finely diced
3 tsp. water chestnuts, finely diced
1 tsp. green onions, chopped

⅛ cup mayonnaise
to taste salt and ground pepper
3 oz. field greens w/dressing of your choice
⅓ medium cucumber, sliced
2 medium Roma tomatoes, sliced

Trim papaya, cut ½" from both ends. Cut in ½, facing narrow end of papaya toward you carefully deseed with a teaspoon. Discard seeds. After thawing, place shrimp in some tap water for a few minutes, drain and squeeze dry thoroughly. Place in mixing bowl. Add onions, celery, water chestnuts and green onions to shrimp and add mayonnaise to your preference, season with salt and pepper. Fill halves of papaya with shrimp mixture. Place on a bed of field greens tossed in dressing and garnish with tomato and cucumbers.

BRAISED LAMB SHANK
(OSSO BUCO)

2 lamb shanks, hind
2 cups port wine
2 cups demi glace, veal
4 oz. onions, small diced ⅛"
2 oz. celery

2 oz. carrots
¼ oz. thyme
pinch rosemary, chopped
parsley, finely chopped
salt and ground pepper

Dry lamb shanks with paper towel. Season shanks with salt, pepper, thyme and rosemary. Reduce port wine by ½. In a thick pot, brown shanks evenly, then remove onto a plate. Drain excess oil, reserving 3 tablespoons. Add onions, celery and carrots. Sauté gently until vegetables are translucent. Replace shanks into pot; add reduced wine and demi glace. Cover pot and place in 300 degree oven until shanks are soft. Shanks are done when a toothpick or skewer is inserted and there is no resistance when pulling out. Serve with fresh mashed potatoes or a risotto.

MA'ALAEA GRILL & CAFÉ O'LEI

With their shared passion and combined talents, husband and wife team Michael and Dana Pastula have created several winning restaurants that are a favorite among locals and a delight for visitors. Their comfortable eateries serve delicious fare, utilizing fresh island products, with influences from Michael's classic French training and Dana's Asian heritage. While serving many of the same great menu selections, each location has its own unique feel and fulfills their desire to offer moderately priced and interesting food.

Ambiance: With its lovely bamboo theme, high ceilings and tropical breezes, **Ma'alaea Grill** will treat you with a view of the harbor and glistening ocean beyond. **Café O'Lei** Lahaina serves guests on a deck right over the ocean with spectacular views and glowing sunsets. Café O'Lei Makawao features alfresco courtyard dining. There is also a Café O'Lei in the lush Iao Valley.

Menu: Lunch items include: Taro Salad with blue cheese, crisp Okinawan sweet potatoes and balsamic vinaigrette, or Blackened Mahi Mahi with fresh papaya salsa, or the popular Crab Club on foccacia.

For dinner appetizers try the Manoa Lettuce Wraps or Fried 'Ahi Stuffed Calamari and for an entrée, Macadamia Nut Roast Ducking, or Grilled Marinated Jumbo Shrimp with basil-macadamia nut pesto. Save room for a homemade dessert: Lilikoi Cheesecake or a dreamy warm individual Pineapple Upsidedown Cake with ice cream. Full bar with tropical cocktails at Ma'alaea and Lahaina locations.

Details: Lunch: $6.95 to $10.95. Dinner: $13.95–22.95. Ma'alaea Grill, lunch daily, dinner Tuesday thru Sunday. Café O'Lei Lahaina, lunch and dinner daily. Café O'Lei Makawao, lunch Monday through Saturday. Café O'Lei Iao, Hawaii Nature Center, Iao Valley, lunch daily depending on the weather.

(808) 243–2206 / 300 MA'ALAEA ROAD, MA'ALAEA HARBOR, MAUI, HI 96793
(808) 661–9491 / OCEANFRONT MARKETPLACE, 839 FRONT STREET, LAHAINA, MAUI, HI 96761
(808) 573–9065 / PANIOLO COURTYARD, 3679 BALDWIN AVENUE, MAKAWAO, MAUI, HI 96768

MANOA LETTUCE WRAP

1 pound ground chicken	2 oz. shiitake mushrooms, sliced
1 oz. chopped garlic	2 oz. hoisin sauce
1 oz. chopped ginger	1 oz. oyster sauce
2 oz. waterchestnuts, chopped	1 oz. chopped cilantro
2 oz. finely chopped onion	24 Manoa lettuce leaves, washed
2 oz. finely chopped carrot	1 Tbsp. red bell pepper, diced

In a large stock pot, heat 1 ounce oil to medium hot; add ground chicken, garlic and ginger. Mix constantly until chicken is lightly browned, about 5 minutes. Add waterchestnuts, onion, carrot and shiitake mushrooms; continue to cook until chicken is done and vegetables have softened. Add hoisin sauce, oyster sauce and cilantro, mix well. To serve arrange 6 Manoa lettuce leaves at the top of a plate, place ¼ of the mixture at the bottom of the lettuce leaves and garnish with diced bell pepper.

Serves 4.

THAI SEAFOOD CURRY

24 oz. Curry Stock, recipe below	8 oz. calamari tubes and tentacles, cleaned
12 oz. coconut milk	8 oz. julienne vegetables: carrots, cucumber,
4 Tbsp. lime juice	and red bell pepper
4 6 oz. lobster tails, cut in ½ lengthwise	2 oz. shoyu
16 jumbo shrimp, peeled, cleaned, tail on	4 sprigs Chinese parsley

In medium stock pot, add curry stock, coconut milk, lime juice and split lobster tails. Place over high heat until liquid boils; add shrimp, calamari, julienne vegetables and shoyu. Mix carefully until all seafood is cooked, about 3 minutes. Turn off heat, divide into 4 individual bowls and garnish with Chinese parsley. Serve with steamed rice on the side.

Serves 4.

CURRY STOCK

3 kaffir lime leaves	24 oz. water
1 piece lemon grass, chopped	¼ cup fish sauce
1 2" piece ginger, chopped	2 Tbsp. chili garlic paste
2 oz. shoyu	

In a medium stock pot, combine lime leaves, lemon grass, ginger, shoyu and water. Bring to a boil and reduce heat to simmer. Simmer for 15 to 20 minutes, add fish sauce and chili garlic paste. Mix well and remove from heat.

MAÑANA GARAGE

Sensual hot colors spice up the industrial decor at **Mañana Garage** while dynamic flavors heat up the sensational Nuevo Latino cuisine created by Chef/Partners Eddie Santos and Scott Idemoto, who was formerly with Haliimaile General Store. After opening in October 2000, locals have developed a passionate love affair with this hip unique restaurant, and tourists are seduced as well. Mañana Garage won the Hale 'Aina award for Restaurants of Distinction Best New Restaurant, 2002. When you visit, you will discover what so many others have found irresistible, unique quality food at reasonable prices, a spirited stylish air and awesome frozen margaritas!

Ambiance: Chic and lively with bold colors on the walls, chrome accents and blown-glass chandeliers along with gas pump door handles, hose clamps for napkins rings and a garage door that lifts to reveal a private dining room. If you prefer, you may dine outside with trade winds and tiki torches. The atmosphere heats up even more with the sensual rhythms of live music Wednesday through Saturday evenings.

Menu: Lunch will entice you with the Chicken Tortilla Epozote Soup, Blackened Fish Tostada or the delicious Adobo BBQ Duck and Sweet Potato Quesadilla. For dinner appetizers the Fried Green Tomatoes, Basil Crusted Crab Cakes, and their signature 'Ahi Ceviche all get rave reviews! Entrées include savory fresh fish specials, Pumpkin Seed Crusted Shrimp, Steak or Vegetarian Fajitas, or Mañana Garage Paella with fresh fish, shrimp, shellfish and calamari (served only on Fridays). Their Sweet Potato Praline Pound Cake Ice Cream Sandwich is so beguiling that *Bon Appétit* requested the recipe!

Details: Open nightly. Dinner entrées: $14.75–26.00. Lunch served Monday–Saturday, $6.95–14.00. Reservations recommended. Late night menu Wednesday–Saturday, 9 p.m. to 10:30 p.m.

(808) 873–0220 / WWW.THEMAÑANAGARAGE.COM
33 LONO AVENUE, KAHULUI, MAUI, HI 96732

'AHI CEVICHE

16 oz. sashimi grade 'ahi
juice of 2 limes
1 large ripe tomato, medium dice
1 small red onion, chopped fine
1 Serrano chili, seeded and chopped fine
1 small bunch cilantro, leaves only,
   chopped rough

2 ripe avocados, firm, cut into ½" cubes
3 oz. coconut milk
salt and white pepper to taste
Garnish
1 green plantain, or vegetable or
   tortilla chips

Cut the 'ahi into ¼" cubes and place in stainless steel or glass bowl. Toss the 'ahi in the lime juice and let stand for 3 minutes. Add the tomato, onion, Serrano chili, and cilantro. Add the avocado and then the coconut milk. Season to taste with salt and white pepper. At the restaurant, we slice the plantain very thin on a slicer and deep fry until crispy for garnish. You can do the same by using a mandolin and then deep frying the plantain slices, or substitute any type of crispy vegetable chip or tortilla chip. Serve in a Margarita glass with a mixture of chili powder and kosher salt on the rim. (Note: If you like more heat, add more chilies!) Serves 4.

ADOBO PULLED PORK WITH EDDIE'S LATIN DIP

1 boneless pork butt
6 dried Ancho chilies, seeded
zest and juice of 4 oranges
1 onion, rough chopped
1 head garlic, chopped

1 tsp. dried oregano
2 oz. cider vinegar
½ tsp. black peppercorns
3 whole cloves
½ tsp. whole cumin seeds

Adobo Marinade: Sauté the Ancho chilies, orange zest, onion, and garlic in a little oil. Add the orange juice, cover the pan and put on low heat until chilies soften. In a dry pan, toast the cumin seeds, black peppercorns and cloves until fragrant, about one minute. Grind in a spice or coffee grinder and add to chili mixture. Add ½ of the cider vinegar and the oregano. Remove from heat and purée in a blender. Allow to cool.

Trim the fat off the pork butt and cut into 3" cubes. Toss with the Adobo Marinade and refrigerate overnight. Roast the pork in a 350 degree oven until brown, about ½ hour. Cover pork with water and put it back in the oven, covered, until pork is tender and falling apart, 2 to 3 hours. Drain the jus from the pork and skim the fat. Reserve for Eddie's Latin Dip.

EDDIE'S LATIN DIP

2 shallots, diced fine
1 Oaxacan pasilla chili (or other smokey
   flavored, dried chili)
1 sprig fresh rosemary
olive oil for sauté
1 bay leaf

2 peppercorns
1 cup red wine
reserved pork jus
2 oz. cider vinegar
2 oz. soy sauce
1 Tbsp. sugar

Sauté shallots, pasilla chili, rosemary sprig, bay leaf and peppercorns in olive oil and deglaze with red wine. Add pork jus, cider vinegar, soy sauce and sugar. Reduce on low heat by ½. Strain.

To finish shred the pork and place in large sauté pan. Add 1 cup of Eddie's Latin Dip and reduce by ⅓, strain and serve with pork.

Chef Eddie Santos

LATIN AMERICAN

MOANA BAKERY & CAFÉ

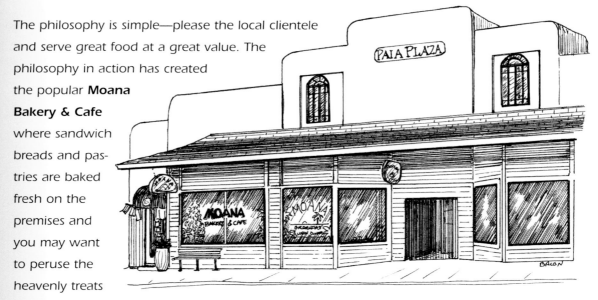

The philosophy is simple—please the local clientele and serve great food at a great value. The philosophy in action has created the popular **Moana Bakery & Cafe** where sandwich breads and pastries are baked fresh on the premises and you may want to peruse the heavenly treats in the pastry case before you order so you'll be sure to save room for dessert! Don Ritchey, the owner and chef (and sometimes dishwasher, he adds) has been cooking for 22 years beginning with Italian cuisine and now incorporating influences from Thailand and Japan with local touches. Growing herbs and exotic fruits himself and using fresh local ingredients, Don caters to what people like to eat and enjoys keeping it simple.

Ambiance: A pleasant bistro atmosphere with high ceilings and local artist's work decorating the walls located in an air conditioned historical building that originally manufactured and sold Hawaiian clothing. The stools lined up at the bar are from the old Singer sewing machines. Live music on Wednesday (vintage Hawaiian), Friday (jazz and blues), and Sunday (Flamenco, Gypsy guitar and violin).

Menu: Popular breakfast recommendations: Loco Moco, Blackened Mahi Mahi, Crab Cake Eggs Benedict among other traditional and local choices. Lunch features a fresh Thai Chicken Salad, Lamb Wahi, Grilled Mahi Mahi sandwich served with Asian slaw, and many other tempting choices. For dinner try Hana Bay Crab Cakes or Lemon Grass Grilled Prawns with Green Papaya Salad for starters, then an entrée of Chili Seared 'Ahi with mango salsa, Rack of Lamb, Thai Red Curry with Coconut Milk or the Fresh Island Catch special. Top off your meal with Creme Brulee, Banana Cream Pie or the delectable Lilikoi Cheesecake. Yum!

Details: Open daily. Breakfast most items under $10.00. Lunch: $6.95–12.95. Dinner entrées: $10.95–26.95. Dinner reservations recommended on weekends.

(808) 579-9999 / WWW.MOANACAFE.COM
71 BALDWIN AVENUE, PA'IA, MAUI, HI 96779

CRISPY VEGGIE SPRING ROLLS
WITH SWEET CHILI SAUCE AND NAMASU

1 cup fresh mushrooms, sliced

1 cup carrots, sliced

1 cup onion, sliced

¼ cup peanut oil

1 tsp. sesame seed oil

2 Tbsp. shoyu

2 cups bean thread noodles (soaked)

¼ cup chopped basil

¼ cup chopped cilantro

lumpia wrappers

cornstarch and water mix

oil for frying

Sauté mushrooms, carrots and onion in peanut oil until soft. Add sesame seed oil, shoyu and bean thread noodles. Mix together and let cool. Add fresh herbs. Wrap about 3 tablespoons of mix in wrappers. Seal with cornstarch and water mix. Prepare Sweet Chili Sauce. Fry spring rolls in hot oil until golden brown. Serve with Sweet Chili Sauce and macadamia nuts.

SWEET CHILI SAUCE

1 pint rice wine vinegar

2 cups sugar

2 Tbsp. chili garlic paste

Reduce vinegar with sugar until thick. Add chili garlic paste.

NAMASU

Marinade

2 cups rice wine vinegar

¾ cup sugar

1 Tbsp. chili paste

2 Tbsp. roasted sesame seeds

seeded cucumbers, julienne

carrots, fine julienne

red onion, fine julienne

Mix marinade ingredients together, add vegetables. Marinate for 3 hours. Serve with Spring Rolls.

NICK'S FISHMARKET MAUI

An enchanting and award–winning restaurant, **Nick's Fishmarket Maui** is situated on the elegant lush grounds of The Fairmont Kea Lani Hotel. Unique features of the this exquisite fine-dining restaurant are the glass-enclosed 2,000 bottle wine display with fine vintages from Italy, France, Germany and California, and a spectacular 800-gallon aquarium. Nick's Fishmarket Maui has been recognized with accolades both nationwide and locally— including the Wine Spectator Award of Excellence and Hale 'Aina awards, both for several consecutive years.

Ambiance: Blending Maui's natural beauty with the romance of a Mediterranean villa, Nick's features an open-air setting where you may dine inside in a booth just for two, or be romanced under stars and vine-covered trellises. For a more casual moment to enjoy an appetizer and drink, try the curving granite bar.

Menu: Innovative, classic cuisine with fresh seafood is the primary focus of Nick's menu, featuring items such as: Live Kona Lobster, Fresh Opakapaka, 'Ahi, Abalone, and Prime Steaks. The Greek Maui Wowie Salad will "wow" your taste buds with fresh zingy flavors. Entrée preparations include Lobster Tails roasted with sweet butter, served with orzo–mushroom risotto, and Potato "Scaled" Mahi Mahi—truffle potatoes, Cabernet–pepper sauce and white truffle oil.

Details: Dinner served nightly. Entrées from $26.95. Call for reservations. Valet parking. Sister restaurants are Sarento's on the Beach, page 118, Sarento's Top of the "I" page 76, and Aaron's Atop the Ala Moana, page 48.

(808) 879-7224 / WWW.TRI-STAR-RESTAURANTS.COM
THE FAIRMONT KEA LANI MAUI, 4100 WAILEA ALANUI DRIVE, WAILEA, MAUI, HI 96753

'AHI "POI POUNDER"

3 oz. sashimi grade 'ahi medallion	1 tsp. tobiko
2 oz. Alaskan king crab meat	½ avocado, sliced
½ oz. mayonnaise	1 oz. shredded nori
¼ tsp. minced chives	1 oz. julienne of cucumber
¼ tsp. minced Kula onion	

Pound 'ahi with a mallet to a thin, carpaccio style consistency. Combine crabmeat, mayonnaise, chives, onion and tobiko. Place in the center of carpaccio. Wrap into a purse, resembling a "poi pounder."

Aioli

¼ cup mayonnaise	1 Tbsp. wasabi paste

Mix mayonnaise and wasabi to taste.

Sauce

¼ cup shoyu	1 tsp. water
1 tsp. cornstarch	

Mix cornstarch and water together. Boil shoyu and add cornstarch mixture until syrupy.

For presentation: Place Aioli and Sauce on plate. Fan slice avocado in the middle. Place "poi pounder" on top of avocado. Garnish with cucumber and nori. Serve immediately.

Serves 1.

Pacific'O

In an era of celebrity chefs, a sense of creative flair and panache brings masterful culinary talent to the table and into the limelight. With these qualities, Executive Chef James McDonald stays on the cutting edge and keeps his customers delighted—from performing his marriage ceremony live over the internet filmed by the webcam at **Pacific'O**, to continually creating innovative dishes, to joining partners Louis Coulombe and Stephan Bel-Robert in an Upcountry farm that grows produce for Pacific'O and their 2 other popular venues (see below). The farm, named O'o, which in Hawaiian means to mature or to ripen, is the brain child of Louis and is run by Robbie Vorfeld. Chef James says he likes to keep his food "light and fresh with the emphasis on fresh fish and blending the different cultures of the islands." Now he has even more creative opportunity with the abundance of fresh, quality produce including some specialty and exotic items grown on the farm.

Pacific'O continually receives many awards including *Wine Spectator's* "Award of Excellence", "A Taste of Lahaina" and *Honolulu Magazine's* Hale 'Aina awards.

Ambiance: Enjoy the open-air setting by the beach with beautiful sunset views over Lana'i. Live jazz Friday and Saturday.

Menu: Everything is made from scratch, including delicious breads that are baked daily. Start with superb Chicken Gyoza or Panko Calamari. For an entrée try the fabulous Painted Fish with Indonesian soy, grilled and served with grilled pineapple and red pepper salsa with ginger sweet and sour sauce, Thai Dye Duck, or Pacific Prawns. Divine desserts include Chocolate Decadence and Banana Pineapple Lumpia.

Details: Open daily for lunch and dinner. Dinner entrées: $22.00–29.00. Reservations recommended. Also, see I'o, page 100 and Feast at Lele, page 94.

(808) 667–4341 / WWW.PACIFICOMAUI.COM
505 FRONT STREET, LAHAINA, MAUI, HI 96761

Thai Chicken Coconut Soup

1 gallon chicken stock
1 gallon coconut milk
2 pounds chicken meat, diced
2 oz. peanut oil
2 Tbsp. red Thai curry paste
6 kaffir lime leaves
¼ cup lemon grass
3 Tbsp. ginger, minced
3 Tbsp. garlic, minced

3 Tbsp. shallots, minced
2 cups sake
2 cups water chestnuts, sliced
2 cups bamboo shoots, sliced
2 cups shiitake mushrooms, sliced
2 cups Chinese straw mushrooms
1 cup cilantro, rough chopped
salt and pepper to taste

In a stock pot set over high heat, add peanut oil, curry, kaffir lime, lemon grass, ginger, garlic, shallots and sauté for 30 seconds. Season chicken and add to pot to lightly brown. Add sake, chicken stock and coconut milk and bring to a boil. Reduce heat to a low simmer; add water chestnuts, bamboo shoots, shiitake, straw mushrooms and let simmer for 30 minutes. Adjust seasoning and add cilantro when serving.

Oysters

50 Pacific oysters on half shell
1 cup Shiso Miso Mignonette (recipe below)

20 lemon wedges
2 cups ogo for garnish

Place some ogo plus 5 oysters on each plate. Drizzle each oyster with Shiso Miso Mignonette and place 2 lemon wedges on each plate.

Makes 10 servings.

Shiso Miso Mignonette

1 cup rice wine vinegar
½ cup white miso paste
8 shiso leaves

2 Tbsp. shallots, rough chopped
½ tsp. tabasco

Purée all in a blender. Reserve chilled.

THE PLANTATION HOUSE

Surrounded by soft emerald hills that glow in the late afternoon sun, **The Plantation House** is situated on the Plantation Course at Kapalua. On chilly winter nights, the glowing fireplace in the dining room creates a warm romantic setting for you to enjoy the bold intense flavors of Executive Chef Alex Stanislaw's cuisine. Deeply influenced by his grandmother's cooking, his Mediterranean ancestry, and Maui's fresh ingredients, he creates food that is bursting with flavor yet is also healthy and light. Partner Chris Kaiwe's knowledge and selection of fine wines is apparent on the wine list, which features many enticing options specifically chosen to complement the cuisine.

Ambiance: Open air and lovely, The Plantation House offers a relaxing plantation-style environment to take in fine food, wine and a spectacular sunset over the Kapalua coast and Moloka'i.

Menu: Specialty fresh fish preparations include: "A Taste of the Mediterranean," Maui onion mustard crusted fish on oven roasted Maui onions with fried caper sauce, and "Sweet Island Breeze," mirin and macadamia nut seared Hawaiian Fish with Jasmine Risotto and Caramelized Chili Sauce. For breakfast and lunch indulge in Crabcake Benedict with Roasted Pepper Hollandaise or Kula Spinach Salad with Wonton Crisps, Sweet Soy Vinaigrette and Seared 'Ahi Sashimi. Dessert selections include the dreamy Chocolate Mousse Torte or Bananas Foster for two.

Details: Breakfast and lunch served from 8 a.m. to 3 p.m. daily: $6.00–14.00. Dinner nightly, entrées: $19.00–30.00. Reservations recommended. Directions: pass the Kapalua exit, turn right on Plantation Estates Drive, then immediately turn left on Plantation Club Drive. Visit sister restaurants, The SeaWatch in Wailea, and The Beach House on Kaua'i (page 18).

(808) 669–6299 / WWW.THEPLANTATIONHOUSE.COM
2000 PLANTATION CLUB DRIVE, KAPALUA, MAUI, HI 96761

Pepper Rubbed 'Ahi Tuna with Heirloom Tomatoes, Arugula and Mediterranean Tomato-Caper Berry Salsa

4   6-7 oz. sashimi quality tuna steaks,
    ¾" thick
1 tsp. kosher salt and
2 tsp. pepper, mixed

8 oz. arugula
4 oz. extra virgin olive oil
2 oz. balsamic vinegar
4 large or 8 small heirloom tomatoes

Prepare salsa (see below). Slice heirloom tomatoes. Chill. Brush 'ahi with olive oil, season with salt and pepper mix. In a **very** hot pan, sear 'ahi for 1 minute per side; remove from pan and chill. Toss arugula with vinegar and olive oil, sprinkle with salt.

Presentation: Place sliced heirloom tomatoes in the center of the plate, top with dressed arugula, top with 'ahi, cover with salsa and drizzle with juice from salsa.

Enjoy with a glass of chilled Rosé or Sauvignon Blanc.

Mediterranean Tomato-Caper Berry Salsa

4 vine ripe tomatoes, seeded and diced
1 small Maui onion, diced
1 bunch flat leaf Italian parsley
1 Tbsp. Hawaiian salt

2 oz. calamata olives, pitted and diced
2 oz. caper berries, stem off, sliced
2 lemons, juiced
4 oz. extra virgin olive oil

Mix together and chill.

Jumbo Diver Scallops with Spinach and Herb Butter

8   2 oz. diver scallops
10 oz. spinach, washed, dried, torn into
    small pieces
8 cloves garlic, finely chopped
3 oz. unsalted butter

1 tomato, seeded and diced
½ bunch Italian parsley, chopped
2 tsp. Hawaiian salt
best crusty bread you can find

Sauté spinach in a hot sauté pan with ½ the garlic and 1 ounce of the butter. Sprinkle with a touch of water to induce wilting, and center on plate or bowl just as it wilts.

On **very** hot pan, brushed with a miniscule amount of oil (we use extra virgin olive oil in a spray can) sear salted scallops 1 minute per side, until rare in the center. Place scallops, 2 per plate, on top of the spinach. In the same pan you sautéed the spinach, sauté the remaining garlic with the remaining butter until the butter and garlic both begin to color, and the garlic smells wonderful. Add the diced tomato and parsley. Toss, sprinkle with the Hawaiian salt. Touch with an ounce of water (careful for the splatter) and pour on the scallops and spinach.

Serve with the crusty bread (to sop up the juice) and a crispy Chardonnay or French Sancere. Enjoy.

SANSEI SEAFOOD RESTAURANT & SUSHI BAR

The winning combination of outstanding food in a friendly upbeat atmosphere continues to impress not only customers, but food critics as well. **Sansei Seafood Restaurant & Sushi Bar** has received recognition and awards both locally and nationally including Honolulu Magazine's coveted Hale 'Aina Awards for 6 years running, "Our favorite Asian Restaurants" in *Bon Appétit* and "America's Best Sushi Bars" in *Travel & Leisure Magazine*, to name a few! Raised on O'ahu, Executive Chef/Owner D.K. Kodama travelled extensively, experiencing many different flavors and culinary styles, before returning to Hawai'i to share his wonderful expertise with us!

Ambiance: Friendly, fun and lively. Sit at the sushi bar and be entertained by watching the chefs create delicious delicacies or enjoy the privacy of your own table. As D.K. says, "Dress casual, bring a smile, relax and enjoy the adventure of dining at Sansei."

Menu: Begin with the excellent award-winning Mango Crab Salad Sushi Roll with Spicy Thai Vinaigrette, and (also award-winning) Asian Rock Shrimp Cake with a Ginger-Lime Chili Butter and Cilantro Pesto. You'll find their selection of sushi and fresh fish specials inspiring. There are also choices for meat lovers such as Tender Scallopini of Pork Tenderloin served over roasted garlic mashed potatoes in an Asian sweet & sour glazed fig chutney. For dessert the Granny Smith Apple Tart with Caramel Sauce served warm with vanilla ice cream is sooo sublime! The wine list is carefully selected to complement the cuisine.

Details: Open nightly. Sushi from $3.95, entrées from $15.95. Please call for reservations. Late night dining Thursday through Saturday, 10 p.m. to 1 a.m. Kapalua location offers late night dining on Thursday and Friday only, and has live karaoke entertainment. Be sure to visit the newest Maui location in Kihei.

(808) 879–0004 / WWW.SANSEIHAWAII.COM / KIHEI TOWN CENTER, KIHEI, MAUI, HI 96753
(808) 669–6286 / THE SHOPS AT KAPALUA, 115 BAY DRIVE, KAPALUA, MAUI, HI 96761
(808) 536–6286 / RESTAURANT ROW, 500 ALA MOANA BLVD., HONOLULU, O'AHU, HI 96813

MACADAMIA NUT CRUSTED TIGER PRAWN TEMAKI
(HAND ROLLED SUSHI)

Vinegar Rice
2 cups sushi quality rice
2 cups + 2 Tbsp. water

¼ cup rice vinegar
2 Tbsp. sugar
½ tsp. salt

Heat sugar in non–aluminum sauce pan until dissolved. Wash rice until water is clear. Transfer to a colander. Set aside, let drain for 1 hour. Measure the water and add to rice in an electric rice cooker. Let cook. When the rice has finished cooking allow 15 minutes afterwards to steam. Remove rice to a large bowl and add vinegar. Cut rice. To incorporate, keep rice at room temperature; cover with a clean cloth.

6 pieces 16/20 tiger prawns or shrimp
   peeled with tail still on, butterfly
½ cup panko (Japanese bread crumbs)
¼ cup macadamia nuts, chopped finely

¼ cup all purpose flour for dusting shrimp
1 egg, beaten
2½ cups vegetable oil for frying

Dust shrimp with flour, dip in egg then mac–nut and panko mixture. Reserve for deep frying. In 350 degree oil, cook shrimp until golden brown, approximately 30 seconds on each side.

6 pieces, halved, sheets of sushi nori
6 pieces cucumber sticks (preferably
   Japanese) cut 4½"x¼"

½ avocado, sliced lengthwise
½ cup sweet Thai chili sauce for dipping

Place piece of nori in hand. Add ¼ cup sushi rice. Press down flat. Then add avocado, cucumber and tiger prawn. Cut in ½ lengthwise. Fold corner of nori over ingredients to shape like a cone. Serve with sweet Thai chili sauce.

Head Sushi Chef Kiefer Takasaki

SANSEI SEARED SCALLOP AND FOIE GRAS

12 pieces whole scallops
4½ oz. foie gras, cut into 12 pieces
2 cups thinly sliced sweet onion
2 oz. fresh arugula, seasoned with lemon
   juice and salt
½ cup Unagi Glaze (Recipe at right)

1 Tbsp. black sesame seeds
1 Tbsp. white sesame seeds
½ Tbsp. lemon juice
Unagi Glaze
2 cups each sake, mirin, soy and water
3 cups sugar

Combine Unagi Glaze ingredients in pot, bring to boil, reduce by ½ on medium heat. Cool and set aside.

Caramelize sweet onion in a sauté pan. Cook until onions are translucent and starting to turn brown. Set aside until presentation. Season scallops with kosher salt and black pepper, sear in sauté pan with butter until medium rare. Remove scallops and drain pan. Season foie gras; cook on each side for 45 seconds in hot pan. For presentation: toss arugula with lemon juice and salt, place in middle of plate. Place 1 teaspoon of onion in 3 places around arugula. Add a scallop on top of the onion, then the foie gras on top of the scallop. Drizzle ⅛ cup Unagi Glaze over scallops, foie gras and greens. Sprinkle plate with sesame seeds, serve immediately.

Executive Chef Eric Arbogast

JAPANESE BASED HAWAIIAN REGIONAL

SARENTO'S ON THE BEACH

With the waves lapping on the sand nearby, a brilliant sunset and sensuous ocean breezes, **Sarento's on the Beach** captures the romance of the islands and enhances it with superb five–star cuisine. The newest of Tri–Star Restaurant Group's four exceptional restaurants, Sarento's has been honored with the 2002 Wine Spectator Award of Excellence, the Hale 'Aina award for Best New Restaurant 2002, and Ilima Awards. Corporate Chef George Gomes, Jr., blends his local boy roots and classic French cuisine training to create intriguing menus for all the Tri–Star restaurants. Complement your dinner with a fine wine from the collection of over 1,500 bottles from France, Germany and California, with a special focus on rare Italian wines.

Ambiance: You can enjoy exceptional service while you luxuriate in this elegant setting right on pristine Keawakapu Beach with views of Molokini, Lanai and Kaho'olawe.

Menu: Sarento's multi–regional Italian cuisine with a Mediterranean flair utilizes the freshest seasonal island ingredients. Specialties include award–winning presentations of homemade pastas, fresh Hawaiian seafood, prime steaks, veal, lamb and more. Begin with Frutta Di Mare—an assortment of chilled seasonal shellfish, or House Smoked Salmon. For your entrée, try the Osso Buco with saffron risotto, Lobster "Cannelloni" or Tonno Alla Griglia—grilled porcini crusted 'ahi, lemon–garlic emulsion and balsamic grilled vegetables.

Details: Dinner served nightly. Entrées from $26.95. Call for reservations. Valet parking. Sister restaurants are Nick's Fishmarket Maui, page 110, Sarento's Top of the "I" page 76, and Aaron's Atop the Ala Moana, page 48.

(808) 875–7555 / WWW.TRI-STAR-RESTAURANTS.COM
2980 SOUTH KIHEI ROAD, KIHEI, MAUI, HI 96753

Kaua'i Shrimp Wrapped in Pancetta
with Fire Roasted Sweet Pepper Sauce & Leeks

30 Kaua'i shrimp, peeled, deveined, heads on   **30 pieces Pancetta bacon, thinly sliced**

First prepare sauce and leeks, recipes below. Then, wrap shrimp tightly with pancetta and sear in hot pan until crispy on all sides. Drain excess oil. Place a spoonful of Sweet Pepper Sauce in the center of a warm plate. Arrange shrimp around the sauce and garnish with leek "fries."

Serves 10 as an appetizer or 6 as an entrée.

Fire Roasted Sweet Pepper Sauce

6 pieces sweet bell pepper, fire roasted,
   peeled and sliced
3 garlic cloves, thinly sliced
3 Tbsp. sherry vinegar
½ tsp. sugar

½ cup extra virgin olive oil
to taste sea salt
to taste freshly ground pepper

Blend peppers, garlic, vinegar and sugar. Purée until smooth. Gradually pour in olive oil in a steady stream until creamy in consistency. Season with salt and pepper and reserve in warm place.

2 large leeks, julienned
2 cups Wondra flour

to taste sea salt
to taste freshly ground pepper

Lightly toss leeks in flour and deep fry until golden brown. Drain on paper towels. Season with salt and pepper and reserve in warm place.

STELLA BLUES CAFÉ

A Kihei favorite for 10 years, **Stella Blues Café** is now in a new spacious and attractive location. With a full bar, a stage for live music, a private banquet room, and lanai seating with mountain views, the new location is a boon and it provides even more

reasons to enjoy the affordable and healthy cuisine at this popular café. The original owners, Janie and Ray Ennis have handed over the restaurant to their son and daughter, Kale and Kindra Ennis and Cindy Anton who will continue serving the great fresh food and hearty portions for which Stella Blues is known.

Ambiance: Casual and relaxed with an open beam ceiling, pleasing decor and an exhibition kitchen. (The former A Pacific Café location.)

Menu: Their large menu keeps customers coming back for more by offering a wide variety of items including many daily specials. For breakfast, try the South of the Border or the Banana Macadamia Nut Pancakes. (People love 'em!) For lunch they have huge gorgeous salads: Cobb or Chicken Caesar, sandwiches, homemade soups, plate lunches, and items such as Grilled Steak Sandwich, and Toby's Tofu Extraordinaire. Dinner features Crispy Crabcakes, Oysters on the Half Shell, Vegetarian Shepherd's Pie, Baby Back Ribs with Tropical BBQ Sauce, pizzas and fresh fish specials such as the Iron Skillet Blackened fish with a cooling cucumber salsa. Divine desserts include Banana Split Cake, and Stella's Pie with an Oreo cookie crust, caramel, chocolate ganache and whipped cream. Wow!

Details: Open daily. Breakfast and lunch under $10.00. Dinner: $9.00–21.95. Appetizers served in the bar until midnight on week days, later on the weekends.

(808) 874–3779 / WWW.STELLABLUESCAFE.COM
1279 SOUTH KIHEI ROAD, AZEKA II MAUKA, KIHEI, MAUI, HI 96753

Stella's Ancho Chicken Chili

1 pound chicken thigh meat

6 Tbsp. ancho chili powder

2 cups celery, diced

2 cups yellow onion, diced

4 Tbsp. garlic, minced

4 cups canned kidney beans

2 cups tomatoes, diced

1 cup beer

4 quarts chicken stock

2 quarts beef stock

1 bunch cilantro

1 bunch green onions

1 Tbsp. chili powder

1 Tbsp. cumin

1 Tbsp. cinnamon

1 Tbsp. cayenne

1 Tbsp. coriander

1 Tbsp. chili flakes

1 Tbsp. oregano

4 Tbsp. flour

4 Tbsp. butter

Sprinkle thigh meat with ancho chili powder to coat well. Roast in a 350 degree oven until just done. Cool.

In a large pot, sweat onion, celery, and garlic. Add dried spices and toast 3 to 4 minutes. Add beer and reduce by ½. Add stocks, tomatoes, and beans. Bring to a boil. Separately, melt butter and add flour; whisk until combined and cook over low heat 5 minutes, stirring often. Add flour mixture to boiling stock and whisk together. Bring back to a boil and simmer until soup begins to thicken. Season with salt and pepper. Remove from heat. When chicken is cool, chop into ¼" cubes. Add to soup along with cilantro and green onions. Cool chili properly and refrigerate. It is better the next day. Enjoy with a glass of beer—it's got a little kick.

The Waterfront Restaurant

The Ma'alaea Waterfront Restaurant will enchant you with a fabulous oceanside setting, warm exceptional service and incredible food. The Waterfront holds a special allure for locals and visitors as it is easy to feel welcome with owners Donna, Gary, and Rick Smith maintaining the philosophy that you are a guest in their home. With Chef Bob Cambra creating award–winning cuisine, they have been honored with "Best Seafood" as well as "Best Service" by *The Maui News* reader poll for several years. Their stellar wine list (which offers 27 wines by the glass!) has received the Award of Excellence from *Wine Spectator* for 8 years. Yet Gary explains, "It's nice to receive awards, but the real reward is the satisfaction we see in our guests' eyes and the fact that they return again and again. That's the best award we could ever receive."

Ambiance: Intimate and romantic whether you sit inside in a booth surrounded by tropical art or on the lanai where ocean breezes and a gorgeous sunset will enhance your dinner.

Menu: We started with the rich Crab Stuffed Mushroom Caps Au Gratinée and then raved over the awesome flavors in the Sesame Pan Seared Sashimi Salad. Five to eight fresh fish selections are available daily, offered with your choice of nine different preparations. I loved the Monchong with Hawaiian Salsa. Lobster, chicken, steak, veal, lamb, and a Lobster Chowder are also offered. Entrées are served with fresh-baked Maui onion bread and homemade Hawaiian beer cheese, fresh vegetables and herbed rice or selected potatoes. For dessert, we moaned over a warm Double Chocolate Brownie with vanilla ice cream and raspberry coulis, and an Upside Down Apple Pecan Pie (recipe at right).

Details: Open nightly. Dinner from $18.95. Call for reservations.

(808) 244–9028 / WWW.WATERFRONTRESTAURANT.NET
MILOWAI CONDOMINIUM, 50 HAUOLI STREET, MA'ALAEA, MAUI, HI 96793

Maui Onion Dressing

2 egg yolks
1 tsp. minced garlic
1 tsp. white pepper
1 oz. tabasco
1 oz. Worcestershire sauce
1 oz. fresh lemon juice

1 tsp. Dijon mustard
5 cups salad oil
1½ cups sugar
1½ cups apple cider vinegar
2 medium Maui onions, diced

In a bowl combine egg yolks, garlic, white pepper, tabasco, Worcestershire sauce, lemon juice and mustard. Emulsify egg yolk mixture and oil together. Add some of the sugar and some of the vinegar intermittently until all the oil, vinegar and sugar are used up. Finish with the diced onions.

Upside-Down Apple Pecan Pie

Bottom

4 oz. brown sugar
8 oz. ground pecans

4 oz. whole butter

Mix all ingredients in a mixer and place in the bottom of a pie pan.

Apples

7 Granny Smith apples
1 oz. lemon juice
½ cup sugar
2 Tbsp. flour
2 tsp. cinnamon

½ tsp. nutmeg
½ tsp. allspice
½ tsp. cloves
pinch of salt

Peel and slice apples. Mix all ingredients in a bowl.

Dough

2 cups flour
½ cup margarine or butter
1 egg

4 oz. ice water
pinch of salt

Mix flour, butter, salt and egg until mixture forms small crumbs. Add water and mix, **do not over mix**. Form two balls.

To assemble: Spread the pecan crust on the bottom. Roll out one of the pie dough balls and place over pecan crust. Place apple mixture on top. Cover with another crust. Cut edges of crust and poke a few slits on top of crust. Bake at 350 degrees for 45 minutes.

Fine Seafood

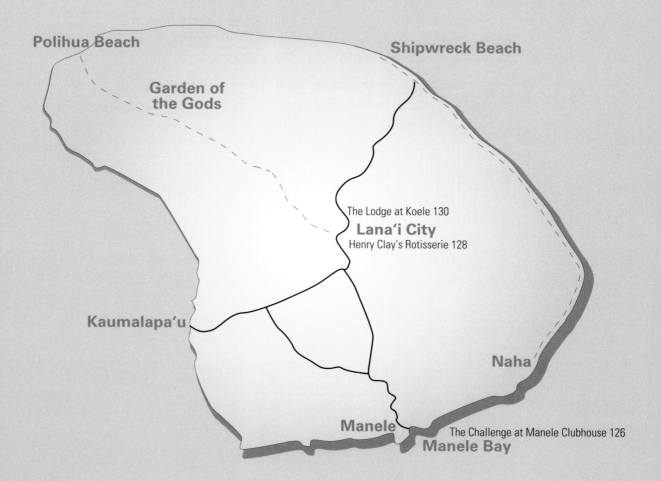

Polihua Beach

Shipwreck Beach

Garden of
the Gods

The Lodge at Koele 130
Lana'i City
Henry Clay's Rotisserie 128

Kaumalapa'u

Naha

Manele
The Challenge at Manele Clubhouse 126
Manele Bay

LANA'I
THE PINEAPPLE ISLAND

Lanaʻi

Restaurant, Page, Type of Cuisine
Recipes Featured

The Challenge at Manele Clubhouse, 126, Island–Inspired
Pan-Seared Salmon with Shallot Spoon Bread, Marinated Cherry Tomatoes and Horseradish–Chive Sauce

Henry Clay's Rotisserie, 128, Country
Seafood Fettuccini in Jalapeño Jack Cream / Eggplant Casserole with Creole Sauce

The Formal Dining Room — The Lodge at Koele, 130, Modern American with an Upscale Feel
Seared Lanai Axis Venison with Root Vegetable Hash, Spinach–Potato Dumplings and Huckleberry Sauce

Majestically perched on the slopes above Hulopo'e Beach, the luxurious **Manele Bay Hotel** is a blend of Mediterranean and *kama'aina* architecture. The elegant interior surrounds you with Oriental artifacts, paintings by local artists and spectacular murals while the stunning landscaping and sweeping views of the grounds will lure you into tranquility. You will discover one of the world's most beautiful golf courses there, the Challenge at Manele, which was designed by Jack Nicklaus. Whether you're touring and exploring or out for a round of golf, **The Challenge at Manele Clubhouse** offers a comfortable place to relax, refresh and enjoy some island-inspired cuisine.

Ambiance: This lovely informal open–air setting offers cliffside dining with views of Maui, Kaho'olawe and the Big Island. During whale season (December through April) it is a prime location to see Humpback whales as well as an occasional school of Spinner dolphins and it is absolutely enchanting during a full moon.

Menu: Lunch features the Grilled Asian Tuna Salad and the Lana'i-Style Mahi Mahi Sandwich. Signature dishes at dinner include the Hulopo'e Firecracker Shrimp, Thai-hitian Seafood Stew and Flank Steak served with Port Blue Cheese, Spinach & Indonesian Blue Crab.

Details: Lunch daily, $12.00–18.00. Dinner Thursday through Monday, entrées: $23.00–29.00. Afternoon Temptations daily from 3:30 to 5:30 p.m. except on Tuesday and Wednesdays until 5:00 p.m. For reservations call extension 2230. Shuttle service available at the Porte Cochre.

(808) 565–2230 / WWW.MANELEBAYHOTEL.COM
MANELE BAY HOTEL GOLF COURSE, LANA'I, HI 96763

Pan-Seared Salmon
with Shallot Spoon Bread, Marinated Cherry Tomatoes and Horseradish–Chive Sauce

4 5-6 oz. fillets of salmon

2 oz. olive oil

salt and pepper to taste

4 cups Shallot Spoon Bread (recipe below)

4 oz. arugula

8 oz. Horseradish–Chive Sauce (below)

2 oz. scallion oil

4 Tbsp. onion chives, chopped

2 cups Marinated Cherry Tomatoes (below)

Season both sides of the salmon fillets. In a large hot oven proof sauté pan, place the olive oil and heat to just under the smoking point. Carefully place the salmon in pan and cook until nicely browned on the presentation side. Turn the salmon over and place in a 400 degree oven to finish cooking.

For presentation, place 1 cup of the Shallot Spoon Bread in the center of the plate. Place a small hole in the center of the spoon bread and pour ½ ounce of the Horseradish–Chive Sauce in the hole. Place the arugula bottoms in the hole and fan out to make a "bed" for the salmon. Place the remaining 1½ ounces per portion of the sauce around the plate. Garnish the sauce with ½ ounce of the scallion oil and the chopped chives. Once the salmon is cooked to your desired degree of doneness, remove and place on the center of the bed of arugula. Cover with the Marinated Cherry Tomatoes. Serves 4.

Shallot Spoon Bread

¾ cup melted butter

1 cup sour cream

1 cup fresh corn (optional)

½ cup shallots, diced and caramelized

¾ cup cream corn (it turns out better if you purée in the blender first)

1 box corn bread mix (3 cups)

Preheat oven to 350 degrees. Spray a 4" half pan with quick release (Pam). First incorporate all the wet ingredients including the corn and shallots, followed by the corn bread mix. Bake at 350 degrees for approximately 30 to 45 minutes or until cake springs back and when you insert a toothpick it comes out clean.

Horseradish–Chive Sauce

1 cup white wine

1 Tbsp. shallots, chopped

¼ cup heavy cream

½ pound butter, cut into cubes

1 Tbsp. prepared horseradish, or to taste

salt and pepper to taste

In saucepan bring the white wine to a boil and reduce by ½. Add cream and return to a boil. Slowly whisk in cold butter. Place in a blender for 2 minutes. Season to taste.

Scallion Oil

4 oz. scallions, chopped, greens only

6 oz. canola oil

In a blender on high speed, add the chopped scallion tops and the oil. Allow to run on high speed for a few minutes. Taste and adjust seasoning with salt and pepper. Strain, either through a very fine mesh strainer or cheesecloth.

Marinated Cherry Tomatoes

2 cups cherry tomatoes, quartered

3 Tbsp. chives, very finely chopped

2 Tbsp. parsley, roughly chopped

2 Tbsp. scallion oil

1 Tbsp. balsamic syrup

1½ tsp. salt

½ tsp. pepper

Combine all ingredients and let sit for a minimum of 2 hours before serving.

Island–Inspired

Henry Clay's Rotisserie

A unique alternative to the resort restaurants on the quiet island of Lana'i, **Henry Clay's Rotisserie** creates a special allure with it's charming character and hearty "soul food." Popular with residents and visitors alike, Henry Clay's is located in the Hotel Lana'i, which was originally built in 1923 by James Dole to accommodate and entertain visiting pineapple executives. Chef/Owner Henry Clay Richardson, originally from French Louisiana, is a family man and creates a feeling of family in his restaurant where you will be served generous portions of food, which he likes to "keep as simple and fresh as possible, keeping it fun." He cooks with his own style and talent inspired by memories of how his mother and grandmother cooked.

Ambiance: The restaurant is warm and cozy with hardwood floors, watercolors by local artists, an exhibition kitchen and a brick fireplace for chilly evenings (they're at 2,000 feet elevation). And, if you'd like to experience the contrast of cool crisp air with warm food, try dining in the peaceful patio under a grove of towering Norfolk pines.

Menu: Rajun Cajun Clay's Shrimp is "to die for" and "extremely habit forming." If you can stop eating the incredible shrimp, you'll have room for Louisiana Style Baby Back Ribs that are down home "Barbeque" cajun seasoned and rotisserie fired, Lana'i's fresh catch of the day, Rotisserie Roasted Chicken, Gourmet Pizza, or the specialty of the house, Lana'i Free Range Axis Deer. Top it all off with a warm and oh-so-good piece of New Orleans Style Pecan Pie.

Details: Open nightly. Entrées: $16.95–30.95. Hotel Lanai offers charming rooms with plantation–style decor and a complimentary continental breakfast. For reservations and information call 1–877–665–2624 or visit their web site.

(808) 565-7211 / WWW.HOTELLANAI.COM
828 LANA'I AVENUE, LANA'I CITY, LANA'I, HI 96763

SEAFOOD FETTUCCINI IN JALAPEÑO JACK CREAM

6 oz. each of fresh scallops, clams, gulf shrimp
   or prawns, and fresh fish (total 24 oz.)
(or substitute your favorite seafood for above)
½ tsp. fresh cracked black peppercorn
¼ tsp. sea salt
2 oz. unsalted butter
1 Tbsp. shallots, finely chopped
1 tsp. garlic, finely chopped
6 slices jalapeño, sliced (add more or less,
   depending on degree of "spicy" desired

1 tsp. flat leaf parsley, chopped
1 Tbsp. red bell pepper, roasted, peeled
   and diced
1 Tbsp. lime juice
8 oz. seafood stock (or substitute good
   clam juice or fish stock with no MSG)
12 oz. heavy cream
2 oz. Monterey Jack cheese, grated
20-24 oz. fettuccini (after cooking)
1 Tbsp. basil, sliced thin

Clean and remove roe from scallops, if still attached. Wash shells of clams. Peel, devein and butterfly shrimp or prawns. Season seafood with cracked black peppercorn and sea salt. Lightly sauté seafood over medium heat. Remove the clams as they begin to open, the shrimp when just turning orange, the fish when opaque, and the scallops when just firming up. Keep all warm to be added back to the sauce. Add shallots, garlic, parsley, bell pepper and jalapeños to pan; sauté until you begin to smell the aroma of the garlic. Deglaze with lime juice, cook until evaporated. Add seafood stock along with any juice in container resulting from cooked seafood. Reduce by ¾. Add heavy cream, reduce by ¼. Now add warm reserved seafood back into the sauce. Cook quickly just to bring the mixture up to temperature. Do not overcook. Away from the heat, add the cheese; stir to melt. Check seasoning, adjust with salt and pepper if needed. Cook fettuccini. When ready, drain and add to sauce. Put back onto the range, heat until just under a simmer. Toss to coat the pasta. Mix basil into entrée. Enjoy!

EGGPLANT CASSEROLE WITH CREOLE SAUCE

Casserole
2 to 3 medium size round eggplants
2 tsp. sea salt
1 tsp. fresh ground pepper (black and white)
2 oz. extra virgin olive oil
4 oz. mushrooms, sliced
2 cloves garlic, minced
2 oz. shallots, chopped
¼ cup chopped herbs: thyme, parsley, tarragon
3 vine ripe tomatoes
4 oz. mozzarella or gouda cheese
8 basil leaves

Sauce
1 red bell pepper, sliced ¼" thick
1 green bell pepper, sliced ¼" thick
2 Maui onions, sliced ¼" thick
1 oz. shallots, chopped
2 cloves garlic, sliced thin
1 Tbsp. lemon juice
¼ tsp. fresh ground pepper
2 Tbsp. white wine
4 oz. vegetable stock
12 oz. fresh tomato sauce or V-8 juice
tabasco or Cajun seasoning to taste

Sauce: Sauté bell peppers in 1 oz. olive oil until they start to brown on edges. Add onions and cook until they begin to caramelize. Add garlic and shallots; cook to release the aroma. Add pepper and Cajun seasoning, deglaze with lemon juice. Add wine, reduce until dry. Add stock, reduce by ¾. Add the tomato sauce or V-8 and reduce by ¼. Check seasoning.

Casserole: Slice eggplant longwise, 3" thick. Layout and brush with oil, season, flip over and repeat. Grill until tender, approximately 2 minutes per side. Do not allow blackening or it will result in a bitter taste. Place on a pan, evenly spaced, and allow to cool. Season and sauté mushrooms over medium heat, until lightly browned. Add shallots and garlic. Continue to sauté until the aroma of the garlic is released. Finish with the herbs, away from the heat. Peel and remove seeds from tomatoes. Cut across into ¼" thick slices. Slice or grate the cheese. Wash and remove stems from basil. In a casserole or lasagna 6"x9" dish, layer eggplant, cheese, mushrooms, tomatoes and basil. Repeat until all is used. Bake at 350 degrees for 20 to 30 minutes until hot throughout. Cover with ½ of the sauce. Bake 5 more minutes. Top with additional sauce and serve.

Travelers from all over the world are seduced by the special qualities of this relaxed, scenic paradise. It is a place where kama'ainas (Hawai'i residents) go to get away. Serene and beautiful, **The Lodge at Koele** offers refinement and grace on the quiet island of Lana'i. It is wonderful to experience the blend of warm aloha from the long-time local residents who make up most of the staff, with the inviting elegance of a top resort. Recognized by *Condé Nast Traveler*, *Zagat*, *Gourmet* and *Bon Appétit* magazines, among others, the Lodge continually receives awards and top ratings. **The Formal Dining Room** offers an exceptional dining experience with outstanding cuisine, first–class service and an elegant setting. Executive Chef Brad Czajka was born in Honolulu and, while he left Hawai'i at a very young age, he is pleased to be back "home." His menus embrace contemporary American cooking and incorporate a variety of local ingredients included in the daily life and celebrations of Hawaiian's.

Ambiance: The beautifully decorated octagonally shaped Formal Dining Room offers extraordinary fine dining and romance enhanced by the glow of a fireplace.

Menu: You may begin with Seared Foie Gras on Mango–Croissant Bread Pudding or House Smoked Salmon. For a salad try the Manchego Cheese Tart and then enjoy the Chef's Fennel Pollen–dusted Hawaiian Sea Bass on Scallop stuffed Portabella "Cannelloni's" with a Wilted–Spinach, Red Onion and Harvest Pear Salad or Pan Roasted Whole Kona Lobster on Foie Gras Mashed Potatoes. Save room for an exquisite dessert.

Details: Dinner only; entrées begin at $42.00. Jacket required.

(808) 565–4580 / WWW.LODGEATKOELE.COM
THE LODGE AT KOELE, LANA'I CITY, LANA'I, HI 96763

Seared Lanai Axis Venison
with Root Vegetable Hash, Spinach-Potato Dumplings and Huckleberry Sauce

venison
Root Vegetable Hash (recipe below)

Spinach-Potato Dumplings (recipe below)
Huckleberry Demi Sauce (recipe below)

Season the venison and pan sear. Finish in oven to desired temperature. Place the hash in the ring mold and sear on the flat top, then finish in oven. Drop the prepared dumplings (see below) into **boiling** salted water. When they float they are ready. Do not over cook. Place them in a hot sauté pan with olive oil and season. Place the hash in the left center of the plate. Slice the venison on a bias and stand up next to the hash facing outwards. Drizzle the sauce around the plate then place dumplings around.

Root Vegetable Hash

10 Idaho potatoes, peeled
5 sweet potatoes, peeled
6 carrots, peeled

6 parsnips, peeled
4 celery roots, peeled
4 onions, peeled

Place all items through the large hole grater. Combine all and mix thoroughly while seasoning. Sear off on a flat top until at least ½ way cooked. Then lay on a sheet pan and reserve.

Spinach–Potato Dumplings

8 cups potatoes
4 cups all purpose flour
4 egg yolks

2 oz. spinach purée, drained
6 egg whites
olive oil and kosher salt

Rinse the potatoes and then towel dry. Coat with olive oil and crust with kosher salt. Place on a sheet pan and bake for 30 to 35 minutes at 375 degrees until almost completely done. Peel the potatoes and run them through a ricer. In a stainless steel bowl, whisk the egg yolks and the spinach together, then fold in the measured out potatoes, mix thoroughly. Sift the flour and then measure in the correct amount. Gently fold in and **do not over mix** as this will make them tough and chewy. Fold in the egg whites and let the dough rest for 30 minutes. Then cut the dough into 8 parts and start rolling out each part into ½" cylinder rolls. Cut them into 1" pieces and lightly dust with flour. Roll them off of a fork, grooved paddle or even a grater. Lay them out on a sheet pan lined with parchment paper and reserve in the freezer until needed. (See cooking instructions in first portion of Venison recipe.)

Huckleberry Demi Sauce

2 cups huckleberries
2 cups dried cranberries
4 cups shallots, diced
1 cup sugar
2 cups carrots, diced
2 cups scallion whites, diced
2 cups celery, diced

2 cups leeks, diced
2 bottles port
3 cups cranberry juice
1 gallon lamb demi
5 thyme sprigs
2 bay leaves

In a sauce pot caramelize the vegetables, then add the sugar. Add the cranberry juice and reduce by ½. Add the port and reduce by ½. Add remaining ingredients and simmer until the consistency is sauce-like. Adjust seasonings and strain.

Modern American with an Upscale Feel

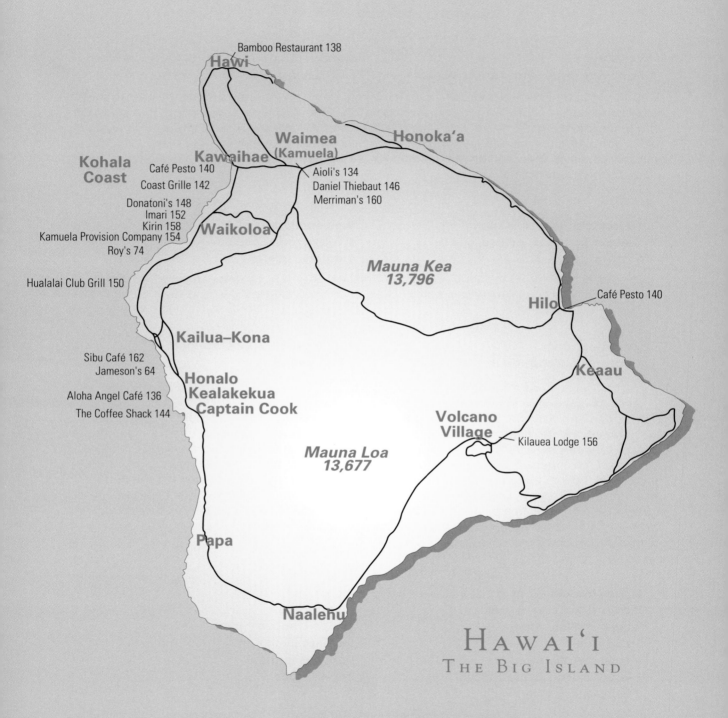

Bamboo Restaurant 138

Hawi

Waimea
(Kamuela)

Honoka'a

Kohala
Coast

Kawaihae

Café Pesto 140

Coast Grille 142

Aioli's 134

Daniel Thiebaut 146

Merriman's 160

Donatoni's 148

Imari 152

Kirin 158

Kamuela Provision Company 154

Roy's 74

Waikoloa

Hualalai Club Grill 150

Mauna Kea
13,796

Hilo

Café Pesto 140

Kailua–Kona

Sibu Café 162

Jameson's 64

Keaau

Aloha Angel Café 136

Honalo
Kealakekua
Captain Cook

The Coffee Shack 144

Volcano
Village

Kilauea Lodge 156

Mauna Loa
13,677

Papa

Naalehu

HAWAI'I
THE BIG ISLAND

HAWAI'I

Restaurant, Page, Type of Cuisine
Recipes Featured

Aioli's Restaurant, 134, Eclectic American
Hawaii Island Goat Cheese Tacos / Wild Mushroom Crepes

Aloha Angel Café, 136, Fresh Island Style
Coconut Split Pea Soup / Aloha Angel Vegan Cookies

Bamboo Restaurant, 138, Fresh Island Style
Green Papaya Salad / Hawaiian Imu Style Pork

Café Pesto, 140, Pacific Rim/Italian
Tempura Mirin Shrimp with Rice Noodles and Shallot Chili Glaze / Thai Roasted Rack of Lamb with Sweet Potato Sauté

Coast Grille, 142, Fresh Seafood
Crispy Soft Shell Crab with Pineapple Jasmine Rice, Grilled Maui Onion and Mint Shallot Sauce

The Coffee Shack, 144, Contemporary Homestyle & Bakery Specialties
Kona Kahlua Cheesecake

Daniel Thiebaut Restaurant, 146, French–Asian
Yellow Fin Tuna, Avocado, Sweet Bell Pepper Tower, Kamuela Field Greens, Thai Curry Vinaigrette
Crispy Chicken Wonton on Asian Stir Fry with Ginger–Soy Mayonnaise

Donatoni's, 148, Northern Italian
Farfalle Con Pollo E Funghi Bow Tie Pasta, Marinated Chicken Breast, Shiitake Mushrooms
& Sun-Dried Tomatoes in White Wine Sauce / Lemon Mascarpone Cheesecake

Hualalai Club Grill, 150, Pacific Club Cuisine
Free Range Lamb Chop with Macadamia Coconut Crust,
White Bean Cassoulet and a Star Anise Drizzle / Plantation Style Crusted Snapper / Cucumber Papaya Salsa

Imari, 152, Traditional Japanese
Maguro Tataki–Seared 'Ahi, Imari Style / Shabu Shabu for Two

Jameson's by the Sea, 64, Fresh Seafood & Steak
Baked Stuffed Shrimp

Kamuela Provision Company, 154, Creative Island/Pacific Rim
Lacquered Salmon / Pacific Style Bouillabaise

Kilauea Lodge, 156, Continental
Prawns Mauna Loa / Macadamia Crusted 'Ahi

Kirin, 158, Genuine Chinese
Kung Bao Chicken / String Beans with Minced Pork

Merriman's Restaurant, 160, Hawai'i Regional
Merriman's Poisson Cru / Sesame Beef Kabobs

Roy's Restaurant, 74, Hawaiian Fusian Style
Coconut Tiger Shrimp Sticks with a Thai Style Cocktail Sauce / Szechwan Baby Back Ribs with a Mongolian Marinade

Sibu Café, 162, Indonesian & Southeast Asian
Ayam Bali — Balinese–Style Fried Chicken / Sayur Tumis — Indonesian Stir Fried Vegetables

AIOLI'S RESTAURANT

A cozy favorite eatery in Waimea, **Aioli's Restaurant** offers "food that is attractive, but not pretentious," says Owner/Chef Jerry Mills. He and Co-owner/Manager Stephen Hall chose the name Aioli's because they like to cook with garlic; it's early in the alphabet and sounds Hawaiian. Later they discovered it means "joyful food" or "joyful sex" in Hawaiian.

Ambiance: Aioli's is intimate, comfortable and friendly. The tables are covered with paper; crayons are offered for artistic expression, some of which is later displayed and then sold for charity. For creative inspiration, you'll enjoy being surrounded by local artists' work, including paintings by Hiroshi Tagami, who is considered a "State Treasure."

Menu: Lunch features homemade soups, salads and sandwiches with bread baked on site. Hot sandwiches include grilled local beef, bison, ostrich, local lamb, chicken and fresh fish as well as their Kobe Waygu burger. With a dinner menu that changes every 3 weeks, Aioli's offers fresh local fish, two vegetarian specials and a unique game dish (alligator, duck, quail), prime rib, steaks and lamb. Fusion dishes often feature Southwest, Cajun and Asian cuisines. For dessert, the Lilikoi Cheesecake is creamy with a perfect flavorful tang. There is no cover charge if you bring your own bottle of wine; drop it by early and they will have it chilled for you.

Details: Lunch under $10.00. Dinner entrées: $11.95–20.95. Open 11 a.m. to 4 p.m. on Tuesday, 11 a.m. to 8 p.m. Wednesday through Thursday; until 9 p.m. Friday and Saturday, and 8 a.m. to 2 p.m. on Sundays. Located behind Merriman's.

(808) 885-6325
OPELO PLAZA, 65-1227 A OPELO ROAD, KAMUELA, HAWAI'I 96743

Hawaii Island Goat Cheese Tacos

8 7″ flour tortillas
1 pound refried beans (refritos)
½ cup sharp cheddar cheese, shredded
1 tsp. powdered cumin
2 Tbsp. finely chopped onion
1 tsp. garlic powder

1 or more pickled jalapeño peppers, diced
4 oz. Monterey Jack cheese, shredded
8 oz. Hawaii Island Goat Dairy chévre cheese
    (other chévre cheese may be substituted)
melted butter

Preheat oven to 400 degrees. Mix the refritos (home made or canned) with the cheddar, cumin, garlic, onion, and jalapeño. Heat the bean mixture either on the range (it may be necessary to add a small quantity of milk to thin the mixture) or in the microwave. Adjust the taste of the refrito mixture, adding more jalapeño peppers if desired. Warm the flour tortillas slightly to make them pliable (you can microwave them for 20-30 sec). Spread a layer of the refrito mixture over half of the tortilla; sprinkle about ½ ounce of the Jack cheese over the beans. Top with about 1 ounce of the goat cheese. Fold the uncovered half of the tortilla over covered side, forming a ½ circle. Butter the exposed top side of the folded tortilla (or spray with oil). Repeat with the other tortillas. At this point the tacos can be covered and refrigerated for up to two days. When ready to bake, place tacos on an oiled cookie sheet (if they have been refrigerated, allow them to return to room temperature) and bake for about 6 to 8 minutes or until crisp and brown on top. Guacamole, avocado, sour cream and salsa are excellent accompaniments. Serves as 4 entrées or can be cut into appetizers for at least 8.

Wild Mushroom Crepes

1½ to 2 pounds total of 3 or more
    types of mushrooms
2 Tbsp. or more butter, as needed to sauté
1 Tbsp. or more of finely chopped garlic
2 Tbsp. cream sherry (a healthy splash)
½ tsp. freshly grated nutmeg

⅓ cup heavy cream
16 oz. chévre goat cheese (preferably
    Hawaiian Island goat cheese)
crepes
sour cream, as needed
Monterey Jack cheese, grated

Preheat oven to 350 degrees. Cut the mushrooms into bite-sized slices. In a large pan sauté each different type of mushroom, one type at a time, in a small amount of butter with medium hot heat until the mushrooms no longer exude liquid. After each type of mushroom has been sautéed, transfer to a large container. When all mushrooms have been sautéed and transferred, add the garlic with a small amount of butter to the pan and sauté for about one minute. Add the mushrooms back to the pan with the garlic, draining the liquid from mushrooms first. Add the cream sherry, the heavy cream, and the nutmeg to the mushroom mixture. Gently heat until the mixture is reasonbly dry. Remove from the heat. At this point, the mushrooms can be refrigerated for several days.

To Prepare: Thinly spread about a teaspoon of sour cream in a 1″ strip about 2″ from the crepe side. Crumble about a tablespoon of the chevre on top of the sour cream, followed by as much of the mushroom mixture as desired. Roll the crepe. (For appetizers, use less mushroom; for an entrée use enough mushrooms to give you a 1½″ inch diameter rolled crepe.) The crêpes can be baked all together, side by side, or they can be baked on an ovenproof plate when they are to be used as an entrée. Top the crepes with a thin layer of sour cream, followed by shredded Jack cheese. (The sour cream helps to keep the cheese from falling off of the crêpe.) Bake until the cheese is melted, about 10-15 minutes. Prepares about 16 crêpes for appetizers or 10 for entrées.

ALOHA ANGEL CAFÉ

Eclectic and inviting, the **Aloha Angel Café** is an all-time favorite you won't want to miss. Serving delicious and hearty fare and utilizing fresh local and organic ingredients whenever possible, this delightful café has been recognized by *Food and Wine*, *Bon Appétit*, *Gourmet Magazine*, and *Zagat Survey*. It is located in the renovated historic Aloha Theatre building, which was completed in 1932 and was originally a silent movie house. After movies evolved from silent to talkies, the Aloha Theatre became a gathering place for the *mauka* (mountain) community. Now, as an arts and cultural center, it features live theater, music, dance and independent films.

Ambiance: Since the last edition of *Tasting Paradise*, they've opened a lovely dining room for dinner guests. During the day, you can dine outside on the long narrow lanai where fresh breezes and sweeping views of pastureland lead out to the ocean.

Menu: Breakfast at the café includes delicious pancakes, fresh fruit, homemade muffins, and fluffy omelets. Lunch features unique homemade soups and fresh baked breads, thick sandwiches, great hamburgers, vegetarian and daily specials. The freshly baked pastries, cakes and cookies are awesome. Dinner entrées include: Fresh Fish Tacos, Lemongrass Grilled Chicken Breast with tropical fruit salsa and Lamb Chops. Espresso drinks, 100% pure Kona coffee, imported and domestic beers and wines are also offered.

Details: Open daily 8 a.m. until 2:30 p.m. Breakfast and lunch average: $8.00. Dinner served from 5 p.m. to 9 p.m. $13.95–24.95.

(808) 322-3383 / WWW.ALOHATHEATRE.COM
79-7384 MAMALAHOA HIGHWAY, KAINALIU, HAWAI'I 96750

Coconut Split Pea Soup

1 medium yellow onion

3 pieces celery

1 carrot

1 each red and green bell pepper

garlic to taste

¼ tsp. thyme

salt and white pepper to taste

¼ cup sherry

2 quarts vegetable stock

1 bag split peas (approximately 2 cups)

2 cups cooked, diced red potatoes

1 can (12.5 oz.) coconut milk

toasted coconut for garnish

Chop onion, celery, carrot and peppers and sauté in olive oil with garlic until brown. Add thyme, salt and white pepper to taste. De-glaze pan with sherry. Add vegetable stock and bring to a boil. Add split peas and cook until almost tender. Add potatoes and finish cooking until peas are completely tender. Whirl 1 to 2 cups of soup in blender and add back to the main pot. Add coconut milk and bring back to temperature. Taste and adjust seasonings to your preference. Garnish with toasted coconut.

Aloha Angel Vegan Cookies

8 cups oats

2 tsp. baking powder

1 tsp. baking soda

2 tsp. cinnamon

1 tsp. nutmeg

4 bananas, ripe

2 cups apple juice

2 cups raisins

Grind the oatmeal in the cuisinart or blender. Add next four ingredients to the ground oatmeal. Blend the banana and apple juice in cuisinart until smooth. Mix all ingredients together including the raisins. Drop two tablespoons of batter on non-stick or parchment lined cookie sheet. Bake 15 minutes at 350 degrees. Will make approximately 15 cookies.

BAMBOO RESTAURANT & GALLERY

Gracious Hawaiian "Aunties" will charm you with aloha as you step back in time in the unique and inviting **Bamboo Restaurant.** While experiencing a bit of Old Hawai'i, you may even be treated to an impromptu hula performance! Since Bamboo opened in 1993, the historical town of Hawi (birthplace of King Kamehameha) has been restored and now has many quaint shops, a center for the arts, and eco-tourism—kayaking, hiking, horseback riding and more. A lovely 30 minute drive from the Kohala Coast resorts, it's definitely worth the drive to Hawi! Residents voted Bamboo "Best Restaurant on the Big Island" in a poll by *Hawai'i Island Journal.* Be sure to visit the Kohala Koa Gallery at Bamboo featuring fine Koa wood furniture, art and hand crafted items.

Ambiance: Relaxing in your wicker chair in this restored historic Hawaiian building, you'll be surround by orchids, palms, and old Hawai'i memorabilia. It's a fun and lively gathering place for the community and a *must* experience for the visitor.

Menu: Featuring fresh fish, organic herbs from their garden and produce from local farmers, Bamboo's fresh Island style cuisine creates a new blend of East and West flavors. Try their Sesame-Nori Crusted Shrimp, Crispy Polenta—goat cheese polenta on greens with grilled fish and roasted red pepper and Thai basil sauce or the popular Chicken Saté Pot Stickers or Kalua Pork Quesadilla. Don't miss their refreshing Passion Fruit (lilikoi) Margaritas.

Details: Open Tuesday through Saturday for lunch: $6.00–10.00 and dinner: $8.00–20.00. Sunday brunch ($5.00-10.00). They are closed Mondays.

Dinner reservations requested.

(808) 889–5555 / www.thebamboorestaurant.com
Akoni Pule Highway 270, Hawi, Hawai'i 96719

GREEN PAPAYA SALAD

Salad

½ green papaya (it should be hard and bright green; the interior papaya flesh will be creamy white)

½ sweet Maui onion

½ cucumber, peeled and seeded

½ ripe but firm tomato

1 small carrot

¼ cup diced green onion

Dressing

½ cup fresh lime juice

½ cup Nam Pla (shrimp sauce)

¾ cup peanut oil

½ cup rice wine vinegar

3 Tbsp. minced fresh garlic

1 Tbsp. sambal

salt and pepper to taste

Garnish lime, cilantro and peanuts

Julienne and mix together all salad ingredients, adding green onion last. Mix dressing ingredients together and marinate the green papaya mixture in the dressing.

When serving, garnish the salad with fresh lime wedges, fresh cilantro and chopped peanuts. The salad can be served vegetarian as a starter on a lettuce leaf, or as a main course. We serve it with grilled pork tenderloin and grilled shrimp at Bamboo, but it also complements fresh fish or steaks.

HAWAIIAN IMU STYLE PORK

At Bamboo, we prepare our pork in the old Hawaiian way—wrapped in ti leaves and baked in an "imu" or underground stone-lined oven for 24 hours. This is as close an approximation we can find that you can make at home.

1 pork butt

1 tsp. Hawaiian kosher salt

1 tsp. liquid smoke

Place the pork in a roaster pan on a rack (this will drain off extra fat). Season the pork with salt and liquid smoke. If you can find ti leaves, cover the pork with the leaves and cover with foil. Do use the foil even if you can't find ti leaves. Roast in a 325 degree oven for 4 hours. When done, the meat should easily shred. Remove the pork butt from the pan and when just cool enough to handle, shred the meat, taking away any fatty portions. At this point, the meat can be bagged and frozen for later use.

CAFÉ PESTO

Serving outstanding innovative cuisine, **Café Pesto** is well known across the islands as a favorite place to enjoy lunch or dinner—whether in historical Hilo Bay or Kawaihae Harbor. Since the first edition of *Tasting Paradise*, this wonderful café has continued to grow in popularity and notability. Some of the awards they've won include: "Hawai'i Top Restaurants," *Zagat Survey Restaurant Guide*; several "Best Big Island Restaurant," *Honolulu Magazine* Hale 'Aina Awards including 2002 and 2003; and "Best of Hawai'i's Hidden Treasures," *Fodor's Travel Guide*.

Ambiance: Café Pesto at Hilo Bay is located in the renovated S. Hata Building in historic downtown Hilo, while the Kawaihae location is tucked in the ocean side of the Kawaihae Shopping Center. Both locations have bold black and white checkered floors, the classic red rose on each table, and have captured the right combination of a casual upbeat atmosphere and outstanding creative island cuisine.

Menu: With a menu that is diverse, fresh and intriguing, you can savor Asian Pacific Crab Cakes with honey-miso vinaigrette and outrageous pizzas such as Chili Grilled Shrimp, shiitake mushrooms, green onions and cilantro creme fraiche. Try the sautéed fresh catch with "passion for mango" sauce, Salmon Alfredo or Island Seafood Risotto. Calzones, distinctive salads, and mouth–watering desserts like Warm Coconut Tart with sweet cream anglaise or Ganache Chocolate torte with raspberry purée complete the menu. For a refreshing local favorite try one of their Specialty Margaritas rimmed with li hing mui.

Details: Open daily. Lunch: $7.95–12.95. Dinner: $7.95–27.95. Dinner reservations suggested.

(808) 969–6640 / WWW.CAFEPESTO.COM / 308 KAMEHAMEHA AVENUE, HILO, HAWAI'I 96720
(808) 882–1071 / KAWAIHAE SHOPPING CENTER, HWY. 270, KAWAIHAE, HAWAI'I 96743

Tempura Mirin Shrimp
with Rice Noodles and Shallot Chili Glaze

20 jumbo shrimp, stretched for tempura
20 cone sushi wrappers
20 green onion stalks, blanched
20 skewers

1 ¼ cups shallot chili glaze
1 packet pancit bihon
mixed baby greens
1 pot fry grade oil

Skewer all of the shrimp. Wrap with sushi wrapper and tie with blanched green onion. Let the shrimp sit over night in the fridge. Fry pancit bihon in 400 degree oil until crispy. Dip shrimp skewers in tempura and fry until crispy. Plate crispy noodles and top with tempura and garnish with shallot chili glaze and baby greens.

Thai Roasted Rack of Lamb with Sweet Potato Sauté

2 racks Kamuela lamb, frenched
2 stalks lemon grass, sliced
4 pieces lime leaf, sliced
1 finger ginger, peeled and chopped
3 cloves garlic, chopped

1 piece shallot, peeled and chopped
1 Tbsp. red curry paste
4 oz. rice wine
4 oz. shallot oil

Sauté lemon grass, lime leaf, ginger, garlic, shallot and curry paste until brown. Deglaze with rice wine and chill. Add shallot oil and marinate lamb racks in curry oil over night. Preheat oven to 350 degrees. Sauté lamb in hot pan browning on all sides and place in oven for 8 minutes.

Sweet Potato Sauté

4 cups sweet potato, boiled, peeled, diced
¼ cup red and yellow pepper, diced
¼ cup zucchini, diced
¼ cup eggplant, diced

¼ cup red onion, diced
1 Tbsp. garlic and shallot, minced
rice wine to deglaze
2 Tbsp. butter

Sauté diced vegetables with olive oil, shallots and garlic. Deglaze pan with rice wine and finish with butter, salt and pepper.

Chutney

1 cup pineapple, diced
1 piece orange, peeled and chopped
2 Tbsp. orange zest, minced
½ Tbsp. garlic, minced
½ Tbsp. shallot, minced

2 cups kukui mango chutney
For Garnish:
4 oz. mixed baby greens or snow pea shoots
¼ cup coconut and macadamia nuts

Place chutney ingredients in a sauce pot with the mango chutney and simmer for 15 minutes. Hold at room temperature.

Place coconut and macadamia nuts on separate pans and toast at 250 degrees until golden brown.

For presentation: Place Sweet Potato Sauté on plate; lean rack of lamb on potatoes. Spoon Chutney over lamb and garnish with greens and toasted coconut and macnuts.

Executive Chef Casey Halpern

Pacific Rim/Italian

COAST GRILLE

With tropical breezes, a view of the sky glowing with color as the sun sinks into the ocean, and the sound of waves rising up from the beach below, **Coast Grille** provides the perfect environment to enjoy a romantic dinner. This fabulous restaurant has been honored with many Hale 'Aina Awards and it's easy to see why—Coast Grille provides an exquisite dining experience from the setting to the service and the phenomenal food. Resort Executive Chef Piet Wigmans has been widely recognized for his flavorful and innovative dishes that utilize fresh local ingredients.

Ambiance: The striking grand architecture is reminiscent of a Frank Lloyd Wright design with large columns and a high circular ceiling; colorful fish painted near the ceiling and large tropical bouquets and plants add a Hawaiian flair.

There is also an impressive marble bar and a marble oyster bar where a variety of exceptionally fresh oysters are served. The restaurant is open air and with three tiers of seating, it offers almost every table a view of beautiful Hapuna beach.

Menu: Pleasing to both the palette and the eye, the Crispy Crab Cakes are a perfect appetizer; Kona Lobster Sushi is unique and remarkably delicious. The Chef's Selection of Fresh Hawaiian Fish offers a sampling of three superb combinations, Sautéed Ono with Lemon Miso cream sauce, Blackened Mahimahi with Asian pear chutney, and Peppery 'Ahi with Mango vinaigrette. (These combinations change daily.) Coast Grille has its own herb garden, and they feature an extensive wine list with an outstanding champagne selection, and sensational desserts.

Details: Call for nights open and reservations. Entrées: $23.00–36.00.

(808) 880–3192 / WWW.HAPUNABEACHPRINCEHOTEL.COM
HAPUNA BEACH PRINCE HOTEL AT MAUNA KEA RESORT, KOHALA COAST, HAWAI'I 96743

CRISPY SOFT SHELL CRAB
WITH PINEAPPLE JASMINE RICE, GRILLED MAUI ONION AND MINT SHALLOT SAUCE

3 pieces crispy soft shell crab
2 rings Maui onion, sliced and grilled
½ cup Grilled Pineapple Rice (recipe below)

2 Tbsp. butter sauce
2 Tbsp. Mint Shallot Sauce

Soft Shell Crab Breading

½ cup corn meal
½ cup all purpose flour
½ cup cornstarch
¼ cup coriander seed
1 Tbsp. kosher salt

2 tsp. cayenne
2 tsp. white pepper
1 cup buttermilk
4 cups peanut oil

In a spice grinder (coffee grinder), freshly grind the coriander seeds, then add to all the dry ingredients.

In a small bowl, soak crab and transfer to bowl of dry ingredients. Heat oil to 350 degrees in a heavy-duty pot. Cook crab for 3 to 4 minutes.

MINT SHALLOT SAUCE

½ cup fresh lime juice
3 shallots, minced
3 cloves garlic, minced
1 cup mint, chopped

¼ tsp. turmeric
1 Tbsp. palm sugar
1 Tbsp. peanut oil

In a small sauce pot heat the oil. Then add shallots and garlic, then cook. Add remaining ingredients and bring to a boil, then purée.

GRILLED PINEAPPLE RICE

1 cup jasmine rice, cooked
¼ cup cilantro, chopped
1 slice grilled pineapple, diced and sliced
to taste kosher salt
to taste table ground pepper
2 Tbsp. grilled Maui onion, diced

Grilled Maui Onion

1 Maui onion, sliced ¼" thick, and grilled
1 tsp. peanut oil
to taste salt and pepper

Season grilled Maui onions with salt, pepper and peanut oil. To assemble the rings: Take the two outside layers of the Maui onion and place on your serving dish. In a medium mixing bowl, combine rice, chopped cilantro, diced pineapple and the middle of the Maui onion, which has been dried. Season with salt and pepper. After mixing the Grilled Pineapple Rice, place inside the two Maui onion rings. Place crab on top of the Pineapple Rice and sauce around crab. You can also garnish with butter sauce, chili oil and cilantro or field greens.

Serves 2.

THE COFFEE SHACK

As you meander along the Mamalahoa Highway heading south from Kona you'll discover expansive views of the coastline from an elevation above 1,000 feet where the climate is cooler and coffee farms thrive. Captain Cook is in the heart of coffee country and that's where you'll find **The Coffee Shack**. A popular place, it is sometimes quite busy, so give yourself time to relax and enjoy the spectacular view when you stop in for a fresh coffee drink, meal or treat. They serve great breakfasts and lunches, along with yummy baked goods in a unique and appealing environment.

Ambiance: It's a rare delight to dine on the open-air deck with a panoramic coastline view (about 26 miles worth!) that includes Kealakekua Bay. You'll also be looking out over the coffee trees that provide the beans for the coffee sold there.

Menu: For breakfast you can try a smoothie with an outrageous cinnamon roll (hard to pass up that heavenly scent!), or for a heartier appetite choose from Eggs Benedict, French Toast, Ham and Cheese Croissant, and more. Lunch features a variety of sandwiches on freshly baked bread and creative daily specials such as Fresh Papaya Salads, Frittatas, Quiches, Coconut Crusted Fresh Fish, or a Burrito with rice and salad. The blended Iced Honey Mocha Latte is so good it's addictive. The tempting selections of homemade desserts and pastries make it hard to decide on just one. I've heard that people make special trips for their homemade Lilikoi Cheesecake and Coconut Cream Pie. Beer and wine served.

Details: 7 a.m. to 4 p.m. daily. Meals: $6.50 to 13.95. Treats: $.95 to 3.50.

(808) 328-9555 / WWW.COFFEESHACK.COM
83-5799 MAMALAHOA HIGHWAY, CAPTAIN COOK, HAWAI'I 96704

Kona Kahlua Cheesecake

First place winner dessert in the 2002 Kona Coffee Recipe Contest.

Crust

7 cups graham cracker crumbs

¾ cup softened butter

½ cup Kona espresso (unbrewed)

½ cup cocoa

Combine dry ingredients; blend in softened butter until all ingredients are moistened. Divide and spread the mixture evenly onto the bottom and sides of two springform pans.

Filling

38 oz. cream cheese (at room temperature)

12 eggs

2½ cups Kahlua

2 cups sugar

In large mixing bowl beat cream cheese until smooth. Add sugar and beat until smooth and creamy. Add eggs, scrape sides, and beat until well blended. Pour in Kahlua and beat just until blended. Pour batter into prepared crust. Set the pan on a baking sheet and bake for 1 hour at 325 degrees or until the edges of the cheesecake are puffed but the center still looks moist and jiggles when the pan is tapped.

Makes 2 10″ cheesecakes.

Topping

3 cups sour cream

3 tsp. vanilla

¾ cup sugar

1½ cups cocoa powder

Whisk together until well blended. Divide and scrape on top of slightly cooled cheesecakes (allow puffiness to recede) spread to smooth and return to oven for 15 minutes, just long enough to set topping. Remove from oven and cool on rack. Refrigerate over night before unmolding.

Sauce

1 cup brewed Kona coffee

1 cup sugar

Cook over medium high heat, stirring until the sugar is dissolved. Increase heat and boil until thickened. Cool and serve over cheesecake slices.

DANIEL THIEBAUT RESTAURANT

The food is tantalizing and fresh, the service warm, friendly and professional, and the restoration of the 100 year old Chock In Store that houses **Daniel Thiebaut Restaurant** is beautifully done. Chef Daniel Thiebaut is passionate about creating excellence. A native of France, his French–Asian cuisine is inspired by world–wide travel and extensive experience combined with fresh local ingredients. You can enjoy his award–winning delicious creations in an atmosphere that holds a special charm, the history of a unique building and personal memories of people in the community.

Ambiance: Warm and friendly, with high ceilings, wood floors and a variety of rooms in which to dine, each with its own story and unique personality: Main Store, Green Room (former beer storage shed), Dress Shoppe, and the Men's Room, which used to be the family garage, to name a few. Antique furnishings and vintage Hawaiian art add to the historical flavor.

Menu: Begin with Hilo Sweetcorn Crabcake with lemongrass-coconut lobster sauce. For an enticing entrée try Miso Glazed Salmon on potato confit; Crab Crusted Monchong on onion mash potatoes or Hunan Style Rack of Lamb. Lunch selections include: New Wave Salad Nicoise with Seared Yellow Fin Tuna and Grilled Local Fish "Kona Style" with Ginger, Soy-Sherry Wine, Green Onions and Jasmine Rice. Their extensive wine list offers over 30 wines by the glass, great for sampling! For your sweet conclusion try the Warm Mango Jubilee with coconut cream ice cream. Sooo good!

Details: Lunch Monday through Friday, most items $7.00–15.00. Dinner served nightly. Entrées: $23.00–39.00. Reservations recommended.

(808) 887-2200 / WWW.DANIELTHIEBAUT.COM
65-1259 KAWAIHAE ROAD, KAMUELA, HAWAI'I 96743

Yellow Fin Tuna, Avocado, Sweet Bell Pepper Tower
Kamuela Field Greens, Thai Curry Vinaigrette

4 oz. tuna, finely diced
1 oz. furikake
2 oz. avocado, finely diced

1 oz. shallot, finely diced
2 oz. sweet pepper, finely diced
2 oz. mixed greens

Alternate in order from bottom; tuna, furukake, avocado and shallot, and sweet pepper (repeat) in a cone mold. Place in center of plate. Mix greens and vinaigrette together and place around tower. Garnish with ogo, curled carrots and daikon.

Thai Curry Vinaigrette

½ cup olive oil
¼ cup rice vinegar
1 tsp. curry powder
1 tsp. red Thai curry paste
¼ cup sesame oil
1 tsp. shallot

1 tsp. ginger
1 tsp. garlic
½ tsp. Dijon mustard
salt and pepper to taste
Garnish: sesame seeds (black and roasted)
ogo, curled carrots and daikon

Mix all ingredients.

Crispy Chicken Wonton on Asian Stir Fry
with Ginger–Soy Mayonnaise

2 chicken breasts
2 Tbsp. Hoisin sauce
1 Tbsp. chopped garlic
16 wonton wrappers

2 Tbsp. chili garlic
3 Tbsp. chopped ginger
1 Tbsp. chopped pepper
1 egg + 2 Tbsp. water

Chop chicken and mix with remaining ingredients, season to taste. Sauté for 5 minutes and let cool. Lay wonton wrapper and put filling in center, lightly brush 2 adjoining edges with egg mixture. Fold the wonton in ½ on the diagonal, making a triangle. Deep fry for 1 minute or until golden, and set on paper towels. Serves 4.

Stir Fry

1 cup julienne carrots
1 cup julienne red bell pepper
½ cup water chestnuts
2 Tbsp. lime juice
1 Tbsp. sesame seeds

1 cup julienne shiitake
1 cup julienne yellow bell pepper
1 cup mung beans
2 Tbsp. cilantro
1 tsp. sesame oil

Sauté vegetables until al dente.

Ginger–Soy Mayonnaise

1 cup mayonnaise
2 Tbsp. soy sauce

1 tsp. chopped ginger

Mix all ingredients together.

Donatoni's

An alluring blend of Hawai'i and Italy, **Donatoni's** greets you with the warmth and grandeur of a lovely Italian villa; the boats drifting by on the lagoon just a step off the terrace are reminiscent of gondolas. You'll be pampered with exceptional and knowledgeable service, and, you'll be in notable company—notice the photos of Tom Cruise, Nicole Kidman, Clint Eastwood, Billy Crystal and others who have dined at Donatoni's. Utilizing fresh local produce, the chef at Donatoni's brings authentic Italian food to Hawai'i, which is tastefully complemented with a bottle of fine wine from their extensive wine list.

Ambiance: Donatoni's is wonderfully romantic with intimate rooms, elegant decor including chandeliers and fine paintings, large comfortable chairs, and an outdoor terrace where you can dine in the balmy tropical night with stars overhead.

Menu: Start with Calamari Fritti, or Pasticcio filled with braised pheasant and porcini mushrooms or the incredible Insalata di Aragosta: sweet lobster tossed with capers and saffron vinaigrette. Entrées include outstanding pasta choices such as Gnocchi di Ricotta with wild boar ragu, fresh fish including Tonno in Crosta d'Olive ('Ahi tuna) and Roasted Rack of Lamb finished with an infusion of figs, mint and saffron. For dessert be seduced by the gorgeous Carnival Mask of Venice resting atop a light bittersweet chocolate marquis on a layer of flourless chocolate cake, served with Frangelico sauce.

Details: Dinner only. Entrées: $23.00–37.00. Call for reservations and nights open.

(808) 886–1234 EXT. 54 / WWW.HILTONWAIKOLOAVILLAGE.COM
HILTON WAIKOLOA VILLAGE, WAIKOLOA, KOHALA COAST, HAWAI'I 96738

Farfalle Con Pollo E Funghi
Bow Tie Pasta, Marinated Chicken Breast, Shiitake Mushrooms & Sun-Dried Tomatoes in White Wine Sauce

6 oz. chicken breast, sliced julienne and
marinated in: olive oil, chopped rosemary,
sage and chopped fresh oregano
2 Tbsp. olive oil
½ tsp. chopped garlic
4 oz. shiitake mushroom

2 oz. white wine
3 oz. sun-dried tomatoes
4 oz. chicken stock
1 Tbsp. butter
10 oz. bow tie pasta
2 oz. grated Parmesan cheese

Sauté the chicken in a hot sauté pan with olive oil at high heat. Add the garlic and julienne sliced mushrooms and let cook for 2 to 3 minutes. Add salt, pepper and the white wine and let the alcohol evaporate. Add sun dried tomatoes and chicken stock and cook for a few minutes. Add butter, check for flavor. In salted boiling water, cook the pasta. When ready, drain the pasta and add to the sauce. Sprinkle with Parmesan cheese.

Lemon Mascarpone Cheesecake

Filling
2 pounds cream cheese
8 oz. mascarpone cheese
1½ cups sugar
2 large eggs
a **little** more than ½ tsp. lemon oil

Crust
powdered sugar
melted butter
anise and nut–
flavored biscotti

Filling: In a mixing bowl, cream together cream cheese, mascarpone cheese and sugar. Scrape bowl thoroughly, add the eggs and lemon oil (there is no substitute for the flavor of pure lemon oil; it is readily available in specialty food stores).

Crust: Grind the biscotti, sweeten with powdered sugar and moisten with melted butter. Par bake the crust until slightly golden brown before you add the cheesecake mixture. Fill your pan and place in a larger pan that contains the water bath.

The trick to cheesecakes is in the baking. Please use a spring form pan. This recipe will make a 9" spring form cheesecake. Pre-heat the oven to 325 degrees. If your oven runs high, reduce heat a bit. The cake must be baked in a water bath, so carefully wrap your spring form pan with a double layer of tin foil to insure that no water leaks into the cake from the bottom. Bake slowly, approximately 1 hour, until the center of the cake begins to solidify. If you over bake it, the texture becomes a little mealy. If you under bake it, it will be runny in the center. You may have to practice by making this recipe a few times.

Serve with Lilikoi (passion fruit) sauce. At Donatoni's this cheesecake is presented with a tiny whimsical marzipan mouse atop, with ears of almond slivers and a long curled tail of chocolate. The chef emphasizes that this cheesecake is "not about the cake, it's about the cheese."

HUALALAI RESORT CLUB GRILLE

Feel the trade winds gently blow through this open-air restaurant as you look out over the palm trees to the glistening waters of the Pacific or a view of the 18th green and manicured lawns. The **Hualalai Resort Club Grille** is located atop the Clubhouse on the 18th green of Hualalai Resort's Jack Nicklaus Signature Golf Course. You will enjoy fare that incorporates local ingredients. The chef explained that all sauces and stocks are made from scratch and the focus is a cuisine that is fresh and light.

Ambiance: Along with the refreshing breezes and views, an exhibition kitchen shows off the action inside, including a brick pizza oven. Reflecting Hualalai Resort's homage to the ancient Hawaiian mariner, an antique koa canoe dating back to the 1880's is suspended in the entry and extensive lounge area.

Menu: Specializing in Pacific Club cuisine they feature brick oven pizzas, fresh pastas, grilled steaks and fresh island fish, with 3 to 5 nightly specials. For starters try the Keahole Lobster Summer Roll, then the Plantation Style Crusted Snapper (recipe on facing page) or Meyers Blackfoot Valley Red Angus with a smoked tomato coulis. Lunch selections include Hirata's Wok Seared 'Ahi Salad, Mango Barbeque Pork Sandwich, Rey's Manila Style Fried Rice or Lobster Pizza with fresh pesto and shiitake mushrooms.

Details: Open daily for lunch and dinner. Reservations are recommended for dinner. Lunch: $10.00–17.50. Dinner entrées: $14.00–38.00.

(808) 325–8525
FOUR SEASONS RESORT, HUALALAI, KAILUA–KONA, HAWAI'I 96745

Free Range Lamb Chop with Macadamia Coconut Crust, White Bean Cassoulet and a Star Anise Drizzle

4 3 oz. lamb chops
broccoli

Crust
½ cup coconut flakes
¼ cup honey
3 Tbsp. Dijon mustard
½ Tbsp. chopped garlic
½ tsp. fresh thyme
½ Tbsp. parsley
½ cup macadamia nuts

White Bean Cassoulet
2 pounds white beans, soak overnight
18 oz. carrots, chopped
14 oz. onions, chopped
10 oz. celery, chopped
2 Tbsp. chopped garlic
½ oz. thyme, tied with butcher twine
4 slices bacon
2 quarts chicken stock

Combine all crust ingredients in mixing bowl. Season the lamb chops with salt and pepper and sear on flat top. Coat each lamb chop with 1½ ounces of crust mixture and finish in the oven at 350 degrees.

White Bean Cassoulet: Sauté bacon over medium heat. Add vegetables and garlic; sauté until onions are translucent. Add stock and thyme sprig. Add beans. Simmer until beans are al denté. Lightly thicken with corn starch to desired thickness.

To serve, arrange steamed broccoli in the center of plate. Place lamb chops, bones to the middle, against the broccoli (to hold them up). Place Cassoulet between each lamb chop. Finish with

Star Anise Drizzle
4 shallots
6 pieces star anise
2 cups red wine
2 bay leaves

1 tsp. peppercorn
4 sprigs thyme
4 cups demi

Blend all ingredients together.

Plantation Style Crusted Snapper

3 2½ oz. pieces of snapper
2 cups brown sugar
½ cup cracked black pepper
1½ cups paprika

½ cup cumin
½ cup salt
¼ cup dried thyme
⅛ cup liquid smoke

Combine all ingredients (except snapper) in a mixing bowl and mix well. Rub the mixture evenly on each piece of snapper. Place each piece, rub down, in a hot oiled skillet until golden brown. Repeat on other side (approximately 90 seconds each). Remove from pan. Serving suggestion: Place one scoop of rice in the center of the plate. Arrange fish at 1, 5 and 9 o'clock on the plate. Place 1 teaspoon of Cucumber Papaya Salsa (recipe below) on each piece and drizzle with balsamic rum.

Cucumber Papaya Salsa

1 papaya, diced
2 cucumbers, diced
1 bell pepper, diced
½ Maui onion, diced
1 jalapeño, diced

½ bunch cilantro, finely chopped
1 tsp. mint, finely chopped
¼ cup peanuts, finely chopped
2 Tbsp. white wine vinegar
3 limes, juiced

Combine all ingredients and toss with vinegar and lime juice. Add salt and pepper to taste.

Pacific Club Cuisine

IMARI

On your way to **Imari**, you'll have the good fortune of strolling from the Hilton lobby through a walkway lined with beautiful fine art. You will know that you have arrived at Imari when you discover the lovely Japanese-tea-room style buildings and a tranquil pond complete with water lilies and koi fish. The delicious Japanese fare at Imari is created by Chef Fumio Inaba.

Ambiance: You'll be greeted by a gracious hostess clad in a kimono who will lead you into a large room with Japanese music, black-lacquer furnishings and a choice of which dining experience you'd like to have. The teppanyaki chefs are talented in both the culinary arts and the performing arts creating a lively, entertaining and incredibly delicious experience. Sushi lovers will be pleased by the excellent sushi bar, or you may be treated to a quiet dinner at your own table.

Menu: The teppanyaki lobster is outstanding as are the Maui onions—so sweet and flavorful! You can choose from an excellent assortment of sushi and delectable fresh sashimi platters. Shabu-shabu, also available, is a traditional Japanese dining experience served table-side and set over an open-flame burner at your table. Dinners, such as the light and tasty Tempura Moriawase (seafood and vegetables) are served with miso shiru, steamed rice and Japanese green tea.

Details: Dinner: $28.00–49.00. A la carte sushi: $6.50–18.00. Call for reservations and nights open.

(808) 886–1234 EXT. 54 / WWW.HILTONWAIKOLOAVILLAGE.COM
HILTON WAIKOLOA VILLAGE, WAIKOLOA, KOHALA COAST, HAWAI'I 96738

Maguro Tataki—Seared 'Ahi, Imari Style

½ to ¾ pound 'ahi block

1 Tbsp. Alaea Hawaiian course salt

1 to 2 Tbsp. shichimi togarashi (Japanese chili peppers)

shredded daikon roots

2 to 4 pieces shiso leaf, for garnish

2 Tbsp. finely chopped scallions

1 oz. ogo seaweed, for garnish, can use wakame seaweed as a substitute)

Sauce

4 Tbsp. soy sauce

8 Tbsp. rice vinegar

1 Tbsp. lemon juice

¾" square kombu seaweed

Sauce: Mix all ingredients together, leave at least overnight or longer.

'Ahi: Sprinkle sea salt and shichimi togarashi over 'ahi block. Let marinate for 15 minutes before searing. Pre–heat a grill or griddle pan. Briefly sear all sides of the block. Spread sliced 'ahi over a plate on top of shredded daikon roots and shiso leaves. Pour sauce on top and sprinkle scallions and ogo seaweed on fish.

Shabu Shabu for Two

kombu seaweed, to taste

5 oz. Chinese cabbage

1 oz. Maui onions

¾ oz. shiitake mushrooms

¾ oz. enoki mushrooms

¼ oz. carrots

½ oz. green onions

¼ oz. bamboo shoots

1/16 tub momen tofu

2½ oz. kishimen noodles

1½ oz. haru same noodles

12 oz. rib eye steak

First boil water and add kombu. Then add ingredients one by one in order of length of time to cook, careful not to over cook items. Once done, dip into Ponzu Sauce (citrus/soy) and enjoy!

KAMUELA PROVISION COMPANY

For fresh and fabulous food in a perfect contemporary Hawaiian setting be sure to visit **Kamuela Provision Company.** Give yourself plenty of time to explore and marvel at the lush grounds of the Hilton Waikoloa Village. Walk through the open breeze ways while admiring the stunning art collection; meander along paths and bridges surrounded by the tropical wonder of pools, gardens, and waterfalls. If you would like a speedier way to get to your destination, catch the tram from the lobby. For a more leisurely and certainly more romantic ride, catch the boat. This is a nice way to end the evening—floating peacefully under the stars.

Ambiance: The setting is elegant yet casual, open-air and lovely. Request a table on the lanai if you want to be steps from the ocean and under the stars while listening to the live solo guitarist. It's quite a treat while sipping your tropical Mai Tai, Piña Colada or cocktail of choice. The last time I was there for the exquisite Hawaiian sunset, many of the other couples dining on the lanai jumped up to capture each other on film in front of the glowing sky and deepening blue ocean.

Menu: Sample a selection of fine wines with your dinner with a wine flight from the wine bar. KPC cuisine utilizes local fresh ingredients whenever possible with an emphasis on clean healthy flavors. The Pupu Platter for Two, appropriately named "Eight Bites", provides an exceptional variety of mouth–watering flavors: Volcano Spiced Charred 'Ahi, Pacific Blue Crab Cakes and Curry Roasted White Shrimp, Tahitian Poisson Cru, Lobster Martini, Limu Poke, and Wasabi Red Potato Salad with Beef Tenderloin Saté. I devoured the deliciously moist and flavorful Lacquered Fresh Pacific Salmon. Meat lovers will be pleased with a selection of steaks, or perhaps the Macadamia Nut Pesto Crusted Pork Chop. Save room for a heavenly dessert!

Details: Dinner only. Entrées: $26.00–42.00. Call for reservations and nights open.

(808) 886–1234 EXT. 54 / WWW.HILTONWAIKOLOAVILLAGE.COM
HILTON WAIKOLOA VILLAGE, WAIKOLOA, KOHALA COAST, HAWAI'I 96738

LACQUERED SALMON

10 3 oz. salmon fillets
⅛ cup soy sauce
⅛ cup sugar
¹⁄₁₆ cup salt

ground ginger to taste
⅛ Tbsp. pepper
¹⁄₁₆ cup peanut oil

Marinate the salmon in the soy sauce, sugar, salt, ground ginger and pepper mixed together. In teflon pan, add peanut oil, place salmon fillets into the pan. Sear until golden brown, turn and brown on other side. Cook until slightly under done. Serve on plum wine sauce.

PACIFIC STYLE BOUILLABAISE

1 46 oz. can clam juice
46 oz. chicken stock
½ pound fennel
1 cup white wine
3 oz. lemon grass
3 oz. ginger root
pinch saffron
½ oz. garlic
5 leaves basil
few sprigs thyme

1 cup lemon juice
2 tomatoes
2 stalks celery
¼ pound carrot
½ pound onion
½ pound leeks
1 tub clam base
1 tub chicken base
1 tsp. red curry paste
to taste salt and pepper

Combine all above ingredients; simmer for ½ hour and strain through fine sieve.

4 oz. leeks, julienne
tomatoes, skinned and cut into 1" chunks
basil, julienne

1 tsp. coconut milk
seafood—fish chunks, lobster, shrimp, clams

In a large pot, combine desired seafood, which has been cut into chunks, with enough stock to cover seafood, topped off with leeks, tomatoes and basil. Cover and simmer until seafood is cooked. Garnish with julienne basil.

CREATIVE ISLAND/PACIFIC RIM

KILAUEA LODGE

Well–loved as a an enchanting romantic get away, locals and visitors are charmed by the warm atmosphere and exceptional cuisine found at **Kilauea Lodge**. During the day you can relax, explore or discover the primordial wonders of Madame Pele (the helpful staff at the lodge can point you to the most recent lava flow area). Owners, Chef Albert and Lorna Jeyte offer winsome overnight accommodations that include a complimentary full breakfast and an abundance of aloha. Before his debut as a talented chef, Albert was an Emmy award–winning make–up artist. His artistry and fine taste is now evident in his popular continental cuisine utilizing local flavors.

Ambiance: Open beam ceilings, hardwood floors, koa tables and a cozy fireplace (for chilly nights) create a feeling of warmth accented with fresh flowers and beautiful original art. People from all over the world have come to the historic "International Fireplace of Friendship" in the Lodge, which was built in 1938.

Menu: Hearty dinners begin with one of the homemade soups of the day, such as the sublime duck vegetable or smooth potato leek, and a salad along with freshly baked bread. Entrées include: Duck l'Orange, a delicious favorite roasted with oranges, pepper and garlic and served with apricot mustard glaze, Hasenpfeffer, Medallions of Venison or the Fresh Catch prepared one of three ways. I enjoyed the 'Ahi broiled and topped with mango chutney glaze and crushed macadamia nuts. Save room for dessert—the Lilikoi Cheesecake is smooth, creamy and tangy. Be sure to peruse their exceptional wine list.

Details: Open nightly. Full dinners (include soup and salad) range from $16.00–43.00. Call for reservations. Located one mile from Volcanoes National Park in Volcano Village.

(808) 967–7366 / www.kilauealodge.com
Old Volcano Road, Volcano, Hawai'i 96785

Prawns Mauna Loa

5 large prawns
2 Tbsp. olive oil
1 tsp. baked garlic, finely chopped
1 tsp. shallots, finely chopped
1 tsp. green onions, finely chopped

1 Tbsp. flour
⅓ cup coconut milk
1 tsp. fresh dill, chopped or (½ tsp. dried)
salt and black pepper to taste

In a sauté pan, add olive oil, garlic, shallots, green onions and sauté at medium heat for about 15 seconds. Whisk in flour. Cook until it forms a roux (a couple of minutes). Pour in coconut milk and stir. Add prawns and seasonings; continue to sauté until prawns turn pink. Serve with rice or pasta.

For an added touch, you can sprinkle roasted coconut flakes over the prawns.

Macadamia Crusted 'Ahi

7 to 8 oz. fillet of 'ahi
¼ tsp. olive oil
pinch of thyme and tarragon
2 Tbsp. macadamia nuts, medium chopped

1 tsp. baked garlic, very finely chopped
1 tsp. shallots, very finely chopped
2 Tbsp. olive oil
salt and black pepper to taste

Rub fish with salt and pepper, ¼ tsp. olive oil, thyme and tarragon. Press one tablespoon of chopped macadamia nuts on each side. Put garlic, shallots and olive oil in sauté pan and heat on high until oil bubbles. Carefully place fish in pan and sear both sides until browned. On high heat, sear about 15 seconds on each side for rare; 30 seconds on each side for medium rare. If you prefer a more "well done" preparation, start at a low heat and saute until done. Serve with your favorite starch and vegetables.

Serves 1. Preparation can be done with mahi mahi or ono.

CONTINENTAL

KIRIN CHINESE RESTAURANT

Kirin creates an authentic Chinese dining experience from the cuisine to the atmosphere. The chefs are from China and Hong Kong and prepare foods true to their region. Kirin is one of the few places outside of Chinatown where you can enjoy Dim Sum, "the art of Chinese tidbits." This special and unique treat is served at lunch and all afternoon as well. Their live seafood specialties are highly recommended; they even have a tank of live fish in the kitchen. That's fresh!

Ambiance: Chinese antiques and hand made items, including beautiful wall hangings that are hand embroidered and a hand-painted mural from China, add an authentic air to Kirin Chinese Restaurant. For enhanced romance in the evening, reserve a table on their outdoor balcony where you'll have candlelight and a view of the lagoon and the ocean's white waves lit up from the moon against the dark night.

Menu: The Dim Sum menu includes delicious delicacies such as "Har Gau"—steamed shrimp dumplings, Deep–fried Mixed Seafood Rolls with seaweed and Barbecued Pork Buns. The main menu features Crispy Spring Rolls, Hot and Sour Soup, Peking Duck and a fresh catch of the day. The Peppery Salt Dungeness Crab (they offer 5 different preparations) has a flavor so outstanding it's addictive!

Details: Ala carte items: $4.00-25.00. Lunch and dinner. Call for days open and reservations. Kirin is located above Donatoni's.

(808) 886–1234 EXT. 54 / WWW.HILTONWAIKOLOAVILLAGE.COM
HILTON WAIKOLOA VILLAGE, WAIKOLOA, KOHALA COAST, HAWAI'I 96738

KUNG BAO CHICKEN

8 oz. chicken meat
2 oz. peanuts, roasted
1 red chili, diced
1 bell pepper, diced
½ Tbsp. mashed garlic
2 oz. bamboo shoots, diced
¼ tsp. salt
2 Tbsp. cornstarch

Seasoning
2 tsp. soy bean paste
½ Tbsp. dark soy sauce
1 tsp. vinegar
1 tsp. salt
2 Tbsp. water

Dice chicken and marinate for 10 minutes in the ¼ teaspoon salt mixed with cornstarch. Stir fry peppers and bamboo shoots in 2 tablespoons oil until cooked. Set aside. Sauté chicken and garlic with 2 tablespoons oil. When chicken is fully cooked, add cooked vegetables. Add seasoning and mix well. Plate and serve.

Makes 2 to 3 servings.

STRING BEANS WITH MINCED PORK

1 pound string beans
½ oz. dried shrimp
3 oz. preserved Szechwan vegetable
3 oz. lean pork
½ Tbsp. ginger, finely miced
½ tsp. sesame oil
oil for frying

Seasoning #1
½ tsp. salt
½ tsp. chicken bouillon
½ tsp. sugar
2 Tbsp. water
Seasoning #2
1 tsp. vinegar
2 stalks green onion, diced

Trim ends of string beans and cut into 2" sections. Wash and drain. Wash dried shrimps; soak and mince. Wash Szechwan vegetables; soak for 20 minutes to remove saltiness. Mince. Mince the pork finely. Place string beans in hot oil for 2 minutes (until skin wrinkles). Set aside. Sauté pork, dried shrimps, ginger and Szechwan vegetable with 3 tablespoons oil. Add string beans; stir fry for a while. Add seasoning #1 and fry until liquid dries up. Add seasoning #2, stir well and add sesame oil. Plate and serve.

Makes 2 to 3 servings.

MERRIMAN'S RESTAURANT

Since 1988, **Merriman's Restaurant** has been luring food aficionados from all over Hawai'i and the world to enjoy delicious, creative and fresh food utilizing locally grown ingredients. "Exciting, regional, tasteful and fun," are words that Chef Peter Merriman uses to describe what a restaurant should be and he is a master at creating exactly what he describes in his restaurants. Called the "Pied Piper of Hawai'i Regional Cuisine" by the *LA Times*, and "a culinary renaissance man" by the *New York Times*—Merriman is the creative genius behind 2 exceptional award-winning restaurants (see Hula Grill page 98). Merriman's Restaurant receives rave reviews in *Zagat Survey*, is consistently honored with *Honolulu Magazine's* Hale 'Aina Award, and won the Ilima Award for Best Big Island Restaurant 2003. Peter Merriman has traveled throughout North America on culinary tours representing the Hawai'i Visitor's Bureau, the Department of Agriculture and Hawaiian Airlines, and has appeared on numerous television shows.

Ambiance: An appealing color scheme, vibrant art and potted palm trees create a comfortable and charming ambiance.

Menu: If you can't decide or simply enjoy variety, try a sampling platter of signature items: Sesame Crusted Fresh Island Fish, Wok Charred 'Ahi, and Kung Pao Fresh Island Shrimp. Appetizers include Wainaku Corn, Macadamia Nut and Shrimp Fritters, and Mauna Kea Goat Cheese Baked in Phyllo. Lunch offers a selection of creative entrées, soups and salads.

Details: Lunch served Monday through Friday, $5.95–12.95. Dinner nightly. Entrées: $18.95–34.95. Reservations recommended.

(808) 885-6822 / WWW.MERRIMANSHAWAII.COM
OPELO PLAZA, HIGHWAY 19, KAMUELA, HAWAI'I 96743

MERRIMAN'S POISSON CRU

1 ½ pounds freshest white or pink fish
⅔ cup lime juice
1 cup diced Maui onion
½ cup green onion tops, sliced ¼"

1 cup tomato, diced
3 cups good quality coconut milk
1 Tbsp. Hawaiian salt

Cut fish into half inch dice. Marinate fish in lime juice for ½ hour. Drain most of the lime juice off of fish. Add remaining ingredients. Chill. Taste carefully for salt and adjust to your taste if necessary.

Makes 8 portions.

SESAME BEEF KABOBS

1 ½ pounds lean beef, such as New York,
    rib eye or sirloin
½ tsp. crushed chilies
2 Tbsp. brown sugar

1 tsp. minced garlic
1 Tbsp. sesame seeds
3 Tbsp. Mountain Gold shoyu (soy sauce)

Cut beef into strips ⅓"x1"x4". Mix all seasonings with beef. Thread beef strips on to twelve skewers. Grill or barbeque on both sides until done to your taste.

Makes 12 kabobs.

SIBU CAFÉ

This fabulous hidden gem is exactly the kind of place that people love to discover! Since 1982, **Sibu Café** has been pleasing customers with its unique and exotic Indonesian food and reasonable prices. I've heard stories of returning visitors rushing straight from the airport to satisfy a craving for Sibu's flavorful fare, and rave reviews for the café continuously show up in a variety of publications and guide books.

Ambiance: Relaxed and casual, you can dine in the courtyard setting enhanced by the subtle sound of water trickling through a lava rock fountain, or at one of the few tables inside where you can examine interesting masks from Indonesia.

Menu: Try Balinese Chicken marinated in tarragon, garlic and onions and served with a peanut sauce; or the traditional Shrimp Laska—shrimp, baby corn, green beans, rice noodles and bean sprouts in a fragrant sauce made with coconut milk, lemongrass and Indonesian spices. For a succulent and spicy dish try the Gading (fish) Panggang Pedis. Beef, Chicken, Vegetable or Shrimp Saté and many more great selections, including lots of choice vegetarian entrées, round out the menu. All food is prepared without MSG or white sugar. Sibu features a short international beer and wine list that is carefully chosen to complement the food flavors.

Details: Lunch and dinner served daily. $10.95–14.95. No credit cards. You'll find Sibu Café in the Banyan Court Mall across from the sea wall (where the waves sometimes splash over onto the road). Park in the lot behind the café, which is accessible from Lakani Street (one–way).

(808) 329–1112
75–5695 ALI'I DRIVE, KAILUA–KONA, HAWAI'I 96740

Ayam Bali — Balinese-Style Fried Chicken

A note from the owner/chef: This dish is pretty darn easy, remarkably delicious and has only one unusual ingredient—dark soy sauce.

1 onion, roughly chopped
2 cloves garlic
1 tsp. fresh chopped ginger
3 fresh red chilies, seeded, roughly chopped
4 macadamia nuts
1 Tbsp. dark soy sauce

2½ pound frying chicken
½ cup frying oil
2 Tbsp. palm sugar or dark brown sugar
2 Tbsp. lemon juice
½ tsp. salt
1 cup coconut milk

Put onion, garlic, ginger, chilies, nuts and soy sauce into an electric blender and blend to a smooth paste. Cut chicken into quarters. Dry well on paper towels. Heat ½ cup of oil (not olive oil) in wok or frying pan and fry the chicken pieces quickly until brown. Remove and drain on paper toweling. Pour off all but 1 tablespoon of the oil, and fry the blended mixture for a few minutes, stirring constantly. Add sugar, lemon juice, salt and coconut milk and keep stirring while the mixture comes to a boil. Return chicken and simmer uncovered for 25 minutes or until chicken is tender and gravy thick. Serve over rice.

Serves 4.

Sayur Tumis — Indonesian Stir Fried Vegetables

A note from the owner/chef: This dish has two somewhat unusual ingredients—light soy sauce and dried shrimp paste, or trasi. Any Southeast Asian grocery should have them. The flavor of trasi is quite strong, and can be challenging to the Western palate, but it is essential to giving this dish its Indonesian flavor.

This recipe works with any kind of vegetable. If using a mixture of vegetables, add first those that take longest to cook. To make it truly Indonesian, try including coarsely shredded cabbage, watercress broken into bite-size lengths, green beans, bean sprouts or celery.

3 cups vegetables, washed, well-drained
2 Tbsp. vegetable oil
1 clove garlic, crushed
1 small onion, finely chopped

scant ¼ tsp. trasi (dried shrimp paste)
1 Tbsp. light soy sauce
salt to taste

Heat oil over medium heat. When hot add the garlic, onions and trasi. Crush trasi with a spoon, stirring constantly. Cook until the onions are soft. Add vegetables and stir fry until lightly cooked but still crisp. Remove from heat and add salt and light soy sauce to taste. Serve immediately.

Bonus Section
Featuring Selected Recipes from the
First Edition of Tasting Paradise

Aloha Angel Café, 165, Papaya Seed Dressing / Tropical Fruit Muffins

Bali Hai Restaurant, 166, Bali Hai Salmon / Peanut Chicken Breast with Curry Sauce

Bamboo Restaurant, 168, Hot Spinach Salad with Papaya Seed Dressing

Brennecke's, 169, Cioppino / Sauce for Clams, Scampi and Pasta

Café Pesto, 170, Poisson Cru with Tropical Fruits Served Over Baby Greens Dressed with an Ohelo Berry Vinaigrette / Lumpia Wrapped Ahi with Fresh Mango

Crouching Lion Inn, 170, Slavonic Steak for Two

Donatoni's, 171, Vitello Ala Sorrentina / Pasta Con Aragosta / Terrina Di Melanzane

Dondero's, 172, Rotolo di Papaya Con Ricotta / Involtini d' Ono Alla Siciliana

Gaylord's at Kilohana, 174, Baked Brie in Filo / Chicken and Rosemary Fettucine

Grandma's Coffee House, 175, Susan's Hawaiian Chicken Curry Stew / Maui Lava Flows

The Hanalei Gourmet, 176, Island Style Shrimp and Sweet Potato Fritters with a Spicy Macadamia Nut Dipping Sauce / Smoked Salmon and Potato Cakes with Dill Cream

Imari, 178, Teriyaki Chicken Breast / Asari Butter Clams

Jameson's by the Sea, 178, Salmon Paté

Kalaheo Coffee Co. & Café, 179, Scones / Kauai Carrot Cake / Butter Cream Cheese Frosting

Kamuela Provision Company, 180, Fire Cracker Scallops / Roasted Red Pepper Aioli / Charred 'Ahi with Three Bean Rice

Kilauea Lodge, 181, Coconut Cream of Celery Soup / Beef Roulades

Koke'e Lodge, 182, Portuguese Bean Soup

Kula Lodge & Restaurant, 182, Baked Cucumbers Stuffed with Opakapaka Mousse / Fresh Spinach with Skillet Roasted Salmon

Merriman's Restaurant, 183, Shrimp with Corn and Black Beans / Wok Charred 'Ahi

Pacific'O, 184, Shrimp Won Ton Served with a Spicy Sweet and Sour Sauce and a Hawaiian Salsa / Banana Imu Style Fish with a Lemon Grass Pesto and Vanilla Bean Sauce

Sarento's Top of the "I", 186, Seafood Fra Diavlo / Key Lime Tarts

Sibu Café, 187, Pais Udang or Shrimp Packages / Fried Tofu with Spicy Lime Sauce

Stella Blues Café, 188, Tofu Scramble with Tahini Sauce / Crab Cakes with Lemon Butter Chive Sauce

Tidepools, 189, Coconut Beer Battered Chicken / Charred 'Ahi with Papaya Relish

Due to many requests for the sold out first edition we've included this special section.

PAPAYA SEED DRESSING

1 cup white wine vinegar
¼ cup + 2 Tbsp. lemon juice
¾ cup honey
½ cup fresh parsley
1 tsp. paprika

1 ½ tsp. salt
5 cloves garlic
1 tsp. pepper
3 cups soybean oil
3 whole, skinned papayas

Put all ingredients in a blender with oil on top. Blend well. Add 2 cups of water. Blend.

TROPICAL FRUIT MUFFINS

1 ½ cups unbleached flour
1 ½ cups baker's bran
1 cup grated coconut
½ cup sesame seeds
1 Tbsp. baking powder
1 Tbsp. baking soda
2 eggs

1 cup honey
½ cup melted butter
2 cups milk
1 cup mashed bananas
1 cup crushed pineapple
Optional: dried fruit, dates, papayas or
  mangos

Mix the dry ingredients together (first 6 ingredients). Mix the wet ingredients together in a separate bowl and stir into dry ingredients. Add optional dried fruits. Bake in a muffin pan at 375 degrees for 30 minutes.

BALI HAI RESTAURANT

BALI HAI SALMON

Duxelle

12 oz. chopped cooked, frozen spinach, thawed and drained

8 oz. cream cheese (room temperature)

1 onion, minced

1 Tbsp. capers, minced

1 oz. Pernod (anise liqueur)

½ tsp. salt

¼ tsp. white pepper

1 Tbsp. olive oil

1 tsp. Worcestershire sauce

Heat oil in a sauté pan over medium high heat. When hot, add onion. Sauté until translucent. Add capers and toss several times. Deglaze with the Pernod. Add spinach and warm. Do not overcook. Add cream cheese, Worcestershire, seasonings, and mix. Keep warm.

Beurre Blanc

1 small shallot, minced

1 cup medium body white wine

¼ cup heavy cream

½ lemon

¼ pound butter (cut in cubes)

In a saucepan, reduce shallot and wine. Add cream and simmer to a large bubble consistency. Add squeeze of lemon and return to large bubble consistency. Stir cubed butter in by thirds. Remove from heat. Hold in double boiler over low heat.

Puff Pastry

8 5x5" puff pastry sheets

1 egg

2 Tbsp. water

Mix egg and water until smooth. Cut pastry to shapes making tops to match with slightly larger bottoms. Lightly brush tops of pastry sheets with egg mixture. Place on sheet pan and bake at 350 degrees until golden brown, approximately 10 minutes depending on product.

Salmon

4 6 oz. salmon fillets (best if approximately the same size for equal cooking times)

Dust with seasoned flour (salt and white pepper to taste). Place into a sauté pan preheated with clarified butter or olive oil. Brown lightly (tops first). Turn. Top each fillet with an equal portion of Duxelle and place pan into a 350 degree oven. Cook until firm but still moist. Place salmon fillet and Duxelle between (cooked) pastry sheets. Place most of sauce underneath each serving and a small amount over the top. Garnish with fresh herbs and lemon. Serves 4.

PEANUT CHICKEN BREAST WITH CURRY SAUCE

8 chicken breasts (boneless, skinless halves)
1 cup panko
½ cup shredded coconut (toasted)
1 cup peanuts (dry roasted, finely chopped)

3 whole eggs (beaten)
2 Tbsp. flour
1 Tbsp. butter
3 Tbsp. oil

Marinade

½ cup water
½ cup shoyu
½ tsp. fresh minced ginger

½ tsp. fresh minced garlic
½ tsp. brown sugar
orange zest (optional)

Trim chicken; combine marinade ingredients, mix well. Add chicken; marinate at least 1 hour. Combine panko, coconut and peanuts. Remove chicken from marinade. Dredge chicken in flour and dip in eggs, coat with panko mixture. In a sauté pan heat butter and oil; sauté chicken over medium heat, turning once. Cook until golden brown, about 6 to 7 minutes. Finish in oven. Serves 4.

Curry Sauce

1 Tbsp. peanut oil
¼ cup chopped onion
2 Tbsp. chopped celery
3 Tbsp. chopped carrot
1 Tbsp. curry paste
1 tsp. whole black peppercorn
1 bay leaf

4 cups chicken stock
1 cup whipping cream
½ cup coconut milk
½ cup chopped banana
½ cup chopped papaya
½ cup orange juice

Heat oil in heavy saucepan over medium heat; add onion, celery, carrot, bay leaf and peppercorns. Sauté until golden brown and tender, about 5 to 6 minutes. Stir in curry paste, cook 2 minutes. Whisk in chicken stock and orange juice; add papaya and banana; bring to a boil, lower heat, simmer. Reduce by half, add coconut milk and whipping cream, simmer until reduced to about 2 cups. Strain. Makes 2 cups.

Bamboo Restaurant

Hot Spinach Salad with Papaya Seed Dressing

Papaya Seed Dressing

2 Tbsp. papaya seeds (fresh)

¼ cup onion, chopped

¾ cup red wine vinegar

1 Tbsp. dry mustard

¾ cup sugar

1 Tbsp. salt

¾ cup canola oil

Blend first 6 ingredients, using 1 tablespoon of the papaya seeds. Add other 1 tablespoon of the seeds, then slowly add oil and adjust to taste. This makes approximately 1 pint which keeps well and can be used as a marinade as well as a dressing.

Spinach Salad

2-3 lbs. fresh spinach

½ papaya, sliced

4 Tbsp. crumbled feta cheese

Sauté the following together in the papaya seed dressing:

½ fresh red pepper, julienned

½ red onion, thinly sliced

½ pound fresh mushrooms, sliced

¼ cup pine nuts

Arrange the fresh spinach leaves on a plate, and when mushrooms are lightly cooked, arrange over the spinach and then pour hot dressing over the salad. Garnish with papaya slices and crumbled feta cheese.

CIOPPINO

⅓ cup olive oil

1 cup finely chopped onion

1 cup finely diced green pepper

1 cup finely diced golden pepper

1 cup finely diced red pepper

1 cup finely diced carrots

3 cloves garlic, crushed

¼ cup balsamic vinegar

1½ Tbsp. fresh parsley, chopped

1 Tbsp. fresh oregano, chopped

1 Tbsp. fresh basil, chopped

1 Tbsp. fresh thyme, chopped

3 pieces bay leaves

¼ cup red wine

2 cans diced tomato (or 1 pound 12 oz. chopped whole tomatoes)

20 pieces Manila clams, washed

1 pound king crab, cut, trimmed, easy to open

1 pound fresh fish ('ahi, ono, mahi, etc.), cut into cubes

1 pound (16–20) shrimp, shelled and cleaned

¼ tsp. white pepper

4 cups stock

salt to taste if preferred

Put all seafood with 1 teaspoon salt into 10 cups of boiling water. Cook for 1 to 2 minutes. Remove all seafood, set aside and refrigerate. Save stock and simmer for 10 to 15 minutes. Strain to have a clear stock. In a 10 quart stock pot (no aluminum please—use stainless steel, enamel, or glass) sauté in olive oil, onion, garlic, carrots, and red, green, and gold peppers. Add tomatoes with juice. Add wine, balsamic vinegar, parsley, oregano, basil, thyme, bay leaves and 4 cups of stock. Bring to boil. Reduce heat and simmer for 20 minutes. Add seafood to simmering vegetables and stock. Let simmer 10 minutes longer. Taste then add salt to your liking. Serve with hot crusty sour dough bread (good for soaking up soup). Serve in wide shallow soup bowls. Serves 6 to 10.

SAUCE FOR CLAMS, SCAMPI AND PASTA

½ cup clarified butter

½ cup flour

½ cup Chablis

1 cup chicken stock

1 cup milk or half and half

½ cup garlic butter

1⅛ tsp. lemon juice

1⅛ tsp. caper juice

Cover bottom of sauté pan with clarified butter, slowly add enough flour to absorb all butter. Cook flour well but do not brown. Add Chablis and slowly stir in chicken stock, slowly add milk, caper juice and lemon juice, and a generous helping of garlic butter. Simmer slowly but do not boil.

Scampi: Add clarified butter into a saucepan with Chablis, add floured shrimp into roux. Add flour gradually into roux with chicken stock and milk. Cook over medium heat, do not burn.

Poipu Pasta: Add chopped veggies into sauce and cook vegetables until slightly crisp and pour over pasta.

Clams: Clean and wash clams before adding into sauce and simmer until shells open.

Sea Bass: Same recipe as scampi. If there is no Seabass in your area, Grouper Bass, or frozen New Zealand Bass will work all the same.

CAFÉ PESTO

POISSON CRU WITH TROPICAL FRUITS SERVED OVER BABY GREENS DRESSED WITH AN OHELO BERRY VINAIGRETTE

1 pound ono (wahoo) or any white fish
½ cup lime juice
1 12 oz. can coconut milk
1 mango, cubed
2 dashes chipolte vinegar (Tabasco)

1 papaya, cubed
2 bananas, cut in chunks
2 kiwi, cut in chunks
salad greens

Cut fish in 1 inch cubes and marinate in lime juice for 1 hour. Drain fish and combine all ingredients and let stand for ½ hour.

Ohelo Berry Vinaigrette

½ cup ohelo berry jam*
⅓ cup red wine vinegar
1 Tbsp. sugar
1 tsp. minced ginger

¼ tsp. fresh cracked pepper
1 cup oil
salt to taste

*Use fresh Ohelo berries cooked and thickened with cornstarch.

In a food processor, combine all ingredients except oil. With machine running, add oil slowly.

LUMPIA WRAPPED AHI WITH FRESH MANGO

8 2 oz. slices of sashimi grade 'ahi
1 fresh mango, peeled and sliced thin
1 Tbsp. wasabi paste (thinned)

2 sheets nori (cut into 8 strips)
salt and pepper
8 lumpia (egg roll) shells

Very lightly baste the top of the 'ahi with wasabi. Place a slice of fresh mango on the 'ahi. Sprinkle lightly with salt and pepper. Wrap the 'ahi and mango with a strip of dampened nori. Place wrapped 'ahi in Lumpia shell and fold into a square. Preheat well-oiled sauté pan at medium-high. Sear 'ahi lumpia until golden brown. Damp off any extra oil and cut lumpias diagonally for presentation. May be served with a mango chutney thinned with rice wine vinegar and spiced with Hawaiian chilies.

CROUCHING LION INN

SLAVONIC STEAK FOR TWO

2 14 oz. tenderloin steaks
salad oil

Italian seasonings
fresh coarsely ground pepper

Marinate the steaks in a mixture of salad oil, Italian seasonings and pepper for 2 hours or to your liking. Charbroil marinated steaks. Serve thinly sliced on a sizzling platter of garlic butter.

VITELLO ALA SORRENTINA

12 2 oz. veal scaloppini
½ cup tomato coulis
4 slices proscuitto
12 slices eggplant, lightly sautéed, sliced

2 oz. olive oil
salt and pepper to taste
1½ tsp. basil chiffonade
12 slices Buffalo mozzarella

Lightly season the veal with salt and pepper. Place basil chiffonade and proscuitto slices on top of the veal. Heat a sauté pan and add olive oil. Sauté the veal on both sides until medium rare. Drain off the oil and cover the top of each scaloppini with the eggplant, then mozzarella. Brown under the broiler. Place tomato coulis on a plate, and display the veal on top of the sauce. Serves 4.

PASTA CON ARAGOSTA

1 pound lobster tail, diced
12 oz. angel hair pasta, cooked
1 cup asparagus stems, pureed
1½ cups cream
2 oz. butter

salt and pepper to taste
chives to taste
olive oil as needed
1 cup asparagus tips, sliced

Heat some olive oil in a non–stick pan, and sauté the pasta. Meanwhile, in another pan, reduce together the cream, asparagus puree, butter, lobster meat and the seasoning. When almost done, add the asparagus tips in the sauce and the warm pasta. When hot, place the pasta in a plate and pour the rest of the sauce over the pasta. Serves 4.

TERRINA DI MELANZANE

1 gelatin sheet
1½ eggplant, sliced ½" thick
1 roasted red pepper
1 roasted yellow pepper
3 oz. balsamic vinaigrette (1 part balsamic vinegar to 3 parts olive oil, salt & pepper)

Garnish
2 Tbsp. Pecorino cheese with truffles
few drops olive oil
½ Tbsp. Italian parsley
2 Tbsp. tomato coulis

Line mold with plastic wrap. In a separate bowl, add gelatin sheet into warm dressing and allow to soften. Roast and peel peppers and remove seeds. Grill eggplant. Fill mold by alternating layers of dressing and vegetables. Cover and refrigerate until firm. Garnish plate with tomato coulis, oil, Pecorino cheese and Italian parsley.

Rotolo di Papaya Con Ricotta

Pasta di Papaya

4 cups unbleached flour
2 eggs
4 tsp. olive oil

pinch salt
2 cups fresh papaya puree

First, make a well with flour. Crack eggs into the well and put in fresh pureed papaya. Add salt and olive oil. Mix with a fork, working the pasta without breaking the walls of flour and slowly form a pasta ball.

Vanilla Sauce

1 cup white wine
1 vanilla bean
2 cups heavy cream

½ cup butter
1 shallot

Reduce white wine with shallot, add whole vanilla bean cut in half, and cream. Reduce until half, add butter slowly.

Vanilla Pine Nut Sauce

½ cup roasted pine nuts
¼ cup walnuts
6 cloves garlic

6 oz. Parmesan cheese
1 ½ cups olive oil

In a blender, grind nuts, and slowly add garlic, cheese, and olive oil until a smooth paste forms. Add slowly into vanilla sauce and serve.

Ripieno for Rotolo

15 oz. ricotta
2 eggs
2 egg yolks
½ cup Parmesan cheese

3 cups spinach, julienne
1 cup sun dried tomatoes, chopped
salt and pepper to taste
1 cup julienne dry papaya

Mix all ingredients together.

After making the pasta, roll it out on cheese cloth to a thickness of about ¹⁄₁₆" with a rolling pin. Spread evenly with ricotta mixture. Carefully roll up the pasta wrapping the cheese cloth around it. Wrap in aluminum foil and tie the ends tightly. Boil for 30 to 40 minutes. Remove, dip in cold water. Drain and let it rest for 10 to 15 minutes. Slowly unwrap, slice, cover with sauce and serve.

Involtini d' Ono Alla Siciliana

16 3 oz. pieces of ono
16 Tbsp. Sicilian Stuffing, recipe below
    (1 Tbsp. for each ono)

3 Tbsp. olive oil
1 cup white wine
salt and pepper to taste

Pound the ono gently to flatten the fish. Then spread Sicilian Stuffing on the fish and roll. Bake with olive oil and white wine at 350 degrees for 6 to 8 minutes. Place on top of Orange Tomato Basil Sauce (Salsa di Pomodoro Arancia e Basilico, recipe below) and serve.

Salsa di Pomodoro Arancia e Basilico (Orange Tomato Basil Sauce)

2½ pounds fresh plum tomatoes, skinned
6 garlic cloves
14 basil leaves

3 oranges
salt and pepper to taste
3 Tbsp. olive oil

Heat olive oil in a pot. Sauté garlic and basil leaves for a few minutes, then add plum tomatoes. Lower the heat, squeeze juice from halved oranges into the pot, then add the oranges. Let cook for 20 minutes. Take out oranges, and puree salsa. Add salt and pepper to taste. Serve with Ono.

Ripieno Alla Siciliana (Sicilian Stuffing for Ono)

1½ cups golden raisins
12 dry figs
1½ cups fresh basil

1½ cups pine nuts (roasted)
12 anchovies
¼ cup Italian parsley

Soak raisins in water for 15 minutes. Put remaining ingredients and raisins in a food processor and grind until you have made a paste. Then spread on Ono and roll into to a bundle.

GAYLORD'S AT KILOHANA

BAKED BRIE IN FILO

1 pound brie round (small)
8 pieces filo

2 whole garlic heads
8 Tbsp. clarified butter

Cut and trim brie so rind is removed. Let stand at room temperature for at least ½ hour to soften. Melt and clarify butter. Let cool. Chop off top of garlic. Roast at 350 degrees for ½ hour or until cloves can be squeezed out easily. Cut filo so that it can be wrapped around entire brie one time. Lay one piece of filo on flat surface, brush with 1 tablespoon butter. Lay another piece directly on top, brush with 1 tablespoon butter, and repeat until all 8 pieces are buttered and layered. Place roasted garlic which has been squeezed out of skin (at least 6 cloves) in the middle of filo, and place brie directly on top. Wrap filo around, folding so that filo is tight against side of brie. Be sure the filo overlaps on bottom so as to make a seal. Cut off any excess dough. Turn brie over so that the seam is on the bottom and garlic on top. Bake at 375 degrees for 25 minutes, or until golden brown. Serve with fresh sliced fruit and sliced french bread or crackers.

CHICKEN AND ROSEMARY FETTUCINE

**12 3 oz. skinless, boneless fresh chicken
   breast pieces**
2 cups flour
24 oz. artichoke hearts (canned are fine)
24 oz. fresh mushrooms, sliced if necessary
1 cup chicken stock
¼ oz. fresh Thai basil (purple) leaves

8 cups cream
2 cups unsweetened coconut milk
sprig lemon grass
½ cup dry white wine
3 Tbsp. clarified butter
48 oz. rosemary fettucine

Reduce the cream by bringing to a boil and boiling slowly for about 20 minutes to reduce to 6 cups. Dredge chicken breasts in flour and sauté in clarified butter. Do not overcook. Remove from pan and set aside. In the same pan, add artichoke hearts, mushrooms and basil to hot pan, sauté until heated through. Splash with white wine to deglaze the pan. Immediately add reduced cream, coconut milk, sprig of lemon grass and chicken broth; simmer for 3 to 4 minutes; remove and discard lemon grass. Add pre-cooked rosemary fettucine and pre-cooked chicken breasts, toss to coat well and simmer about a minute to heat through. Arrange fettucine and 2 chicken breast pieces per plate, cover with sauce and garnish with purple basil or Italian parsley. Serves 6.

SUSAN'S HAWAIIAN CHICKEN CURRY STEW

5 pounds boneless, skinless chicken thighs
3 cups cubed cut Maui Kula onions
3 cupscut carrots
3 cups potatoes, peeled and cubed
1½ cups chopped green bell pepper
1½ cups chopped celery
2 Tbsp. curry powder

2 oz. fresh Hawaiian ginger, chopped
1 whole clove garlic, chopped
8 cups water
3 Tbsp. flour, to thicken gravy
3 tsp. ground black pepper or to taste
3 tsp. sea salt, or to taste

Slice chicken thighs into thirds, sauté to brown, then add seasonings including ginger and garlic. Add potatoes, carrots, and water. Simmer over moderate heat for 35 minutes. Then add the rest of the vegetables and simmer for approximately 10 more minutes. Note that all measurements are approximate and may be adjusted to taste.

MAUI LAVA FLOWS

Crust

¾ cup unsalted butter
2 cups unbleached flour

1 cup packed Maui raw sugar

Mix for approximately 2 minutes. Spread over lightly greased 9x13" pan. Bake at 350 degrees for 20 to 25 minutes until dark brown.

Filling

1½ cups packed Maui raw sugar
4 eggs
4 Tbsp. unbleached flour
2 tsp. salt

2 tsp. pure vanilla
2 cups chocolate chips
1½ cups chopped pecans

Blend all ingredients (except chocolate chips and pecans) in mixer until light and fluffy. Add chocolate chips and pecans, and mix 1 minute. Pour over crust. Bake at 350 degrees 20 to 25 minutes.

Frosting

3 Tbsp. unsalted butter
4 Tbsp. cocoa
4 Tbsp. water

1 tsp. Grandma's Maui Coffee espresso
2 cups powdered sugar

Mix first 4 ingredients in sauce pan over medium heat. Bring to a boil and put in mixer. Add sugar and beat until smooth and thick. Drizzle over bars to look like lava flows.

ISLAND STYLE SHRIMP AND SWEET POTATO FRITTERS WITH A SPICY MACADAMIA NUT DIPPING SAUCE

Sauce

2 cloves garlic, crushed

1 fresh red chili pepper, finely minced

2 Tbsp. sugar

2 Tbsp. lime juice

¼ cup rice vinegar

¼ cup Nuoc Mam (Vietnamese fish sauce)

3 Tbsp. toasted macadamia nuts, ground

2 Tbsp. chopped fresh cilantro

Combine sugar and garlic in a mortar and pestle, grind to a paste. Mix in lime juice and vinegar. Stir to dissolve sugar. Combine remaining ingredients. Stir well. Let stand at room temperature for 1 hour to combine flavors. Note: This sauce is somewhat pungent. A few tablespoons of water may be added to achieve desired taste.

Fritters

24 shrimp, head on preferred

1 Tbsp. fish sauce (Nuoc Mam)

4 cloves garlic, minced

2 cups flour

2 Tbsp. dark brown sugar

1 Tbsp. salt

2 tsp. baking powder

1 Tbsp. Madras curry powder

1 large sweet potato

¼ red onion, julienned paper thin

2 scallions, finely sliced

3 Tbsp. fresh cilantro, coarsely chopped

Peel the shrimp, leaving the heads and tails on 16 for a garnish. Cut the remaining shrimp into pieces. Marinate the shrimp in the fish sauce and garlic.

Combine the flour, brown sugar, salt, baking powder and curry powder in a bowl. Make a well in the center and whisk in 1 to 1¼ cups cold water to form a light batter.

In a larger bowl, combine the red onion, scallions and cilantro. Peel the sweet potato, slice into paper thin rounds, then cut the rounds into a fine julienne. Combine with the onion and scallion mixture. Add the chopped shrimp and about ¾ of the batter. Mix well. Heat 2 to 3 inches of peanut oil in a wok to 370 degrees. Form the fritter mixture on a wide spatula, about 2 tablespoons batter per fritter. Place a whole shrimp in the center and press firmly to secure. Take a long thin knife and gently slide the fritters into the oil and fry, turning once, until golden brown. Transfer to a platter lined with paper towels and keep warm in a 375 degree oven until ready to serve. Serve the fritters on bibb lettuce with the dipping sauce.

Yield: 16 cakes (approximately).

SMOKED SALMON AND POTATO CAKES WITH DILL CREAM

Dill Cream

½ cup low fat plain yogurt
1 clove garlic, chopped fine
⅛ tsp. cayenne

3 Tbsp. chopped fresh dill
½ cup sour cream

Stir in bowl all together, cover and chill.

Salmon Cakes

3 large Idaho potatoes, peeled, cut into
   coarse chunks
1 tsp. olive oil plus 3 tsp. for frying patties
6 scallions, sliced very thin
10 oz. smoked salmon, minced
½ cup chopped fresh dill

1 Tbsp. fresh lemon juice
1 Tbsp. low fat plain yogurt
few drops Tabasco sauce
2 large eggs plus 2 egg whites
⅛ tsp. cayenne
¾ tsp. salt
2 tsp. unsalted butter

Cook potatoes in boiling, salted water about 15 to 20 minutes, until very tender. Drain, return to pan, place on low heat to fry, about one minute. Put potatoes through a food mill, ricer, or transfer to bowl and mash. Cover. Chill at least 1 hour or over night. Heat 1 teaspoon olive oil in non-stick skillet. Sauté scallion. Set aside. Beat eggs and whites together until smooth, add potatoes, scallions, salmon, dill, lemon juice, yogurt, cayenne, Tabasco. Mix lightly. Chill if not using right away. Just before serving, heat ½ teaspoon of butter and ½ teaspoon olive oil in non-stick skillet over medium-high heat. Gently form potato mixture into 12 patties, 2 inches wide, ½ inch thick (or 24 patties for hors d'oeuvres). Place 4 patties in pan, lower heat to medium and cook, shaking pan to prevent sticking, about 4 to 5 minutes. Gently flip until golden brown 3 to 4 minutes. Repeat twice. Keep patties warm in oven at 200 degrees. Serve hot with dab of dill cream and fresh sprig of dill or parsley. Serves six or 12 hors d'oeuvres.

Imari

Teriyaki Chicken Breast

4 8 oz. boneless chicken breasts
salt and pepper to taste
2 oz. tempura flour
2 oz. sterling oil

½ cup mirin
½ cup sake
4 oz. Teriyaki Sauce (recipe below)
2 Tbsp. chopped green onions

Teriyaki Sauce
½ cup soy sauce
¾ cup mirin

3 Tbsp. sake
4 tsp. tamari sauce

Season chicken breast with salt and pepper, dredge in flour. Heat oil, brown chicken, and deglaze with mirin and sake. Simmer until chicken is done.

In a separate pan, mix together ingredients for Teriyaki Sauce and bring to a simmer. Place chicken on a plate and sauce with Teriyaki Sauce. Sprinkle with green onions. Serve with steamed rice. Serves 4.

Asari Butter Clams

4 doz. clams
1 ½ cups dashi
2 oz. shoyu

3 Tbsp. green onions, chopped
½ cup butter

Place clams with dashi and shoyu in a sauté pan and steam clams open. Add all of the butter and whisk in broth. Sprinkle with green onions before serving.

Jameson's by the Sea

Salmon Paté

1 ¾ pounds sockeye salmon
1 pound cream cheese
2 Tbsp. sour cream
2 Tbsp. horseradish

2 Tbsp. minced white onion
¼ cup lemon juice
1 Tbsp. salt or to taste
¼ Tbsp. liquid smoke

Put all ingredients (except salmon and cream cheese) in a blender and blend thoroughly. In a KitchenAid mixer with a dough hook, put: 1 ¾ pound sockeye salmon (canned–remove all bones, skin, and blood line) and cream cheese. Blend together until completely mixed. When mixed, add blended ingredients and thoroughly mix. Put mixture in 2 quart containers (old milk containers) and freeze. When you need Salmon Paté simply cut off the desired amount and serve with a dab of sour cream on top, chopped onion and capers. Use Diamond Soda Crackers.

Kalaheo Coffee Co. & Café

Scones

3–5 Tbsp. fresh orange juice
½ orange, zest only
½ cup raisins/currants
3 cups flour
⅓ cup sugar
1 Tbsp. baking powder
½ tsp. salt
½ cup unsalted cold butter, cut into small pieces
¾ cup buttermilk
Egg Wash
1 egg yolk plus 1 Tbsp. milk

Sift flour, sugar, baking powder and salt into a bowl. Work butter into dry ingredients until nut size balls are formed. Make a well in the center, add wet ingredients and raisins. Work dough as in biscuits. Combine **without over working the dough.** Form into balls by pulling the dough and **don't over work**. (At this point, the dough can be frozen for future use.) Wash with egg wash before baking. Bake at 350 degrees for 20 minutes. Note: Other fruit may be used in place of raisins. Soak dry fruits in the orange juice or add fresh, frozen, or canned fruit in the same amount to the recipe in the same sequence. A slight adjustment of more flour may be needed if fruit is quite moist. Yields 10 medium size scones.

Kauai Carrot Cake

4 eggs
1¼ cups oil
2 cups sugar
2 tsp. vanilla
2 cups flour
2 tsp. baking powder
1 tsp. baking soda
¼ tsp. salt
2½ tsp. cinnamon
2½ cups carrots, grated
8 oz. can pineapple, crushed, drained
½ cup coconut flakes
1 cup walnuts, chopped

Beat together first 4 ingredients until blended. Beat in the next 5 ingredients until blended. Stir in the remaining ingredients. Divide batter between 2 greased 9" tube pans and bake in a 350 degree oven for about 40 minutes, or until a cake tester, inserted in center, comes out clean. When cool, frost with Butter Cream Cheese Frosting. Each cake serves 8. Makes 2 cakes.

Butter Cream Cheese Frosting

½ cup butter, softened
8 oz. cream cheese
1 tsp. vanilla
3 cups sifted powdered sugar

Beat butter and cream cheese until blended. Beat in remaining ingredients until blended.

Kamuela Provision Company

Fire Cracker Scallops

20 large scallops
4 1" thick pineapple slices with skin on
8 Tbsp. Roasted Red Pepper Aioli (recipe below)
2 lemons
1 tsp. butter

salt and pepper to taste
1/3 tsp. red curry paste
1/3 tsp. lemon grass, finely chopped
1/2 tsp. garlic, minced
1/2 tsp. ginger, minced

First prepare the Aioli (recipe below).

Season scallops with salt and pepper, red curry paste, lemon grass, garlic and ginger. Sauté in hot butter. When cooked, place on pineapple slice and drizzle with Roasted Red Pepper Aioli; garnish with lemon. Serves 4.

Roasted Red Pepper Aioli

1 red bell pepper
2 Tbsp. onions
1/2 tsp. chopped garlic
1/2 tsp. chopped shallots

1 1/2 oz. white wine
1 1/2 oz. chicken stock
salt and pepper to taste
6 oz. mayonnaise

Roast, seed and peel pepper. Return to large saucepan. Combine garlic, onions, shallots, (all finely chopped) white wine and chicken stock. Reduce until all liquid is gone. Blend until puree is smooth. Cool, then add mayonnaise and mix well. Put aside.

Charred 'Ahi with Three Bean Rice

4 'ahi blocks, 3 oz. each
1 1/2 cups Three Bean Rice (recipe below)
4 Tbsp. clarified butter
2 Tbsp. blackening spice

1 Tbsp. wasabi mustard
2 lemons
4 oz. soy sauce

Dip 'ahi in clarified butter. Sprinkle with blackening spice. Char all sides very lightly in very hot cast iron pan. Slice and serve over Three Bean Rice. Garnish with lemon, wasabi and soy sauce in eye cup. Serves four.

Three Bean Rice

1 cup converted rice, cooked
1 cup wild rice, cooked
1 Tbsp. red bell pepper, diced
1 Tbsp. green bell pepper, diced
1 Tbsp. Maui onion, diced
1 Tbsp. cilantro, chopped
1/3 tsp. cumin

1/3 tsp. coriander
salt and pepper to taste
1/2 cup kidney beans, cooked
1/2 cup navy beans, cooked
1/2 cup black beans, cooked
1 tsp. garlic
3 oz. Cabernet Dressing (recipe below)

Cook rice and cool. Cook beans and cool. Mix all ingredients in large container. Add Cabernet Dressing last. Mix well.

Cabernet Dressing

3 oz. soy bean oil
1 oz. Cabernet Sauvignon
1 oz. wine vinegar

1 tsp. sugar
1 tsp. corn syrup
salt and pepper

COCONUT CREAM OF CELERY SOUP

10 cups chicken broth

3 pounds celery stalk, cubed

2 pounds Russet potatoes, peeled, cubed

17 fluid oz. milk

½ cup heavy cream

½ cup coconut syrup

1½ tsp. celery salt

1 tsp. white pepper

8 oz. unsalted butter

parsley, finely chopped

Pour chicken stock into 4 quart pot. Bring to a boil. Puree celery and potato in food processor until very fine. Add puree into boiling chicken broth and beat with whip for 2 minutes. Add milk, heavy cream, and coconut syrup. Stir. Bring to a fast boil, then reduce heat to low and let simmer. Add celery salt and white pepper. Stir. Cover pot and let simmer for 40 minutes. Stir frequently. Remove pot from stove. With a 2 ounce ladle force liquid through a fine sieve into a 4 quart bowl. Discard heavy puree in sieve. Cut butter into ½ inch cubes. Add to cream of celery in the bowl. Whip until butter has dissolved. Sprinkle a little parsley on each serving. Serve cold or hot. For 8 to 10 people. Serve hot or cold.

BEEF ROULADES

8–10 slices top round beef (each ¼" thick)

Dijon mustard

salt

black ground pepper

1 cup diced bacon

3 spears dill pickle, diced

1 cup diced onion

4 oz. bacon fat

2 quarts water

4 tsp. cornstarch

2 Tbsp. cold water for cornstarch

toothpicks

Lay out the slices of beef on a table or large cutting board and pound lightly with mallet. Sprinkle with salt and black pepper and spread a little mustard. Add teaspoon each of diced onion, bacon, and dill pickle. Fold in on both sides and roll up tightly. Push in 2 toothpicks. Put aside until all slices are done.

Heat up bacon fat in large enough pot to hold the roulades on the bottom plus 2 quarts of water. Add the roulades and brown on all sides. After browning, add one pint of water slowly from the side first. Add additional water to cover the roulades just to the top. Cover with lid and simmer for 1½ to 2 hours. Roulades should be soft. Replace water as needed. When roulades are soft, remove and place on a plate.

In a small bowl mix water with cornstarch. Add to simmering sauce and let thicken. Stir. Add roulades again and simmer for 5 more minutes. Stir. Remove toothpicks and serve. Serves 4.

KOKEʻE LODGE

PORTUGUESE BEAN SOUP

8 oz. dry kidney beans
1 pound ham hock
1 pound soup bone
1 onion, chopped
2 whole cloves
½ pound celery, sliced
2–3 carrots, sliced
1 salad potato, cubed

½ green pepper, minced
12 oz. hot Portuguese sausage, sliced
1 small cabbage, chopped
1 clove garlic, minced
1 bunch parsley, minced
3 peppercorns
1 bay leaf
8 oz. tomato sauce

Soak beans overnight in 1 quart water and 1 teaspoon salt. Drain. Add remaining ingredients, except sausage and cabbage, with 8 cups water. Simmer, partially covered, 4 to 5 hours, adding water as necessary. Add sausage and simmer 30 minutes. Remove ham hock and soup bone. Pick off meat and return to stock pot. Refrigerate to degrease, if possible. Reheat, add cabbage and more water, if necessary, and simmer 30 minutes.

KULA LODGE & RESTAURANT

BAKED CUCUMBERS STUFFED WITH OPAKAPAKA MOUSSE

3 cucumbers
16 oz. fresh opakapaka
2 egg whites
½ tsp. salt
½ tsp. paprika

cayenne pepper
1 cup heavy cream
1 Tbsp. macadamia nuts
2 Tbsp. melted butter
1 cup Beurre Blanc (recipe below)

Cut cucumbers into 1¼" pieces. Scoop out the seeds with a small melon ball cutter. Blanch in boiling salted water for 2 minutes and submerge in ice water. Drain well on a paper towel. In a food processor, puree the opakapaka and add egg whites, salt, cayenne pepper, and paprika. Pour in the heavy cream slowly and the macadamia nuts until well mixed. Place the cucumber cup in a buttered baking dish. Preheat oven to 350 degrees. Fill cucumbers with the Opakapaka Mousse. Bake for 20 minutes. Place the cucumbers in a serving dish and serve with Beurre Blanc.

Beurre Blanc

4 shallots, chopped
3 Tbsp. white vinegar
1 cup white wine

1½ cups unsalted butter, cut into small chunks
salt and ground white pepper to taste

Combine shallots, vinegar, and wine in a non–reactive saucepan. Bring to a boil and cook until liquid reduces to 2 tablespoons. Reduce heat to low and whisk in butter, a few chunks at a time until all of the butter has been incorporated. Season with salt and white pepper to taste.

FRESH SPINACH WITH SKILLET ROASTED SALMON

black peppercorns
8 oz. salmon
6 Tbsp. unsalted butter

2 Tbsp. sesame oil
1 pound fresh spinach
coarse sea salt

Press black peppercorns into salmon filet. Heat butter and oil in a skillet over medium heat. Add salmon fillets, skin side down, and cook without turning for about 15 minutes. Melt butter in a pot. Add spinach and sprinkle with salt and pepper. Cook the spinach over medium high heat for a few minutes until liquid in skillet evaporates. Place spinach on a serving platter and salmon on the top of the spinach, skin side down. Sprinkle salmon with coarse sea salt and serve.

SHRIMP WITH CORN AND BLACK BEANS

1 pound (16–20) shrimp, peeled, deveined

1½ Tbsp. vegetable oil

2 ears fresh corn, cut from the cob

1 tsp. fresh garlic, minced

1 tsp. shallots, minced

¼ cup Chinese salted black beans

2 tsp. fresh ginger, minced

½ tsp. sugar

1 Tbsp. butter

½ cup green onion tops, cut on the bias

2 Tbsp. cilantro

½ tsp. salt, or to taste

2 cups mixed salad greens

1 tomato, cut into wedges

Heat vegetable oil in a 10" sauté pan. Add shrimp and sear on both sides until just pink. Remove from pan. Add the corn, ginger, garlic, and shallots and sauté until corn is just cooked, about 2 minutes. Add the shrimp and black beans, butter, and sugar. Toss and cook 1 minute. Add the green onions and toss. Add salt to taste. Arrange the greens on 4 plates. Place the shrimp mixture on top of the greens, and garnish with cilantro and tomato wedges.

An appetizer for 4.

WOK CHARRED 'AHI

½ cup clarified butter

2 tsp. fresh grated ginger

2 tsp. chopped shallots

2 tsp. crushed chilies

1 tsp. fresh chopped thyme

2 tsp. crushed garlic

1 tsp. fresh chopped marjoram

½ tsp. cayenne pepper

1 tsp. salt

½ lemon, juice only

2 pieces 8 oz. 'ahi logs, scored on top for cutting logs, cut 4" long by 1¼" square

Mix together clarified butter, ginger, shallots, chilies, thyme, garlic, marjoram, cayenne pepper, salt, and lemon juice. Heat wok until metal begins turning white. Dredge 'ahi logs in butter mixture, then sear in wok 20 seconds on each side. Slice and serve. Note: The sauce we use is 4 parts Shoyu (soy sauce), 1 part Mirin, 1 part lime juice and Wasabi to taste. Wasabi must be made into a thick paste with water first; ¼ cup Wasabi to 2 cups Shoyu (this is the Sashimi dip). Fresh tropical fruit makes an excellent accompaniment.

SHRIMP WON TON SERVED WITH A SPICY SWEET AND SOUR SAUCE AND A HAWAIIAN SALSA

Won Ton Marinade

1 cup low salt soy sauce

1 cup sesame oil

1 cup loosely packed fresh cilantro

2 stalks chopped lemon grass

2 bulbs ginger root

1 egg

Place all ingredients in a blender and process. Pour over peeled shrimp and let stand for 15 minutes.

Sweet and Sour Sauce

1 cup sugar

1 cup red wine vinegar

1 Tbsp. low salt soy sauce

1 tsp. red chili flakes

1 stick cinnamon

1 tsp. ground cinnamon

Place all ingredients in a sauce pot and simmer for 20 minutes.

Hawaiian Salsa

2 large ripe mangos, peeled and diced
  (papaya or pineapple may be substituted)

1 medium onion, peeled and diced

½ cup loosely packed fresh cilantro, coarsely
  chopped

Place all ingredients in a bowl and mix gently.

Won Ton

24 won ton wrappers

6 oz. hoisin sauce, in a squirt bottle

24 leaves fresh sweet basil

24 large shrimp, peeled, tails on

oil for deep frying

Lay won ton wrappers on a table. Place one leaf of basil on each. Place one shrimp on each piece of basil. Roll won ton closed around shrimp. Deep fry at 350 degrees until won ton becomes crisp and shrimp is lightly cooked, 1½–2 minutes. Arrange shrimp on a plate. Ladle some Sweet and Sour Sauce over. Place a spoon full of Hawaiian Salsa on shrimp. Finish by squirting some hoisin sauce over the shrimp and plate.

Serves 6.

BANANA IMU STYLE FISH WITH A LEMON GRASS PESTO AND VANILLA BEAN SAUCE

Lemon Grass Pesto

3 cloves garlic

1 bunch fresh basil leaves

1 cup olive oil

½ cup toasted macadamia nuts

1 large stalk lemon grass, smashed and coarsely chopped

Place all items in a blender and process into a smooth paste. Can be stored in the refrigerator for up to one month.

Vanilla Bean Sauce

1 fresh vanilla bean, split lengthwise

1 stalk lemon grass, smashed

1 bulb ginger, smashed

3 cloves garlic, smashed

1 small basil bunch, coarsely chopped

1 small cilantro bunch, coarsely chopped

1 tsp. turmeric

1 cup rice wine vinegar

1 tsp. honey

2 cups clam juice

2 tsp. cornstarch mixed with

1 Tbsp. water

In a sauce pot, dry sauté first 7 ingredients for approximately 2 minutes, stirring frequently. Add vinegar and honey, then reduce by half. Add clam juice and bring to a boil. Add cornstarch mixture and thicken. Reduce heat and simmer on low heat for 20 minutes. Strain mixture through a China cap and reserve. Cut white fish filet into 2 to 3 ounce pieces. Cut banana leaf into 3 inch wide strips. Lay out strips of banana leaf and place a piece of fish on each. Spread a small amount of Lemon Grass Pesto on each and roll in leaf. Place on grill and cook until fish is half cooked. Turn over and continue cooking until done. Time of cooking depends on type of fish used. Fish may be baked in an oven. Ladle sauce on plate garnished with rice and stir fried vegetables. Place fish on top of the sauce.

Seafood Fra Diavlo

1 lobster tail (remove from shell and dice into 1" pieces)
2 oz. white wine
8 oz. linguine
12 oz. Marinara Sauce (recipe below)
1 large pinch of crushed red pepper
6 med/large shrimp
6 blue gold mussels
4 oz. olive oil
4 oz. chopped basil
4 oz. garlic butter (recipe below)

Sauté all seafood in olive oil. Add white wine, red pepper, fresh basil, then reduce. Add marinara and garlic butter. Simmer 3 to 5 minutes. Toss with cooked linguine and serve. Serves 2.

Marinara Sauce

¼ cup olive oil
1 large diced onion
¼ cup minced garlic
3 15 oz. cans plum tomatoes, hand squeezed
8 oz. can tomato paste
1 cup red wine
3 Tbsp. oregano
1 Tbsp. thyme
1 Tbsp. basil
½ tsp. red pepper
½ tsp. black pepper
1 oz. salt
1 oz. sugar
2 tsp. rosemary
2 bay leaves

Sauté onions in olive oil. Add spices, wine, garlic, tomatoes and paste. Simmer ½ hour. Yield: 1 gallon of sauce. Sauce can be stored up to 1 month in refrigerator.

Garlic Butter

2 lbs. butter, softened
1 Tbsp. garlic powder
1 Tbsp. minced fresh garlic
½ tsp. Worcestershire sauce
½ tsp. bitters
dash Tabasco sauce
2 Tbsp. white wine
1 tsp. brandy
2 Tbsp. chopped parsley

Place butter in mixer. Add all dry ingredients, blend. Add all liquids, blend.

Key Lime Tarts

Crust

1 pound graham cracker crumbs
½ cup sugar
¼ cup clarified butter

Mix all ingredients until well blended.

Filling

4 cups sweetened condensed milk
6 sugared egg yolks
½ cup key lime juice

In a mixer, mix milk and yolks until blended. Add lime juice and mix until well blended.

Meringue

6 egg whites
¼ cup sugar

Heat sugar and egg whites constantly stirring until sugar dissolves. Whip in mixer until stiff peaks form. Press crust mixture into round tart molds (approximately 3" in diameter). Fill crusts with filling. Bake tarts at 350 degrees for 12 minutes; remove from oven and let cool. Top with meringue. Yield: 12 tarts.

Pais Udang or Shrimp Packages

2 pounds large shrimp or prawns
6 macadamia nuts
1 oz. ginger root
½ tsp. turmeric
3 jalapeños (or other hot chilies)
6 green onions or scallions

1 medium lime
1 fresh sprig of basil or mint
1 bay leaf
salt
1 banana leaf (or aluminum foil)

Clean, wash and drain the shrimp, put in a bowl, sprinkle lightly with salt, and set aside. In a food processor (or mortar and pestle), place the mac nuts, ginger and turmeric and grind them together until fine. Seed the chilies and slice them finely. Slice the lime into thin rounds, discarding the seeds. Chop the green onion into ½ inch pieces. Mix all these ingredients together with the shrimp, add a little more salt and that's the filling. Place some of the mixture on a piece of banana leaf (or aluminum foil), lay the herbs on top and fold into an oblong package. Toothpicks work nicely to hold the package closed. Steam or bake (at 350 degrees) for 15 minutes then transfer the package to a hot skillet and cook it for 5 to 10 minutes in order to reduce some of the liquid.

Serves 4 to 6.

Fried Tofu with Spicy Lime Sauce

tofu cut into ½ or ⅝ inch squares
2 cloves garlic
1½ hot red seeded chilies
½ cup water

2 Tbsp. fish sauce
½ cup fresh lime juice
3 Tbsp. brown sugar

For the dipping sauce, combine the garlic, chilies and water in blender or food processor until the ingredients are minced. Combine the fish sauce, lime juice and sugar in a bowl. Add the contents from the food processor. Deep fry the tofu in a wok or deep pan until the cubes are slightly puffy and a little browned. Stick each cube with a toothpick and dip.

STELLA BLUES CAFÉ

TOFU SCRAMBLE WITH TAHINI SAUCE

2 cups firm tofu cut in small pieces
½ cup broccoli heads, diced
½ cup mushrooms, sliced
½ cup green onions, sliced

1 cup Jack cheese, shredded
½ cup Tahini Sauce (recipe below)
2 Tbsp. butter

Sauté vegetables and tofu in butter. Add Tahini Sauce and toss. Add Jack cheese and cook until cheese is melted. Serve hot. Serves 2.

Tahini Sauce

1 cup toasted sesame tahini
¾ cups water
1 lemon, juiced
3 cloves garlic, minced

1 tsp. cumin
2 tsp. soy sauce
¼ cup fresh parsley, minced
dash cayenne

Mix together. Makes 1 cup.

CRAB CAKES WITH LEMON BUTTER CHIVE SAUCE

1 shallot, minced
3 Tbsp. butter
2 beaten eggs
½ cup heavy cream
1 cup fresh bread crumbs

2 cups crab meat, shredded
1 Tbsp. lemon juice
1 tsp. fresh dill, minced
½ tsp. salt
½ tsp. paprika

Sauté the shallots in 2 tablespoons of the butter, simmer 3 minutes, reserving 1 tablespoon butter and ½ cup bread crumbs. Combine the remaining ingredients and add the shallots. Chill this mixture 2 hours.

Shape into 6 3" cakes and roll in bread crumbs. Melt 1 tablespoon butter in a sauté pan and quickly brown on both sides. Lower the heat and simmer the cakes slowly about 7 minutes longer. Serves two.

Lemon Butter Chive Sauce

2 shallots, minced
¼ cup butter
½ cup dry white wine

1 Tbsp. lemon juice
¼ cup heavy cream
2 Tbsp. chives, finely chopped

Sauté shallots in butter. Stir in other ingredients.
Cover the bottom of the plates with sauce and place 3 cakes per plate.

COCONUT BEER BATTERED CHICKEN

½ pound flour

6 oz. beer

6 oz. water

1 ½ oz. oil

1 egg yolk

pinch salt

pinch sugar

2 egg whites

shredded, unsweetened coconut

Place flour in bowl, add beer, water, oil, yolk and seasoning. Blend. In separate bowl beat whites until stiff, but not dry and fold gently into flour mixture. Dip chicken strips in flour, shake off excess. Dip in batter, then into shredded unsweetened coconut, and fry in hot oil. Serve with Guava Sauce.

Guava Sauce

6 oz. guava jelly

½ tsp. chopped ginger

½ cup water

¼ lemon, juice only

1 clove chopped garlic

1 cinnamon stick

2 peppercorns

½ lime, juice only

Combine all. Simmer ½ hour. Let sit 2 hours. Strain.

CHARRED 'AHI WITH PAPAYA RELISH

7 oz. 'ahi, cut into 2x2x6" blocks

2 oz. Papaya Relish (recipe below)

¼ oz. sunflower sprouts

1 oz. blackened seasoning

salt and pepper to taste

1 oz. soy sauce

2 oz. soft butter

Heat cast iron skillet or other heavy duty skillet on medium high heat for 5 minutes. Sprinkle blackened seasoning on 'ahi. Place butter in skillet until melted. Place 'ahi in skillet and cook on all 4 sides approximately 30 seconds each. Let cool. Slice into ¼" slices and arrange on a platter with sunflower sprouts and papaya relish. Serve with soy sauce.

Papaya Relish

1 papaya, large dice

⅓ pineapple, large dice

½ red bell pepper, medium dice

¼ red onion, medium dice

¼ bunch cilantro, minced

1 lemon, juice only

2 limes, juice only

Mix all ingredients. Add salt and white pepper to taste.

Glossary

`Ahi — very popular, often served as sashimi. `Ahi is the Hawaiian name for yellowfin and bigeye tuna. It is red in color when raw and turns almost white when cooked.

Aku — also known as skipjack tuna, may be eaten raw as sashimi or cooked.

Bok Choy — a Chinese cabbage with dark green leaves and a white stem.

Cilantro* — Chinese parsley.

Coconut Milk* — made from coconut meat and water. Available canned or frozen.

Daikon* — in the turnip family with a similar flavor to a radish.

Dashi* — Japanese soup stock.

Fish Sauce* — a thick, brown, salty sauce made from anchovies.

Furikake* — a Japanese seasoning mix of dried seaweed and sesame seeds.

Ginger — a rhizome (similar to a root). Peel the outer skin, then finely chop or grate. It has a spicy flavor.

Green Papaya — see Papaya.

Guava — a plum size tropical fruit primarily used for juices, jellies and sauces.

Hoisin Sauce* — a sweet , spicy, fermented soybean sauce.

Jicama — a root similar to a turnip. Crunchy and flavorful raw. Can also be cooked.

Kaffir Lime Leaves* — often used in Thai cooking, they produce a citrus flavor and aroma.

Kiawe Wood — similar to mesquite.

Lehi — a delicately flavored pink snapper.

Lemon Grass — long greenish-gray stalks that add a lemony flavor to dishes.

Lilikoi* — passion fruit. Available in frozen concentrate form, which is often used in recipes.

Lumpia* — used to wrap egg rolls and other items.

Lychee — a delicious fruit with soft, sweet, juicy meat surrounded by a reddish woody shell that needs to be removed before eating the fruit.

Mahi mahi — dolphin fish (unrelated to the mammal). White, delicately flavored meat. Very popular.

Mango — a sweet tropical fruit that is yellow with some orange and red. In some recipes peaches my be used as a substitute.

Maui Onion — a sweet and mild onion grown in the cooler climate of Kula, the upcountry region of Maui.

Mirin* — a sweetened rice wine. One teaspoon of sugar may be substituted for one teaspoon of Mirin.

Miso* — a thick fermented soybean paste commonly used to make miso soup, which is light and brothy.

Monchong — a moist, mild and tender fish.

Nori* — sheets of dried, compressed seaweed often used for wrapping sushi rolls.

Ogo — seaweed.

Onaga — a delicately flavored red snapper. Snapper, monkfish and orange roughy may be substituted for onaga.

Ono/Wahoo — similar to mackerel or tuna with white, delicate, flaky meat. Often used as a substitute for mahi mahi.

Opah/Moonfish — pink to orange flesh. Suitable for a variety of preparations.

Opakapaka — Hawaiian pink snapper with a delicate flavor and moist meat. Snapper may be used as a substitute.

Panko* — crispy Japanese bread crumbs used for breading.

Papaya — a very popular pear shaped fruit with yellow skin when ripe. The melon-like flesh is sweet and mild. When used unripe, it is called green papaya and is usually shredded for salads.

Papio — a flaky, tender white fish with a mild flavor.

Poke — pieces of raw fish in a flavorful marinade including seaweed and sesame oil.

Pupu — Hawaiian for appetizer, hors d' oeuvre.

Sake* — Japanese rice wine.

Sambal Olek — red chili paste.

Sashimi — thin slices of extremely fresh raw salt water fish. `Ahi is most commonly used for sashimi.

Shichimi — a Japanese spice blend.

Shiitake Mushrooms* — large mushrooms with dark caps. Available dried or fresh.

Shoyu/Soy Sauce* — a salty liquid flavoring made from soybeans.

Taro — a tuberous vegetable. Taro is a staple food of the Hawaiian culture and is used to make poi (a thick starchy paste). The flesh is a light purplish-gray. Taro is now being used by many chefs in a way similar to potatoes (chips, hash browns, etc.).

Tobiko* — often used in sushi, it is the orange-redish roe of the flying fish.

Tofu — white soybean curd with a mild flavor. Blocks of tofu, which are packed in water (drain and rinse tofu before using) are available in most supermarkets.

Uku — gray snapper.

Wasabi* — similar to horseradish. May be purchased as a paste, or in powder form and mixed with water to make a paste. Served with sushi.

*May be found in Asian food stores or the Asian section of most supermarkets.

Recipe Index

A

Adobo Pulled Pork with Eddie's Latin Dip, 107
Agedashi Tofu, 71
'ahi
    'Ahi Ceviche, 107
    'Ahi "Poi Pounder", 111
    'Ahi Spring Rolls, 61
    Charred 'Ahi with Papaya Relish, 189
    Charred 'Ahi with Three Bean Rice, 180
    Fresh Oysters with 'Ahi Tartare & Lilikoi Mignonette, 49
    Garlic Shichimi 'Ahi with Ponzu Vinaigrette, 71
    Hawaiian 'Ahi Poke, 95
    Kamakazi Wrap, 21
    Lumpia Wrapped 'Ahi with Fresh Mango, 170
    Macadamia Crusted 'Ahi, 157
    Macadamia Nut Breaded 'Ahi with Green Apple
        Guava Sauce, 27
    Maguro Tataki–Seared 'Ahi, Imari Style, 153
    Pepper Rubbed 'Ahi Tuna with Heirloo Tomatoes, Arugula
        and Mediterranean Tomato-Caper Berry Salsa, 115
    Seared Peppered 'Ahi With Wasabi Aioli, 89
    Wok Charred 'Ahi, 183
    Yellow Fin Tuna, Avocado, Sweet Bell Pepper Tower,
        Kamuela Field Greens, Thai Curry Vinaigrette, 147
'Ahi Ceviche, 107
'Ahi "Poi Pounder", 111
'Ahi Spring Rolls, 61
Aloha Angel Vegan Cookies, 137
Asari Butter Clams, 178
Ayam Bali — Balinese–Style Fried Chicken, 163

B

bacon
    Bacon Wrapped Shrimp with Lobster Cream Sauce, 81
    Kaua'i Shrimp Wrapped in Pancetta with Fire Roasted
        Sweet Pepper Sauce & Leeks, 119
Baguette, 53
Baked Brie in Filo, 174
Baked Cucumbers Stuffed with Opakapaka Mousse, 182
Baked Stuffed Shrimp, 65
Bali Hai Salmon, 166
banana (*also see fruit*)
    Banana Foster, 63
    Banana Imu Style Fish with a Lemon Grass Pesto and
        Vanilla Bean Sauce, 184
barbeque
    Pineapple BBQ Ribs, 73
beans
    Charred 'Ahi with Three Bean Rice, 180
    Hawaii Island Goat Cheese Tacos, 135
    Free Range Lamb Chop with Macadamia Coconut Crust,
        White Bean Cassoulet and a Star Anise Drizzle, 151
    Portuguese Bean Soup, 182
    Stella's Ancho Chicken Chili, 121
    Wok Charred Soy Beans with Garlic and Chilies, 73
beef (*see meat*)
    Beef Roulades, 181
Braised Lamb Shank (Osso Buco), 103
bread
    Baguette, 53
    Shallot Spoon Bread, 127
Buerre Blanc, 39
Butter Cream Cheese Frosting, 179

C

Caesar Salad, 63
cakes
    Kauai Carrot Cake, 179
Charred 'Ahi with Papaya Relish, 189
Charred 'Ahi with Three Bean Rice, 180
cheese
    Baked Brie in Filo, 174
    Goat Cheese Crab Cakes, 101
    Hawaii Island Goat Cheese Tacos, 135
    Rotolo di Papaya Con Ricotta, 172
cheesecake
    Kona Kahlua Cheesecake, 115
    Lemon Mascarpone Cheesecake, 149
    Mascarpone Cheese Cake, 25
chicken
    Ayam Bali — Balinese–Style Fried Chicken, 163
    Chicken and Rosemary Fettucine, 174
    Chicken Buona Sera, 55
    Chicken Macadamia, 57
    Coconut Beer Battered Chicken, 189
    Crispy Chicken Wonton on Asian Stir Fry with
        Ginger–Soy Mayonnaise, 147
    Curried Chicken and Grapes in a White Wine
        Cream Sauce, 27
    Farfalle Con Pollo E Funghi Bow Tie Pasta, Marinated
        Chicken Breast, Shiitake Mushrooms & Sun-Dried
        Tomatoes in White Wine Sauce, 149
    Kung Bao Chicken, 159
    Manoa Lettuce Wrap, 105
    Okinawan Potato Hash, 25
    Peanut Chicken Breast with Curry Sauce, 167
    Stella's Ancho Chicken Chili, 121
    Susan's Hawaiian Chicken Curry Stew, 175
    Teriyaki Chicken Breast, 178
    Thai Chicken Coconut Soup, 113
chili
    Kokee Lodge Chili, 37
    Stella's Ancho Chicken Chili, 121

chocolate
    Chocolate Creme Brulée, 23
    Chocolate Sauce, 41
Chunky Chocolate Mac Nut Bars, 35
Cioppino, 169
Citrus Herb Vinaigrette, 101
Clam Chowder, 45
coconut/coconut milk
    Ayam Bali — Balinese–Style Fried Chicken, 163
    Coconut Beer Battered Chicken, 189
    Coconut Cream of Celery Soup, 181
    Coconut Lobster Soup, 43
    Coconut Split Pea Soup, 137
    Coconut Tiger Shrimp Sticks with a Thai Style Cocktail
        Sauce, 75
    Lemon Grass Coconut Curry Sauce, 43
    Thai Chicken Coconut Soup, 113
coffee
    Mokihana Coffee, 37
cookies
    Aloha Angel Vegan Cookies, 137
    Chunky Chocolate Mac Nut Bars, 35
    Maui Lava Flows, 175
crab cakes
    Crab Cakes with Lemon Butter Chive Sauce, 188
    Goat Cheese Crab Cakes, 101
Cream of Cocoa Sauce, 53
Creme Anglaise, 41
creme brulee
    Creme Brulee, 89
    Chocolate Creme Brulée, 23
crepes
    Wild Mushroom Crepes, 135
Crispy Chicken Wonton on Asian Stir Fry with Ginger–Soy
    Mayonnaise, 147
Crispy Shrimp in a Blanket with Ogo Vinaigrette, 29
Crispy Soft Shell Crab with Pineapple Jasmine Rice,
    Grilled Maui Onion and Mint Shallot Sauce, 143
Crispy Veggie Spring Rolls with Sweet Chili Sauce and
    Namasu, 109
Cucumber Papaya Salsa, 151
curry
    Curried Chicken and Grapes in a White Wine Cream
        Sauce, 27
    Curried Seafood and Saffron Rissotto with Achote Chili
        and Cilantro Chive Oils, 17
    Lemon Grass Coconut Curry Sauce, 43
    Peanut Chicken Breast with Curry Sauce, 167
    Susan's Hawaiian Chicken Curry Stew, 175
    Thai Seafood Curry, 105
    The Willows Curry, 81

D

desserts
    Banana Foster, 63
    Creme Brulee, 89
    Kauai Carrot Cake, 179
    Key Lime Tarts, 186
    Macadamia Cheese Mousse, 29
    Peach Cobbler, 45
    Pepper Pineapple Dessert, 53
    Plantation Gardens Banana Lumpia, 41
    Tiramisu, 77
    Upside-Down Apple Pecan Pie, 123
dressings
    Mango Dressing
    Maui Onion Dressing, 123
    Papaya Seed Dressing, 165, 168
    Sesame Miso Dressing, 61

E

eggplant
    Eggplant Casserole with Creole Sauce, 129
    Eggplant Tapenade, 77
    Scallop Stir Fry with Baby Eggplant, 59
    Terrina Di Melanzane, 171

F

Farfalle Con Pollo E Funghi Bow Tie Pasta, Marinated
    Chicken Breast, Shiitake Mushrooms & Sun-Dried
    Tomatoes in White Wine Sauce, 149
Firecracker Fish Soup, 99
Fire Cracker Scallops, 180 Roasted Red Pepper Aioli, 180
fish
    Baked Cucumbers Stuffed with Opakapaka Mousse, 182
    Bali Hai Salmon, 166
    Banana Imu Style Fish with a Lemon Grass Pesto and
        Vanilla Bean Sauce, 185
    Charred 'Ahi with Papaya Relish, 189
    Charred 'Ahi with Three Bean Rice, 180
    Firecracker Fish Soup, 99
    Fresh Spinach with Skillet Roasted Salmon, 182
    Garlic Shichimi `Ahi with Ponzu Vinaigrette, 71
    Involtini d' Ono Alla Siciliana, 173
    Island Bouillabaisse, 53
    Island Carpaccio du jour, 101
    Lacquered Salmon, 155
    Macadamia Crusted `Ahi, 157
    Macadamia Nut Crusted Mahi Mahi, 99
    Maguro Tataki–Seared `Ahi, Imari Style, 153
    Merriman's Poisson Cru, 161
    Pan Seared Opakapaka and Kona Prawns Sweet Chili
        Beurre Blanc, Green Papaya Slaw and Fermented
        Black Beans, 85
    Pan-Seared Salmon with Shallot Spoon Bread, Marinated
        Cherry Tomatoes and Horseradish–Chive Sauce, 127

Pepper Rubbed `Ahi Tuna with Heirloom Tomatoes, Arugula and Mediterranean Tomato-Caper Berry Salsa, 115
Plantation Gardens Seafood Lau Lau, 41
Plantation Style Crusted Snapper, 151
Roasted Sea Bass with Serrano Ham & Rosemary, 67
Salmon Paté, 178
Salt Baked Moi, 67
Seared Peppered `Ahi With Wasabi Aioli, 89
Smoked Salmon and Potato Cakes with Dill Cream, 177
Togarashi Calamari with Guava Cocktail Sauce, 19
Yellow Fin Tuna, Avocado, Sweet Bell Pepper Tower, Kamuela Field Greens, Thai Curry Vinaigrette, 147
Five Spiced Seared Scallops, 79
Free Range Lamb Chop with Macadamia Coconut Crust, White Bean Cassoulet and a Star Anise Drizzle, 151
Fresh Oysters with `Ahi Tartare & Lilikoi Mignonette, 49
Fresh Spinach with Skillet Roasted Salmon, 182
Fried Tofu with Spicy Lime Sauce, 187
frosting
    Butter Cream Cheese Frosting, 179
fruit
    Banana Foster, 63
    Cucumber Papaya Salsa, 151
    Grandma's Banana Macadamia Nut Scones, 97
    Green Papaya Salad, 139
    Guava Cocktail Sauce, 19
    Hawaiian Salsa, 184
    Huckleberry Sauce, 131
    Keko Berry Fruit Smoothie, 31
    Key Lime Tarts, 186
    Lilikoi Mignonette, 49
    Lumpia Wrapped 'Ahi with Fresh Mango, 170
    Macadamia Nut Breaded `Ahi with Green Apple Guava Sauce, 27
    Mango Dressing
    Mountain Apple Salad with Lilikoi Dijon Vinaigrette, 19
    Oatmeal Fruit Scones, 35
    Papaya Relish, 189
    Papaya Salsa, 31
    Papaya Seed Dressing, 165
    Papaya Shrimp Salad, 103
    Peach Cobbler, 45
    Pepper Pineapple Dessert, 53
    Plantation Gardens Banana Lumpia, 41
    Poisson Cru with Tropical Fruits Served Over Baby Greens Dressed with an Ohelo Berry Vinaigrette, 170
    Rotolo di Papaya Con Ricotta, 172
    Tropical Fruit Muffins, 165
    Upside-Down Apple Pecan Pie, 123

G

Garlic Prawn Pita with Mango Dressing, 87
Garlic Shichimi `Ahi with Ponzu Vinaigrette, 71

Ginger Caramel Sauce, 29
Goat Cheese Crab Cakes, 101
Grandma's Banana Macadamia Nut Scones, 97
Green Apple Guava Sauce, 27
Green Papaya Salad, 139
Guava Cocktail Sauce, 19

H,I

Hawaii Island Goat Cheese Tacos, 135
Hawaiian `Ahi Poke, 95
Hawaiian Grilled Beef Papadam, 87
Hawaiian Imu Style Pork, 139
Honey Garlic Shrimp, 55
Horseradish–Chive Sauce, 127
Hot Spinach Salad with Papaya Seed Dressing, 168
Huckleberry Demi Sauce, 131
Involtini d' Ono Alla Siciliana, 172
Island Bouillabaisse, 53
Island Carpaccio du jour, 101
Island Style Shrimp and Sweet Potato Fritters with a Spicy Macadamia Nut Dipping Sauce, 176

J,K

Jade Sauce, 39
Jumbo Diver Scallops with Spinach and Herb Butter, 115
Kamakazi Wrap, 21
Kaua'i Carrot Cake, 179
Kaua'i Shrimp Wrapped in Pancetta with Fire Roasted Sweet Pepper Sauce & Leeks, 119
Keko Berry Fruit Smoothie, 31
Key Lime Tarts, 186
Kokee Lodge Chili, 37
Kona Kahlua Cheesecake, 115
Kung Bao Chicken, 159
Kung Pao Shrimp, 59

L

Lacquered Salmon, 155
lamb *(also see meat)*
    Lamb Osso Buco, 91
lau lau
    Plantation Gardens Seafood Lau Lau, 41
lemon grass
    Banana Imu Style Fish with a Lemon Grass Pesto and Vanilla Bean Sauce, 185
    Lemon Grass Coconut Curry Sauce, 43
    Lemon Grass Cream Sauce, 33
    Shrimp and Clams with Chili Lemon Grass Black Bean Sauce, 51
Lemon Mascarpone Cheesecake, 149
lilikoi *(also see fruit)*
    Lilikoi Dijon Vinaigrette, 19

Linguine Diavola, 55
lobster *(also see shellfish)*
   Coconut Lobster Soup, 43
   Lobster and Hearts of Palm Salad, 85
Lucy's Pick–it Salad, 69
Lucy's Szechwan Prawns with Spicy Black Bean Cream Sauce, 69
Lumpia Wrapped 'Ahi with Fresh Mango, 170

M, N

macadamia nuts
   Ayam Bali — Balinese–Style Fried Chicken, 163
   Chicken Macadamia, 57
   Free Range Lamb Chop with Macadamia Coconut Crust, White Bean Cassoulet and a Star Anise Drizzle, 151
   Grandma's Banana Macadamia Nut Scones, 97
   Island Style Shrimp and Sweet Potato Fritters with a Spicy Macadamia Nut Dipping Sauce, 176
   Macadamia Cheese Mousse, 29
   Macadamia Crusted 'Ahi, 157
   Macadamia Nut Breaded 'Ahi with Green Apple Guava Sauce, 27
   Macadamia Nut Crusted Mahi Mahi, 99
   Macadamia Nut Crusted Tiger Prawn Temaki (Hand Rolled Sushi), 117
   Mountain Apple Salad with Lilikoi Dijon Vinaigrette, 19
Maguro Tataki–Seared 'Ahi, Imari Style, 153
mahi mahi *(see fish)*
mango *(see fruit)*
Manoa Lettuce Wrap, 105
Mascarpone Cheese Cake, 25
Maui Lava Flows, 175
Maui Onion Dressing, 123
meat
   Beef Roulades, 181
   Braised Lamb Shank (Osso Buco), 103
   Free Range Lamb Chop with Macadamia Coconut Crust, White Bean Cassoulet and a Star Anise Drizzle, 151
   Hawaiian Grilled Beef Papadam, 87
   Hawaiian Imu Style Pork, 139
   Lamb Osso Buco, 91
   Pineapple BBQ Ribs, 73
   Seared Lanai Axis Venison with Root Vegetable Hash, Spinach-Potato Dumplings and Huckleberry Sauce, 131
   Sesame Beef Kabobs, 161
   Slavonic Steak for Two, 170
   String Beans with Minced Pork, 159
   Szechwan Baby Back Ribs with a Mongolian Marinade, 75
   Thai Roasted Rack of Lamb with Sweet Potato Sauté, 141
   Uncle Chris's Sweet and Sour Spareribs, 97
   Vitello Ala Sorrentina, 171
Merriman's Poisson Cru, 161
Miso Vinaigrette, 39
Mokihana Coffee, 37

Mountain Apple Salad with Lilikoi Dijon Vinaigrette, 19
muffins
   Tropical Fruit Muffins, 165
mushrooms
   Farfalle Con Pollo E Funghi Bow Tie Pasta, Marinated Chicken Breast, Shiitake Mushrooms & Sun-Dried Tomatoes in White Wine Sauce, 149
   Shiitake Mushroom Relish, 39
   Wild Mushroom Crepes, 135

O

Oatmeal Fruit Scones, 35
Octopus Lobster Salad, 95
ogo
   Crispy Shrimp in a Blanket with Ogo Vinaigrette, 29
   Hawaiian 'Ahi Poke, 95
   Maguro Tataki–Seared 'Ahi, Imari Style, 153
   Octopus Lobster Salad, 95
oils
   Achote Chili Oil, 17
   Cilantro Chive Oils, 17
   Scallion Oil, 127
Okinawan Potato Hash, 25
Okinawan Sweet Potato Ravioli, 33
ono *(see fish)*
opakapaka *(see fish)*
osso buco
   Braised Lamb Shank (Osso Buco), 103
   Lamb Osso Buco, 91
   Veal Osso Buco, 23
Oysters, 113

P, Q

Pacific Style Bouillabaise, 155
Pais Udang or Shrimp Packages, 187
Pan Seared Opakapaka and Kona Prawns Sweet Chili Beurre Blanc, Green Papaya Slaw and Fermented Black Beans, 85
Pan-Seared Salmon with Shallot Spoon Bread, Marinated Cherry Tomatoes and Horseradish–Chive Sauce, 127
papaya *(also see fruit)*
   Papaya Salsa, 31
   Papaya Seed Dressing, 165
   Papaya Shrimp Salad, 103
pasta
   Chicken and Rosemary Fettucine, 174
   Chicken Buona Sera, 55
   Farfalle Con Pollo E Funghi Bow Tie Pasta, Marinated Chicken Breast, Shiitake Mushrooms & Sun-Dried Tomatoes in White Wine Sauce, 149
   Linguine Diavola, 55
   Lucy's Szechwan Prawns with Spicy Black Bean Cream Sauce, 69
   Pasta Con Aragosta, 171

Rotolo di Papaya Con Ricotta, 172
Sauce for Clams, Scampi and Pasta, 169
Seafood Fettuccini in Jalapeño Jack Cream, 129
Seafood Fra Diavlo, 186
Peach Cobbler, 45
Peanut Chicken Breast with Curry Sauce, 166
pecans
    Upside-Down Apple Pecan Pie, 123
Pepper Pineapple Dessert, 53
Pepper Rubbed `Ahi Tuna with Heirloom Tomatoes,
    Arugula and Mediterranean Tomato-Caper Berry Salsa, 115
pies
    Upside-Down Apple Pecan Pie, 123
pineapple *(also see fruit)*
    Pineapple BBQ Ribs, 73
Pistachio Crust for Mascarpone Cheese Cake, 25
Plantation Gardens Banana Lumpia, 41
Plantation Gardens Seafood Lau Lau, 41
Plantation Style Crusted Snapper, 151
poisson cru
    Merriman's Poisson Cru, 161
    Poisson Cru with Tropical Fruits Served Over Baby
        Greens Dressed with an Ohelo Berry Vinaigrette, 170
pork *(see meat)*
Portuguese Bean Soup, 182
potatoes
    Island Style Shrimp and Sweet Potato Fritters with a
        Spicy Macadamia Nut Dipping Sauce, 176
    Okinawan Potato Hash, 25
    Okinawan Sweet Potato Ravioli, 33
    Smoked Salmon and Potato Cakes with Dill Cream, 177
    Thai Roasted Rack of Lamb with Sweet Potato Sauté, 141
Prawns Mauna Loa, 157
Quail Saltimboca, 91

R

ravioli
    Okinawan Sweet Potato Ravioli, 33
relishes
    Papaya Relish, 189
    Shiitake Mushroom Relish, 39
rice
    Charred 'Ahi with Three Bean Rice, 180
    Crispy Soft Shell Crab with Pineapple Jasmine Rice,
        Grilled Maui Onion and Mint Shallot Sauce, 143
    Curried Seafood and Saffron Rissotto with Achote Chili
        and Cilantro Chive Oils, 17
    Kamakazi Wrap, 21
    Lemon Grass Coconut Curry Sauce, 43
    Tequila Shrimp with Firecracker Rice, 93
Roasted Red Pepper Aioli, 180
Roasted Sea Bass with Serrano Ham & Rosemary, 67
Root Vegetable Hash, 131
Rotolo di Papaya Con Ricotta, 172

S

Saffron Coconut Clams, 79
salads
    Caesar Salad, 63
    Green Papaya Salad, 139
    Hot Spinach Salad with Papaya Seed Dressing, 168
    Lobster and Hearts of Palm Salad, 85
    Lucy's Pick-it Salad, 69
    Mountain Apple Salad with Lilikoi Dijon Vinaigrette, 19
    Octopus Lobster Salad, 95
    Papaya Shrimp Salad, 103
salmon *(see fish)*
    Salmon Paté, 178
salsas
    Cucumber Papaya Salsa, 151
    Hawaiian Salsa, 184
    Mediterranean Tomato-Caper Berry Salsa, 115
    Papaya Salsa, 31
Salt Baked Moi, 67
Sansei Seared Scallop and Foie Gras, 117
sauces
    Cheese Sauce, 65
    Chocolate Sauce, 41
    Cream of Cocoa Sauce, 53
    Dill Cream, 177
    Fire Roasted Sweet Pepper Sauce & Leeks, 119
    Ginger Caramel Sauce, 29
    Ginger-Soy Mayonnaise, 147
    Green Apple Guava Sauce, 27
    Guava Cocktail Sauce, 19
    Hollandaise Sauce, 65
    Horseradish-Chive Sauce, 127
    Huckleberry Sauce, 131
    Jade Sauce, 39
    Lemon Butter Chive Sauce, 188
    Lemon Grass Coconut Curry Sauce, 43
    Lemon Grass Cream Sauce, 33
    Lobster Cream Sauce, 81
    Macadamia Cheese Mousse, 29
    Mint Shallot Sauce, 143
    Orange Tomato Basil Sauce, 173
    Pineapple BBQ Sauce, 73
    Plantation Gardens Banana Lumpia, 41
    Roasted Red Pepper Aioli, 180
    Sauce for Clams, Scampi and Pasta, 169
    Spicy Sweet and Sour Sauce, 184
    Sweet Chili Sauce, 109
    Tahini Sauce, 188
    Vanilla Bean Sauce, 185
    Wasabi Aioli, 89
Sauce for Clams, Scampi and Pasta, 169
Sautéed Jumbo Sea Scallops, 39
Sayur Tumis — Indonesian Stir Fried Vegetables, 163
Scallop Stir Fry with Baby Eggplant, 59

Scones, 179
   Grandma's Banana Macadamia Nut Scones, 97
   Oatmeal Fruit Scones, 35
Seafood Fettuccini in Jalapeño Jack Cream, 129
Seafood Fra Diavlo, 186
Seared Lanai Axis Venison with Root Vegetable Hash,
   Spinach-Potato Dumplings and Huckleberry Sauce, 131
Seared Peppered `Ahi With Wasabi Aioli, 89
Sesame Beef Kabobs, 161
Sesame Miso Dressing, 61
Shabu Shabu for Two, 153
Shallot Spoon Bread, 127
shellfish
   'Ahi "Poi Pounder", 111
   Asari Butter Clams, 178
   Bacon Wrapped Shrimp with Lobster Cream Sauce, 81
   Baked Stuffed Shrimp, 65
   Cioppino, 169
   Clam Chowder, 45
   Coconut Lobster Soup, 43
   Coconut Tiger Shrimp Sticks with a Thai Style Cocktail
     Sauce, 75
   Crab Cakes with Lemon Butter Chive Sauce, 188
   Crispy Shrimp in a Blanket with Ogo Vinaigrette, 29
   Crispy Soft Shell Crab with Pineapple Jasmine Rice,
     Grilled Maui Onion and Mint Shallot Sauce, 143
   Curried Seafood and Saffron Rissotto with Achote Chili
     and Cilantro Chive Oils, 17
   Fire Cracker Scallops, 180
   Five Spiced Seared Scallops, 79
   Fresh Oysters with `Ahi Tartare & Lilikoi Mignonette, 49
   Garlic Prawn Pita with Mango Dressing, 86
   Goat Cheese Crab Cakes, 101
   Honey Garlic Shrimp, 55
   Island Bouillabaisse, 53
   Island Style Shrimp and Sweet Potato Fritters with a
     Spicy Macadamia Nut Dipping Sauce, 176
   Jumbo Diver Scallops with Spinach and Herb Butter, 115
   Kaua`i Shrimp Wrapped in Pancetta with Fire Roasted
     Sweet Pepper Sauce & Leeks, 119
   Kung Pao Shrimp, 59
   Lucy's Szechwan Prawns with Spicy Black Bean Cream
     Sauce, 69
   Macadamia Nut Crusted Tiger Prawn Temaki (Hand
     Rolled Sushi), 117
   Octopus Lobster Salad, 95
   Oysters, 113
   Pacific Style Bouillabaise, 155
   Pais Udang or Shrimp Packages, 187
   Pan Seared Opakapaka and Kona Prawns Sweet Chili
     Beurre Blanc, Green Papaya Slaw and Fermented
     Black Beans, 85
   Papaya Shrimp Salad, 103

Pasta Con Aragosta, 171
Plantation Gardens Seafood Lau Lau, 41
Prawns Mauna Loa, 157
Saffron Coconut Clams, 79
Sansei Seared Scallop and Foie Gras, 117
Sauce for Clams, Scampi and Pasta, 169
Sautéed Jumbo Sea Scallops, 39
Scallop Stir Fry with Baby Eggplant, 59
Seafood Fettuccini in Jalapeño Jack Cream, 129
Seafood Fra Diavlo, 186
Shrimp and Clams with Chili Lemon grass Black Bean
   Sauce, 51
Shrimp with Corn and Black Beans, 183
Shrimp Won Ton Served with a Spicy Sweet and Sour
   Sauce and a Hawaiian Salsa, 184
Tempura Mirin Shrimp with Rice Noodles and Shallot
   Chili Glaze, 141
Tequila Shrimp with Firecracker Rice, 93
Thai Seafood Curry, 105
Wok Seared Tiger Shrimp, 43
Shiitake Mushroom Relish, 39
Shiso Miso Mignonette, 113
shrimp *(also see shellfish)*
   Shrimp and Clams with Chili Lemongrass Black Bean
     Sauce, 51
   Shrimp with Corn and Black Beans, 183
   Shrimp Won Ton Served with a Spicy Sweet and Sour
     Sauce and a Hawaiian Salsa, 184
Slavonic Steak for Two, 170
Smoked Salmon and Potato Cakes with Dill Cream, 176
smoothies
   Keko Berry Fruit Smoothie, 31
spring rolls
   'Ahi Spring Rolls, 61
   Crispy Veggie Spring Rolls with Sweet Chili Sauce and
     Namasu, 109
soups
   Cioppino, 169
   Clam Chowder, 45
   Coconut Cream of Celery Soup, 181
   Coconut Lobster Soup, 43
   Coconut Split Pea Soup, 137
   Firecracker Fish Soup, 99
   Island Bouillabaisse, 53
   Pacific Style Bouillabaise, 155
   Portuguese Bean Soup, 182
   Thai Chicken Coconut Soup, 113
Spinach–Potato Dumplings, 131
Stella's Ancho Chicken Chili, 121
String Beans with Minced Pork, 159
Susan's Hawaiian Chicken Curry Stew, 175
sweet potatoes *(see potatoes)*
Szechwan Baby Back Ribs with a Mongolian Marinade, 75

T

tacos
Hawaii Island Goat Cheese Tacos, 135
Tempura Mirin Shrimp with Rice Noodles and Shallot Chili Glaze, 141
Tequila Shrimp with Firecracker Rice, 93
Teriyaki Chicken Breast, 178
Terrina Di Melanzane, 171
Thai Chicken Coconut Soup, 113
Thai Roasted Rack of Lamb with Sweet Potato Sauté, 141
Thai Seafood Curry, 105
Tiramisu, 77
tofu
Agedashi Tofu, 71
Fried Tofu with Spicy Lime Sauce, 187
Tofu Scramble with Tahini Sauce, 188
Togarashi Calamari with Guava Cocktail Sauce, 19
Tropical Fruit Muffins, 165

U,V

Uncle Chris's Sweet and Sour Spareribs, 97
Upside-Down Apple Pecan Pie, 123
veal (also see meat)
Veal Osso Buco, 23
vegetarian
Agedashi Tofu, 71
Aloha Angel Vegan Cookies, 137
Crispy Veggie Spring Rolls with Sweet Chili Sauce and Namasu, 109
Eggplant Casserole with Creole Sauce, 129
Eggplant Tapenade, 77
Fried Tofu with Spicy Lime Sauce, 187
Hawaii Island Goat Cheese Tacos, 135
Linguine Diavola, 55
Okinawan Sweet Potato Ravioli, 33
Rotolo di Papaya Con Ricotta, 172
Sayur Tumis — Indonesian Stir Fried Vegetables, 163
Terrina Di Melanzane, 171
Tofu Scramble with Tahini Sauce, 188
Wild Mushroom Crepes, 135
The Willows Curry, 81
Wok Charred Soy Beans with Garlic and Chilies, 73
vinaigrettes
Citrus Herb Vinaigrette, 101
Lilikoi Dijon Vinaigrette, 19
Miso Vinaigrette, 39
Ohelo Berry Vinaigrette, 170
Red Wine Vinaigrette, 69
Thai Curry Vinaigrette, 147
Vitello Ala Sorrentina, 171

W,X,Y,Z

Wild Mushroom Crepes, 135
The Willows Curry, 81
Wok Charred 'Ahi, 183
Wok Charred Soy Beans with Garlic and Chilies, 73
Wok Seared Tiger Shrimp, 43
won ton
Crispy Chicken Wonton on Asian Stir Fry with Ginger–Soy Mayonnaise, 147
Shrimp Won Ton Served with a Spicy Sweet and Sour Sauce and a Hawaiian Salsa, 184
wraps
Kamakazi Wrap, 21
Manoa Lettuce Wrap, 105
Yellow Fin Tuna, Avocado, Sweet Bell Pepper Tower, Kamuela Field Greens, Thai Curry Vinaigrette, 147

Note: *Chefs and restaurant owners chose the recipes that they wished to contribute. Some represent items from the menu, others are specials that are served occasionally or seasonally.*

The recipes have not been kitchen tested by the author. Effort has been made to make the recipes clear and easy to follow and they have been proofread three times. Be adventuresome, experiment and enjoy!

RESTAURANT INDEX

Aaron's atop the Ala Moana, Honolulu, O'ahu 48

Aioli's Restaurant, Kamuela, Hawai'i 134

Alan Wong's Restaurant, Honolulu, O'ahu 50

Aloha Angel Café, Kainaliu, Hawai'i 136

Bali by the Sea, Honolulu, O'ahu 52

Bali Hai, Princeville, Kaua'i 16

Bamboo Restaurant, Hawi Hawai'i 138

Bay Club, The, Kapalua, Maui 84

Beach House, The, Po'ipu, Kaua'i 18

Brennecke's, Po'ipu, Kaua'i 20

Buona Sera Italian Restaurant, Kailua, O'ahu 54

CJ's Deli & Diner, Ka'anapali, Maui 86

Café Pesto, Hilo and Kawaihae, Hawai'i 140

Café Sauvage, Lahaina, Maui 88

Capische?, Kihei/Wailea, Maui 90

Challenge at Manele Clubhouse, The, Manele Bay, Lana'i 126

Coast Grille, Kohala Coast, Hawai'i 142

Coffee Shack, The, Captain Cook, Hawai'i 144

Crouching Lion Inn, Ka'a'awa, O'ahu 56

Daniel Thiebaut Restaurant, Kamuela, Hawai'i 146

David Paul's Lahaina Grill, Lahaina, Maui 92

Donatoni's, Kohala Coast, Hawai'i 148

Dondero's, Po'ipu, Kaua'i 22

Feast at Lele, The, Lahaina, Maui 94

Gaylord's at Kilohana, Lihu'e, Kaua'i 24

Golden Dragon, Honolulu, O'ahu 58

Grandma's Coffee House, Keokea, Maui 96

Hale'iwa Joe's Seafood Grill, Hale'iwa and Kaneohe, O'ahu 60

Hanalei Gourmet, The, Hanalei, Kaua'i 26

Hawaiian Classic Desserts Restaurant & Bakery, Lihu'e, Kaua'i 28

Hawai'i's Java Kai, Hanalei, Kapa'a, Maui and Honolulu, O'ahu 30

Henry Clay's Rotisserie, Lana'i City, Lana'i 128

Hualalai Club Grill, Kailua-Kona, Hawai'i 150

Hukilau Lanai, Kapa'a, Kaua'i 32

Hula Grill, Ka'anapali, Maui 98

Hy's Steakhouse, Honolulu, O'ahu 62

Imari, Kohala Coast, Hawai'i 152

I'o, Lahaina, Maui 100

Jameson's by the Sea, Hale'iwa, O'ahu and Kailua-Kona, Hawai'i 64

Kalaheo Coffee Company & Café, Kalaheo, Kaua'i 34

Kamuela Provision Company, Kohala Coast, Hawai'i 154

Kilauea Lodge, Volcano, Hawai'i 156

Kirin, Kohala Coast, Hawai'i 158

Koke'e Lodge, Koke'e, Kaua'i 36

Kula Lodge & Restaurant, Kula, Maui 102

Le Bistro, Honolulu, O'ahu 66

Lemongrass Grill and Seafood & Sushi Bar, Kapa'a, Kaua'i 38

Lodge at Koele, The, Lana'i City, Lana'i 130

Lucy's Grill 'n Bar, Kailua, O'ahu 68

L'Uraku Restaurant, Honolulu, O'ahu 70

Ma'alaea Grill & Café O'Lei, Ma'alaea, Makawao, Lahaina, Wailuku, Maui 104

Mañana Garage, Kahului, Maui 106

Merriman's Restaurant, Kamuela, Hawai'i 160

Moana Bakery & Café, Pa'ia, Maui 108

Nick's Fishmarket Maui, Wailea, Maui 110

Pacific'O, Lahaina, Maui 112

Pineapple Room, The, Honolulu, O'ahu 72

Plantation Gardens Restaurant & Bar, Po'ipu, Kaua'i 40

Plantation House Restaurant, The, Kapalua, Maui 114

Roy's Restaurant, Hawai'i Kai/Honolulu, O'ahu, Kahana and Kihei, Maui, Po'ipu, Kaua'i and Waikoloa, Hawai'i 74

Sansei Seafood Restaurant & Sushi Bar, Kapalua and Kihei, Maui and Honolulu, O'ahu 116

Sarento's on the Beach, Wailea, Maui 118

Sarento's top of the "I", Honolulu, O'ahu 76

Sibu Café, Kailua-Kona, Hawai'i 162

Stella Blues Café, Kihei 120

Tidepools, Po'ipu, Kaua'i 42

Tiki's Grill & Bar, Honolulu, O'ahu 78

Waterfront Restaurant, The, Ma'alaea, Maui 122

Willows, The, Honolulu, O'ahu 80

Wrangler's Steakhouse, Waimea, Kaua'i 44

MAIL ORDER SOURCES

The Coffee Shack (Featured on page 144.)
83–5799 Mamalahoa Highway, Captain Cook, Hawai'i 96704
(808) 328–9555 **coffeeshack.com**
Hawaiian grown coffees.

Grandma's Coffee House (Featured on page 96.)
9232 Kula Highway, Keokea, Maui, Hawai'i 96790
1-800-375-7853 808-878-2140 **grandmascoffee.com**
Organic Hawaiian grown coffees.

Hawaiian Vintage Chocolate Company
1050 Bishop Street, Suite 162, Honolulu, Hawai'i 96813
808-735-8494 **hawaiianvintagechocolate.com**
Vintage chocolates made from chocolate grown on the Big Island of Hawai'i.

Hawai'i's Java Kai (Featured on page 30.)
P.O. Box 6335, Santa Barbara, California 93160
1-866-JAVAKAI (toll free) (808) 245–6704 **javakai.com**
Hawaiian grown coffees.

Kalaheo Coffee Company & Café (Featured on page 34.)
2-2426 Kaumualii Highway, #A-2, Kalaheo, Kaua'i, Hawai'i 96741
1-800-255-0137 808-332-5858 **kalaheo.com**
Hawaiian grown and international coffees.

Mamane Street Bakery & Café
Mamane Street, Honoka'a, Hawai'i 96727
808-775-9478 **mamanebakery.com**
*Coffee, fresh roasted macadamia nuts, Hawaiian Sweet Bread, Hawaiian gourmet butters,
jams, jellies, chutney and honey.*

Maui Jelly Factory
1464 Lower Main Street, Suite 104, Wailuku, Maui, Hawai'i 96793
1-800-803-8343 808-242-6989 Fax 808-242-8389
Jams, jellies, mustards, sauces, syrups, salad dressings and candies.

Take Home Maui, Inc.
121 Dickenson Street, Lahaina, Maui, Hawai'i 96761
1-800-545-MAUI 808-661-8067 Fax 808-661-1550
Maui grown pineapples, Maui onions, papayas and macadamia nuts.

To order more copies of

Tasting Paradise III

Restaurants & Recipes of the Hawaiian Islands

THIRD EDITION

Send $18.95 per book plus $4.00 for shipping.

(Shipping includes up to 10 books per address.)

COASTAL IMPRESSIONS PRESS, LLC

P.O. Box 1006, Kula, HI 96790-1006

Remember Tasting Paradise is a great gift for
cooking and traveling friends. Bon Appétit!